A Treasury of
COOKBOOK
Classics

Chef's Dedication:
To my girls

Acknowledgements:
The publisher wishes to thank the following people and organizations for their kind assistance in the development of this book:
Christine Babiuk, John Barlow, Bob Brown, Loretta Brown, Chintz and Company, Bill Hole, Don King, John Klingle, Ed Klippstein, Terry O'Neill, Brian Skelly, Pinna Staan, Stokes, Arlyn Sturwold, Tim Wood.

Very special thanks to:
Kim Banks, Creative Assistant; Al Birkbeck, Creative Assistant;
Staff and Management of Creative Edge Graphic Design;
Linda Gibbons, J. Ennis Fabrics; Duane Kalmbach, Builders Wholesale Appliances;
Darren Jacknisky, Fred Walker, Oneida Canada.

Pictured on the front cover: Classic Roast Beef Au Jus (page 154)

Published by Creative Publishing Inc.
17206 - 106A Avenue
Edmonton, Alberta, Canada T5S 1E6 Ph. (403) 486-4461 Fax (403) 486-0146

Editor: Lori Hannah
Assistant Editor: Dawn Prescott
Design Director: Scott MacAuley
Food Styling and Recipes: John Butler
Photography: Darren Jacknisky
Creative Publishing Studios
Color Separations, Design and Film Production:
Creative Edge Graphic Design

Canadian Cataloguing in Publication Data

Butler, John, 1947–
A treasury of cookbook classics
Includes index.
ISBN 1-896938-08-6
1. Cookery. I. Title
TX714.B88 1998 641.5 C98-900456-2

The recipes in this book have been carefully tested by the author and have been edited by the publisher. The author and the publisher cannot be held liable for any adverse effects resulting from use of this information or for recipe errors.

This 1998 edition exclusive to

(949) 587-9207

IMPORTED BY/IMPORTE PAR
DS-MAX CANADA
RICHMOND HILL, ONTARIO
L4B 1H7

ENGLAND
WENTWALK LTD.
278A ABBEYDALE ROAD, WEMBLEY
MIDDLESEX, HA0 1NT

MALAYSIA
PRO ENTERPRISE SDN BHD
LOT 605, SS13/1K, OFF JLN.
KEWAJIPAN, 47500 SUBANG JAYA
SELANGOR D.E., MALAYSIA

DS-MAX
IRVINE, CA 92618
IMPORTER: #16-1241510
949-587-9207

Printed in China

10 9 8 7 6 5 4 3 2 1

A Treasury of COOKBOOK Classics

By Master Chef

John Butler

In association with

CREATIVE

PUBLISHING INC.

Foreword

Photo credit: Rosina Solylo

What are the ingredients of a great cookbook?

In my experience as a chef and teacher, I have identified the key elements that make a cookbook effective. With these features in mind, I have created this collection of recipes designed to help you use simple ingredients to make delicious food.

Photographs are a valuable cookbook resource, illustrating so much more than words alone can. Pictures describe, inform, suggest and entice. They show the reader what the finished dish looks like and how to prepare it. And photographs also help you decide if a recipe is something you would like to try. There are color pictures on almost every page of this book, helping you identify recipes that will suit your tastes and your lifestyle.

Have you ever happened upon the perfect recipe only to be disappointed when you could not find one of the ingredients? I have tried to use ingredients that are commonly found in most pantries and refrigerators, with a few interesting items thrown in for variety. Yes, there are a few exotic ingredients in some of my recipes. But once you try these dishes, you will understand what makes these ingredients so special. The continual blending of different cultural cooking styles has produced a wide variety of new culinary techniques and procedures. The fusion of international cuisines provides the home cook with a limitless supply of new tastes. Although not an international cookbook per se, this book does include a variety of dishes from across the globe, intended to introduce new, exciting flavors into your kitchen.

Like many other people, you may be concerned about what you eat. Perhaps a member of your family is on a calorie restricted diet. Maybe sodium or cholesterol intake is a concern. In response to an increasing awareness and appreciation for personal health, the recipes in this book have been analyzed for their caloric, protein, carbohydrate, fat, cholesterol and sodium content. I feel today's cook should be able to choose recipes based not only on appearance and taste, but on health and well-being considerations as well.

My wish is that you enjoy this book and find it a practical addition to your collection. I know it will provide you with many years of pleasant food experiences to share with those dear to you.

John Butler

Contents

Appetizers

Antipasto Plate

An Italian snack so easy to prepare.

INGREDIENTS

1 cup	**(250 mL) marinated artichoke hearts**
4 oz	**(115 g) Italian sausage, sliced**
4 oz	**(115 g) prosciutto ham, shaved**
4 oz	**(115 g) green olives**
4 oz	**(115 g) black olives**

METHOD

1. Arrange all ingredients on a platter or on 8 individual serving plates.
2. Serve with fresh bread or salad greens.

8 servings

Tip:

- *Fresh vegetables, such as carrots, celery, zucchini or cucumbers, and pickled vegetables are suitable additions to the antipasto plate.*

Approximate nutritional analysis per serving
Calories 180, Protein 9 g, Carbohydrates 10 g, Fat 12 g, Cholesterol 21 mg, Sodium 1047 mg

Savory Cheese Log

Makes any occasion extra special.

INGREDIENTS

8 oz	**(225 g) cream cheese, softened**
3 tbsp	**(45 mL) butter, softened**
1 tbsp	**(15 mL) capers, chopped**
1 tsp	**(5 mL) paprika**
1 tbsp	**(15 mL) fresh parsley, chopped**
1 tsp	**(5 mL) lemon juice**
1 tbsp	**(15 mL) onion, minced**

METHOD

1. In a medium bowl, combine cream cheese and butter using a wooden spoon.
2. Add capers, paprika, parsley, lemon juice and onions to cream cheese mixture. Mix thoroughly.
3. Spoon mixture onto wax paper. Roll and shape into a log.
4. Roll log in plastic wrap. Finish shaping.
5. Refrigerate for 1 hour.
6. Remove plastic wrap and wax paper from cheese log.
7. Slice and serve with assorted breads or crackers.

4 servings

Variation:

- *Before refrigerating the cheese log, roll in dry herbs or spices.*

Approximate nutritional analysis per serving
Calories 268, Protein 5 g, Carbohydrates 3 g, Fat 28 g, Cholesterol 80 mg, Sodium 594 mg

Savory Cheese Log

Jalisco Refried Bean Dip

It's party time, Mexican style!

INGREDIENTS

2 tbsp	**(30 mL) vegetable oil**
1 cup	**(250 mL) onion, chopped**
2	**garlic cloves, minced**
½ cup	**(125 mL) tomato sauce**
1 tsp	**(5 mL) chili powder**
1 tsp	**(5 mL) Mexican-style taco seasoning**
14 oz	**(398 mL) canned refried beans**
4 oz	**(125 mL) canned green chilies, chopped**
½ tsp	**(2 mL) salt**
½ tsp	**(2 mL) pepper**

METHOD

1. In a skillet, heat oil over medium heat.
2. Add onions and garlic. Cook until soft, about 5 minutes.
3. Add tomato sauce, chili powder, taco seasoning and refried beans.
4. Cook for 5 minutes, stirring occasionally.
5. Add chilies. Cook for 5 minutes.
6. Season with salt and pepper.
7. Serve with tortilla or corn chips, salsa, sour cream and grated Cheddar cheese.

3 cups (750 mL)

Approximate nutritional analysis per ½ cup (125 mL) serving
Calories 135, Protein 5 g, Carbohydrates 18 g, Fat 5 g, Cholesterol 0 mg, Sodium 702 mg

Seasoned Onion Rings

A crowd-pleaser with flavor to spare.

INGREDIENTS

2	**large onions**
2 cups	**(500 mL) all-purpose flour**
2 tsp	**(10 mL) salt**
1 tsp	**(5 mL) white pepper**
½ cup	**(125 mL) cornstarch**
1 cup	**(250 mL) cold water**
2	**large egg yolks**
	vegetable oil for deep frying
1	**lemon, cut into wedges**

METHOD

1. Slice onions into rings.
2. In a medium bowl, combine ½ cup (125 mL) flour with salt and pepper.
3. Dredge onion rings in seasoned flour.
4. In a medium bowl, combine remaining flour, cornstarch, water and egg yolks to make a smooth batter.
5. Heat oil to 350°F (175°C).
6. Dip floured onion rings into batter. Drain off excess batter.
7. Deep fry onion rings for 2-3 minutes, until golden brown.
8. Remove from oil and drain on paper towels.
9. Garnish with lemon wedges.
10. Serve with sour cream, salsa, ketchup or plum sauce for dipping.

4 servings

Tips:

- *Onion ring batter may be flavored with dried herbs and spices.*
- *How To Make Seasoned Flour: Combine 1 cup (250 mL) all-purpose flour, 4 tsp (20 mL) salt and 2 tsp (10 mL) white pepper. Keep a plastic bag of seasoned flour on hand for later use.*

Approximate nutritional analysis per serving
Calories 359, Protein 9 g, Carbohydrates 72 g, Fat 3 g, Cholesterol 106 mg, Sodium 2141 mg

Seasoned Onion Rings

Beef Satay

Succulent skewers of beef complemented by spicy-sweet peanut sauce.

INGREDIENTS

8 oz	**(225 g) bottom round steak**

Marinade

2 tsp	**(10 mL) light soy sauce**
2 tsp	**(10 mL) rice wine**
1 tsp	**(5 mL) sesame oil**
½ tsp	**(2 mL) salt**
½ tsp	**(2 mL) white pepper**
½ tsp	**(2 mL) sugar**
1	**garlic clove, minced**
1 tsp	**(5 mL) ginger root, peeled and minced**
1 tbsp	**(15 mL) green onion, chopped**
1 tsp	**(5 mL) cornstarch**

Peanut Sauce

4 tbsp	**(60 mL) crunchy peanut butter**
2 tsp	**(10 mL) peanut oil**
½ tsp	**(2 mL) sesame oil**
1	**garlic clove, minced**
1 tsp	**(5 mL) lemon juice**
1	**small chili pepper, chopped**
1 tbsp	**(15 mL) light soy sauce**
1 tsp	**(5 mL) curry paste**
¼ cup	**(50 mL) coconut milk or hot water**

Step 1. Cut beef across grain into 2 x 1-inch (5 x 2.5 cm) strips.

Step 10. Thread beef strips lengthwise onto bamboo skewers.

METHOD

1. Cut beef across grain into 2 x 1-inch (5 x 2.5 cm) strips.
2. Place beef strips in a medium bowl.
3. In a small bowl, combine all marinade ingredients.
4. Pour marinade over beef strips and toss together.
5. Cover with plastic wrap and refrigerate for 2 hours.
6. Heat broiler.
7. In a small bowl, combine all sauce ingredients except coconut milk.
8. Place sauce in a double boiler. Heat gently, stirring occasionally. If sauce becomes too thick, add a small amount of coconut milk.
9. Remove beef strips from marinade.
10. Thread beef strips lengthwise onto bamboo skewers.
11. Place skewers on a baking sheet.
12. Broil for 1 minute per side.
13. Serve hot with sauce as an accompaniment.

4 servings

Approximate nutritional analysis per serving
Calories 267, Protein 22 g, Carbohydrates 6 g, Fat 17 g, Cholesterol 54 mg, Sodium 672 mg

Beef Satay

Antipasto

Keep this popular favorite in the refrigerator for unexpected guests.

INGREDIENTS

1 cup	**(250 mL) olive oil**
6	**garlic cloves, crushed**
1	**large cauliflower head, cut into flowerets**
14 oz	**(398 mL) pitted black olives, drained and chopped**
12 oz	**(341 mL) pimiento-stuffed green olives, drained**
24 oz	**(682 mL) pickled onions, drained and chopped**
20 oz	**(568 mL) canned mushroom stems and pieces, drained**
8 oz	**(250 mL) canned cut green beans, drained**
2	**large green peppers, chopped**
8 oz	**(250 mL) pimiento, drained and chopped**
7½ cups	**(1.8 L) ketchup**
1¾ cups	**(425 mL) hot ketchup**
32 oz	**(1 L) sweet mixed pickles, chopped, liquid reserved**
3 oz	**(85 g) canned anchovies, chopped**
21 oz	**(590 g) canned solid white tuna, chopped**
12 oz	**(340 g) canned small shrimp, drained**
3 tsp	**(15 mL) cinnamon**
3 tsp	**(15 mL) salt**
3 tsp	**(15 mL) black pepper**

METHOD

1. In a large, non-corrosive pot, heat oil over medium-high heat.
2. Add garlic and cauliflower. Reduce heat to medium and cook for 2 minutes.
3. Add olives and pickled onions. Cook for 10 minutes, stirring constantly.
4. Add mushrooms, green beans, green peppers, pimento, ketchups and mixed pickles. Simmer for 10 minutes, stirring constantly.
5. In a medium bowl, mix together anchovies, tuna and shrimp.
6. Rinse vegetable mixture with boiling water. Drain well.
7. Stir anchovies, tuna and shrimp into vegetable mixture.
8. Season to taste with cinnamon, salt and pepper. If mixture appears dry, add some of the reserved sweet mixed pickle liquid to moisten.
9. Transfer mixture to sterilized jars.
10. Serve with fresh bread, crackers or pita bread.

28 cups (7 L)

Tips:

- *To save time, use a food processor to chop the black olives, green olives and the sweet mixed pickles.*
- *This recipe may be frozen for up to 3 months.*

Approximate nutritional analysis per ½ cup (125 mL) serving
Calories 138, Protein 6 g, Carbohydrates 17 g, Fat 6 g, Cholesterol 14 mg, Sodium 958 mg

Antipasto

Salmon Pâté

A rich, smooth dip ready in minutes.

INGREDIENTS

7½ oz	**(213 g) canned pink salmon, drained, bones and skin removed**
1 lb	**(450 g) cream cheese, softened**
3 oz	**(85 g) smoked salmon**
⅓ cup	**(75 mL) ketchup**
1 tsp	**(5 mL) lemon or lime juice**

METHOD

1. In a food processor, blend salmon, cream cheese and smoked salmon.
2. Add ketchup to color and season.
3. Add lemon or lime juice.
4. Serve as a dip or pipe onto rye bread pieces, table water biscuits or melba toast.

3⅓ cups (825 mL)

Approximate nutritional analysis per ½ cup (125 mL) serving
Calories 332, Protein 15 g, Carbohydrates 6 g, Fat 28 g, Cholesterol 99 mg, Sodium 722 mg

Sole Fingers with Dill

Crispy treats from the sea.

INGREDIENTS

2 cups	**(500 mL) all-purpose flour**
½ cup	**(125 mL) cornstarch**
2 tsp	**(10 mL) salt**
1 cup	**(250 mL) ice water**
1¼ lbs	**(565 g) sole fillets**
½ cup	**(125 mL) fresh dill, chopped**
	vegetable oil for deep frying
1 tsp	**(5 mL) baking soda**
	salt and white pepper
1	**lemon or lime, cut into wedges**

METHOD

1. In a medium bowl, sift 1 cup (250 mL) flour with cornstarch and salt.
2. Stir in water to form a smooth batter.
3. Cover with plastic wrap and allow batter to rest for 1 hour.
4. Cut sole fillets on the bias into 4-inch (10 cm) strips.
5. Toss sole strips in dill.
6. Heat oil to 350°F (175°C).
7. Just before cooking, sprinkle batter with baking soda. Mix until well blended.
8. Place remaining flour in a medium bowl. Season with salt and pepper.
9. Dust sole strips with seasoned flour, then dip into batter.
10. Deep fry for 2-3 minutes, until crisp.
11. Remove from oil and drain on paper towels.
12. Garnish with lemon or lime wedges. Serve hot.

6 servings

Approximate nutritional analysis per serving
Calories 462, Protein 15 g, Carbohydrates 59 g, Fat 19 g, Cholesterol 30 mg, Sodium 1302 mg

Sole Fingers with Dill

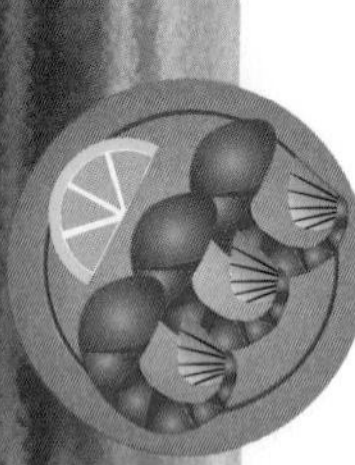

Beggars' Purses

These delectable bundles complement both formal and casual gatherings.

INGREDIENTS

6	**green onion tops**
2	**medium eggs**
2 cups	**(500 mL) milk**
¾ cup	**(175 mL) whole wheat flour**
3 tbsp	**(45 mL) vegetable oil**
2 tbsp	**(30 mL) honey**
pinch	**salt**
1½ cups	**(375 mL) cooked, seasoned rice, kept warm**

Step 13. Place 1 tbsp (15 mL) of rice in center of each crêpe.

Step 14. Gather edges of each crêpe around filling.

Step 15. Tie each bundle with a strand of green onion.

METHOD

1. Place green onions in hot water for 1 minute to soften. Drain.
2. Slice each green onion in half lengthwise to make two strips.
3. In a medium bowl, whisk together eggs and milk.
4. Gradually whisk in flour until thoroughly combined.
5. Add oil, honey and salt.
6. Heat a 9-inch (22 cm) skillet over medium heat.
7. Holding pan off heat, brush lightly with oil. Return to heat.
8. Place 2 tbsp (30 ml) batter in pan. Swirl batter to spread evenly over bottom of pan.
9. Cook until top of crêpe is dry, about 30 seconds.
10. Flip crêpe over and cook for 10 seconds.
11. Slide crêpe out of pan onto a dry surface. Keep warm.
12. Repeat steps until all of batter has been used.
13. Place 1 tbsp (15 mL) of rice in center of each crêpe.
14. Gather edges of each crêpe around filling.
15. Tie each bundle with a strand of green onion.
16. Serve warm.

6 servings

Variation:

- *1½ cups (375 mL) of any savory filling, such as scrambled eggs or a mixture of cooked spinach and cheese, may be substituted for the rice.*

Approximate nutritional analysis per serving
Calories 287, Protein 9 g, Carbohydrates 38 g, Fat 12 g, Cholesterol 73 mg, Sodium 150 mg

Beggars' Purses

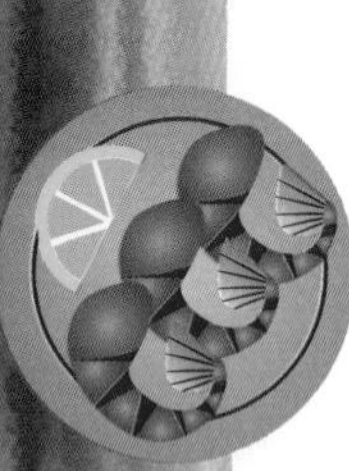

Tea Eggs

Take these along on your next picnic.

INGREDIENTS

6	**medium eggs**
1 tbsp	**(15 mL) orange peel, grated**
1 tbsp	**(15 mL) black tea leaves**
¼ cup	**(50 mL) dark soy sauce**
1	**whole star anise pod**
2 tsp	**(10 mL) black peppercorns**
1 tbsp	**(15 mL) sugar**
1 tsp	**(5 mL) salt**

METHOD

1. Gently place eggs in a large saucepan.
2. Add enough cold water to cover eggs.
3. Bring eggs to a boil. Reduce heat and simmer for 15 minutes.
4. Remove eggs from water and cool under cold, running water.
5. Gently tap eggs all over with the back of a spoon. Do not remove the shells.
6. Place remaining ingredients in a large saucepan.
7. Add eggs to saucepan. Add enough water to cover eggs.
8. Bring eggs to a boil. Reduce heat.
9. Gently simmer eggs for 45 minutes, until they turn a rich brown color.
10. Remove saucepan from heat.
11. Leaving eggs in cooking liquid, refrigerate overnight.
12. Remove shells from eggs.
13. Serve as is or use as a garnish.

6 servings

◄ Approximate nutritional analysis per serving
Calories 102, Protein 7 g, Carbohydrates 8 g, Fat 5 g, Cholesterol 187 mg, Sodium 683 mg

Artichoke Frittata

Great for brunch with fresh bread.

INGREDIENTS

3 tbsp	**(45 mL) butter**
1	**medium onion, diced**
1	**medium red pepper, diced**
10 oz	**(284 mL) canned artichoke hearts, drained**
6	**large eggs**
2 tsp	**(10 mL) fresh basil, chopped**
3 tbsp	**(45 mL) fresh parsley, chopped**
¼ cup	**(50 mL) Parmesan cheese, grated**
	salt and pepper

METHOD

1. Preheat broiler.
2. In an ovenproof skillet, melt butter over medium heat.
3. Add onions and peppers. Cook for 2 minutes until softened, stirring occasionally.
4. Add artichoke hearts. Stir gently until artichokes are coated with butter.
5. In a medium bowl, lightly beat eggs. Add basil, parsley and 2 tbsp (30 mL) Parmesan cheese. Season with salt and pepper. Stir until combined.
6. Pour eggs over artichoke mixture in skillet.
7. Cook over medium heat, without stirring, for 3-4 minutes until edges are golden brown.
8. Sprinkle with remaining Parmesan cheese. Broil for 1 minute, until frittata is just set.
9. Cut into 6 wedges and serve.

6 servings

Approximate nutritional analysis per serving
Calories 226, Protein 14 g, Carbohydrates 8 g, Fat 16 g, Cholesterol 380 mg, Sodium 279 mg

Artichoke Frittata

Salmon Cakes with Tarragon Butter

Salmon, chives and tarragon — a mouth-watering combination.

INGREDIENTS

3 tbsp	**(45 mL) mayonnaise**
2 tbsp	**(30 mL) ketchup**
1 tbsp	**(15 mL) lemon juice**
1 tsp	**(5 mL) dry mustard**
dash	**hot pepper sauce**
½ cup	**(125 mL) fresh chives, minced**
2 tsp	**(10 mL) salt**
1 tsp	**(5 mL) black pepper**
1 lb	**(450 g) salmon fillets, minced**
1 cup + 2 tbsp	**(280 mL) fresh bread crumbs**
½ cup	**(125 mL) butter**
1 cup	**(250 mL) dry white wine**
1 tbsp	**(15 mL) lime juice**
½ cup	**(125 mL) fresh tarragon, minced**
	salt and pepper

Step 3. Shape salmon mixture into equal-sized cakes.

Step 4. Dust salmon cakes with remaining bread crumbs.

METHOD

1. In a large bowl, combine mayonnaise, ketchup, lemon juice, dry mustard, hot pepper sauce, chives, salt and pepper.
2. Add salmon and 1 cup (250 mL) bread crumbs. Mix well.
3. Shape salmon mixture into 4 equal-sized cakes.
4. Dust salmon cakes with remaining bread crumbs.
5. Place cakes on a tray and refrigerate for 1 hour.
6. In a skillet, melt ¼ cup (50 mL) butter over medium heat.
7. Reduce heat to low. Fry salmon cakes for 5 minutes per side, or until lightly browned. Remove cakes from skillet and keep warm.
8. Wipe out skillet.
9. Add wine and lime juice to skillet. Bring to a boil over medium-high heat.
10. Reduce heat to low. Whisk in remaining butter 1 tbsp (15 mL) at a time.
11. Remove skillet from heat and add tarragon.
12. Season with salt and pepper to taste.
13. Serve tarragon butter as an accompaniment to the salmon cakes.

4 servings

Approximate nutritional analysis per serving
Calories 541, Protein 26 g, Carbohydrates 12 g, Fat 39 g, Cholesterol 131 mg, Sodium 1573 mg

Salmon Cakes with Tarragon Butter

Oriental Scrambled Delight

A fresh variation on scrambled eggs.

INGREDIENTS

¼ cup	**(50 mL) vegetable oil**
2 cups	**(500 mL) tofu, drained and diced**
8	**eggs**
2 tbsp	**(30 mL) soy sauce**
4 tbsp	**(60 mL) edible flower petals, washed thoroughly and drained**
2 tbsp	**(30 mL) green onions, chopped**

METHOD

1. In a large skillet, heat oil over medium heat.
2. Add tofu. Sauté for 5 minutes until golden brown, stirring occasionally.
3. In a medium bowl, beat eggs with soy sauce. Add to tofu in skillet.
4. Cook for 4 minutes, until eggs are almost set, stirring occasionally.
5. Sprinkle with petals and green onions. Serve.

8 servings

Tip:

- *Edible flowers include pansies, nasturtiums, roses and chrysanthemums.*

Approximate nutritional analysis per serving
Calories 237, Protein 16 g, Carbohydrates 3 g, Fat 18 g, Cholesterol 361 mg, Sodium 369 mg

Crab-Filled Mushrooms

Two types of mushrooms in this favorite.

INGREDIENTS

8	**large white mushrooms**
4	**large portabella mushrooms**
1 tbsp	**(15 mL) olive oil**
4	**shallots, finely chopped**
1 cup	**(250 mL) fresh white bread crumbs**
1 tbsp	**(15 mL) parsley, chopped**
½ cup	**(125 mL) cooked crab meat or baby shrimp**
pinch	**dried tarragon**
	salt and pepper
2 tbsp	**(30 mL) Parmesan cheese, grated**
1 tbsp	**(15 mL) butter, melted**

METHOD

1. Preheat oven to 375°F (190°C).
2. Gently remove mushroom stems, reserving caps.
3. Finely chop mushroom stems.
4. Rinse mushroom caps. Set on a baking sheet.
5. In a skillet, heat oil over medium heat. Sauté shallots in oil for 2 minutes.
6. Add mushroom stems and cook for 3 minutes.
7. Add bread crumbs, parsley and crab meat to skillet. Cook for 1 minute to heat through.
8. Add tarragon, salt and pepper. Remove from heat.
9. Fill mushroom caps with seasoned filling.
10. Sprinkle Parmesan cheese on top of mushrooms. Drizzle with melted butter.
11. Bake for 10 minutes and serve hot.

12 appetizers

Approximate nutritional analysis per appetizer
Calories 46, Protein 2 g, Carbohydrates 3 g, Fat 3 g, Cholesterol 9 mg, Sodium 60 mg

Crab-Filled Mushrooms

Seafood Phyllo Horns

Creamy seafood in buttery phyllo pastry — a delicate blend of flavors.

INGREDIENTS

3	**sheets phyllo dough**
¼ cup + 2 tbsp	**(80 mL) butter**
¼ cup	**(50 mL) onion, finely chopped**
2 tbsp	**(30 mL) all-purpose flour**
⅓ cup	**(75 mL) milk**
1 tsp	**(5 mL) white wine**
4 oz	**(115 g) cooked seafood, such as lobster, crab or shrimp**
⅓ cup	**(75 mL) Parmesan cheese, grated**
½ tsp	**(2 mL) lemon juice**
¼ tsp	**(1 mL) salt**
¼ tsp	**(1 mL) pepper**
dash	**hot pepper sauce**

Step 4. Brush one sheet of phyllo dough with butter.

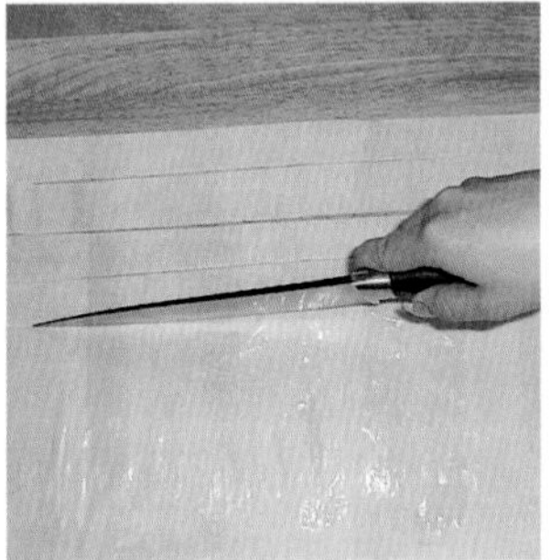

Step 6. Cut layered phyllo dough into 1-inch (2.5 cm) wide strips.

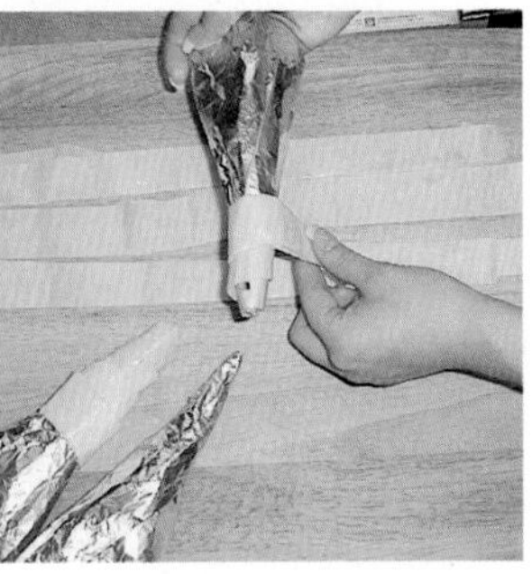

Step 7. Wrap dough strips in a spiral around prepared molds.

METHOD

1. Preheat oven to 400°F (205°C).
2. Lightly grease 12 metal horn molds.
3. Melt ¼ cup (50 mL) butter.
4. Brush one sheet of phyllo dough with butter.
5. Place second sheet of phyllo dough on top of first layer. Brush with butter. Repeat with last sheet of phyllo dough.
6. Cut layered phyllo dough into 1-inch (2.5 cm) wide strips.
7. Wrap dough strips in a spiral around prepared molds.
8. Brush with butter and place on a baking sheet.
9. Bake for 12-15 minutes, until golden brown. Cool.
10. In a saucepan, melt remaining butter over medium heat.
11. Add onions. Sauté until tender, about 4 minutes. Do not brown.
12. Stir in flour.
13. Slowly add milk. Stir constantly, until sauce thickens.
14. Add wine and seafood. Reduce heat to low.
15. Simmer mixture for 5 minutes, until seafood is heated through.
16. Add remaining ingredients. Stir well to blend flavors.
17. Carefully remove phyllo horns from molds. Handle gently as they are fragile.
18. Fill open end of each horn with seafood filling.
19. Serve hot.

12 pieces

Tip:

- *If you do not have metal horn molds on hand, you may make your own by molding sheets of aluminum foil into cone shapes.*

Approximate nutritional analysis per piece
Calories 131, Protein 4 g, Carbohydrates 9 g, Fat 9 g, Cholesterol 31 mg, Sodium 201 mg

Seafood Phyllo Horns

Parmesan Baked Chicken Wings

Tender chicken in a crunchy coating.

INGREDIENTS

2½ cups	**(625 mL) fresh bread crumbs**
¾ cup	**(175 mL) Parmesan cheese, freshly grated**
¼ cup	**(50 mL) fresh parsley, chopped**
1 tsp	**(5 mL) salt**
1 tsp	**(5 mL) black pepper**
¼ tsp	**(1 mL) red pepper flakes**
1 tsp	**(5 mL) garlic powder**
24	**chicken wings, tips removed**
1 cup	**(250 mL) butter, melted and cooled**

METHOD

1. Preheat oven to 350°F (170°C).
2. In a large bowl, mix bread crumbs, Parmesan cheese, parsley, salt, pepper, pepper flakes and garlic powder.
3. Split wings in half lengthwise.
4. Lightly brush wings with melted butter.
5. Dip wings in bread crumb mixture to coat.
6. Arrange wings on a baking sheet. Drizzle with remaining butter.
7. Bake for 30-40 minutes until golden brown.
8. Serve hot.

48 pieces

◀ Approximate nutritional analysis per piece
Calories 120, Protein 6 g, Carbohydrates 4 g, Fat 9 g, Cholesterol 31 mg, Sodium 137 mg

Creamy Eggs in Tomato-Filled Baskets

A tasty, hot appetizer or brunch item.

INGREDIENTS

4	**crusty rolls**
6 tbsp	**(90 mL) butter, melted**
4	**green onions, chopped**
8	**eggs, lightly beaten**
	salt and white pepper
3 tbsp	**(45 mL) heavy cream**
2	**medium tomatoes, blanched, peeled, seeded and chopped**

METHOD

1. Preheat oven to 375°F (190°C).
2. Carefully slice tops off rolls. Hollow out soft centers leaving ¼-inch (0.6 cm) shells. Reserve tops of rolls.
3. Generously brush tops and insides of shells with melted butter.
4. Place hollow shells on a baking sheet. Bake for 2-3 minutes until golden brown. Remove from oven and keep warm.
5. In a large skillet, sauté green onions in remaining butter over medium-low heat for 2-3 minutes, stirring occasionally.
6. Add eggs to skillet. Season with salt and pepper.
7. Cook eggs over medium heat for 4-5 minutes, until they begin to set.
8. Add cream to eggs. Stir until eggs are smooth and creamy.
9. Spoon tomatoes into warm shells. Top with egg mixture.
10. Replace tops of rolls and serve.

4 servings

Approximate nutritional analysis per serving
Calories 421, Protein 14 g, Carbohydrates 17 g, Fat 33 g, Cholesterol 439 mg, Sodium 266 mg

Creamy Eggs in Tomato-Filled Baskets

Tangy Deviled Eggs

Rich and zesty — a classic.

INGREDIENTS

4	**hard-boiled eggs**
1 tsp	**(5 mL) prepared mustard**
1 tbsp	**(15 mL) ketchup**
2 tbsp	**(30 mL) mayonnaise**
dash	**Worcestershire sauce**
	salt and white pepper

METHOD

1. Slice eggs in half lengthwise. With a spoon, carefully remove yolks, reserving egg whites.
2. Blend egg yolks in a food processor.
3. Add next 4 ingredients to food processor. Season with salt and pepper.
4. Place mixture in a pastry bag.
5. Pipe filling into egg halves and serve.

8 pieces

Tip:

- *Garnish deviled eggs with any of the following: fresh dill, sliced olives, pickle slices, chopped peppers, capers, chopped cucumbers or chopped radishes.*

Approximate nutritional analysis per piece
Calories 65, Protein 3 g, Carbohydrates 1 g, Fat 5 g, Cholesterol 109 mg, Sodium 88 mg

Tortellini Treats

A colorful party favorite.

INGREDIENTS

1 lb	**(450 g) tri-color tortellini**
¼ cup	**(50 mL) olive oil**
1 tbsp	**(15 mL) hot pepper flakes**
½ cup	**(125 mL) Parmesan cheese, grated**
	salt and black pepper

METHOD

1. Cook tortellini according to package directions. Drain well.
2. In a medium bowl, mix olive oil, pepper flakes and Parmesan cheese.
3. While still hot, toss tortellini in Parmesan cheese mixture. Season with salt and pepper.
4. Thread tortellini on wooden skewers or toothpicks and serve.

6 servings

Approximate nutritional analysis per serving
Calories 264, Protein 11 g, Carbohydrates 17 g, Fat 17 g, Cholesterol 104 mg, Sodium 318 mg

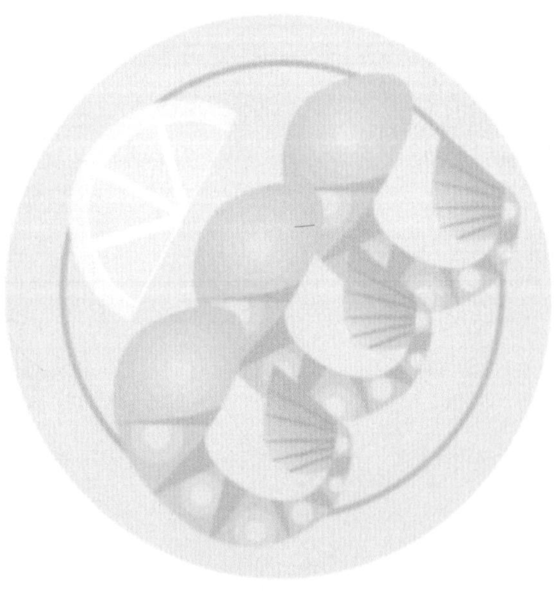

Tortellini Treats

Feta-Stuffed Grape Leaves

Feta cheese, dill and grapes are the perfect filling for this Mediterranean classic.

INGREDIENTS

⅓ cup	**(75 mL) olive oil**
1 cup	**(250 mL) green onions, chopped**
1 cup	**(250 mL) seedless black grapes, sliced**
1 cup	**(250 mL) feta cheese, crumbled**
½ cup	**(125 mL) fresh dill, chopped**
1 tbsp	**(15 mL) lemon juice**
	black pepper
16	**grape leaves, rinsed thoroughly**
1 cup	**(250 mL) canned chicken broth**
1	**lemon, cut into wedges**

Step 8. Place 2 tsp (10 mL) filling on bottom of leaf. Roll leaf one turn around filling.

Step 9. Fold in side tips of leaf to enclose filling.

Step 10. Finish rolling leaf around filling, folding side tips in.

METHOD

1. In a medium skillet, heat oil over low heat.
2. Add green onions and sauté for 3 minutes. Remove skillet from heat.
3. Add grapes, feta cheese and dill to green onions.
4. Season filling mixture with lemon juice and pepper to taste.
5. Blanch grape leaves in boiling water for 2-3 minutes or until pliable. Cool leaves under cold, running water.
6. Snip stems from grape leaves with scissors.
7. Lay out grape leaves with leaf tips facing away from you.
8. Place 2 tsp (10 mL) filling on bottom of leaf. Roll leaf one turn around filling.
9. Fold in side tips of leaf to enclose filling.
10. Finish rolling leaf around filling, folding side tips in.
11. Repeat steps until all grape leaves have been rolled.
12 Place rolled leaves, seam edges down, in a large skillet.
13. Add chicken broth and cover. Cook over medium heat for 5 minutes.
14. Serve hot or cold with lemon wedges.

16 pieces

Approximate nutritional analysis per piece
Calories 104, Protein 4 g, Carbohydrates 6 g, Fat 8 g, Cholesterol 13 mg, Sodium 282 mg

Feta-Stuffed Grape Leaves

Samosas

Savory turnovers filled with potatoes, peas and exotic spices.

INGREDIENTS

3 cups	**(750 mL) all-purpose flour**
¼ cup	**(50 mL) clarified butter, melted**
pinch	**salt**
¾ cup	**(175 mL) cold water**
1 tbsp	**(15 mL) vegetable oil**
1	**small onion, diced**
1 tsp	**(5 mL) ginger root, peeled and grated**
4	**potatoes, peeled, boiled, diced into small pieces**
2 cups	**(500 mL) frozen peas, thawed**
¼ tsp	**(1 mL) coriander**
¼ tsp	**(1 mL) garam masala**
	vegetable oil for deep frying

METHOD

1. In a large bowl, combine flour, butter and salt.
2. Add enough water to make a smooth dough.
3. Knead dough for 3-4 minutes. Allow dough to rest for 1 hour.
4. In a skillet, heat oil over medium heat.
5. Sauté onions and ginger for 3-4 minutes.
6. Add potatoes and peas to heat through.
7. Stir in coriander and garam masala. Remove from heat.
8. Knead dough and form into 12 small balls.
9. Flatten each ball into a 4-inch (10 cm) circle.
10. Fold dough circles in half to make semicircles.
11. Roll semicircles out thinly.
12. Place 1 tbsp (15 mL) filling on one side of each semicircle.
13. Fold dough over filling to form triangle shapes.
14. Moisten edges with water and pinch to seal.
15. Heat oil to 350°F (175°C).
16. Deep fry pieces for 2 minutes, until golden brown.
17. Remove from oil and drain on paper towels.
18. Serve hot or cold.

12 pieces

Step 10. Fold dough circles in half to make semicircles.

Step 12. Place 1 tbsp (15 mL) filling on one side of each semicircle.

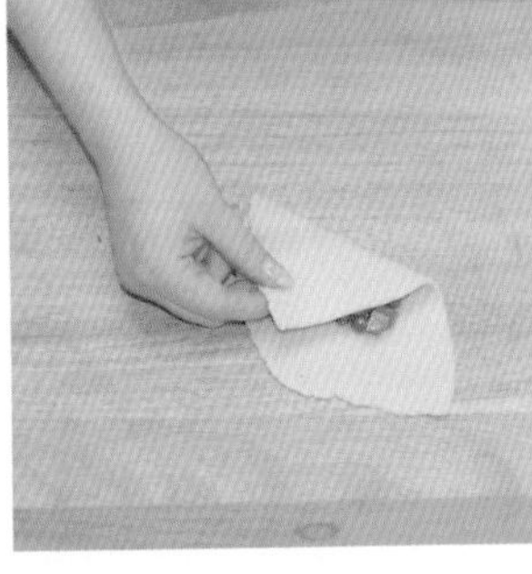

Step 13. Fold dough over filling to form triangle shapes.

Approximate nutritional analysis per piece
Calories 221, Protein 5 g, Carbohydrates 37 g, Fat 6 g, Cholesterol 11 mg, Sodium 32 mg

Samosas

Seviche of White Fish

A special hors d'oeuvre sure to please.

INGREDIENTS

1½ lbs	**(675 g) sole, halibut or whitefish**
½ cup	**(125 mL) lime juice**
1	**medium red onion, chopped**
1	**medium green pepper, diced**
1	**medium red pepper, diced**
¼ cup	**(50 mL) celery, finely diced**
1 tsp	**(5 mL) fresh thyme**
1 tsp	**(5 mL) cumin**
¼ cup	**(50 mL) olive oil**
2 tsp	**(10 mL) hot pepper sauce**
3 tbsp	**(45 mL) cilantro, chopped**

METHOD

1. Combine all ingredients in a large glass or porcelain bowl.
2. Cover with plastic wrap and refrigerate for 24 hours.
3. Flake fish into bite-sized pieces with a fork.
4. Place fish and dressing on a bed of salad greens. Serve chilled.

4 servings

Spinach Dip in Crusty Bread

An all-time favorite.

INGREDIENTS

1 lb	**(450 g) frozen spinach, thawed, chopped and squeezed dry**
1 cup	**(250 mL) mayonnaise**
1 cup	**(250 mL) sour cream**
3 oz	**(85 g) dry onion soup mix**
4	**green onions, chopped**
1 cup	**(250 mL) sunflower seeds**
	black pepper
1	**round loaf French or Italian crusty bread, 10-inch (25 cm) diameter**

METHOD

1. Mix first 7 ingredients together in a medium bowl. Chill overnight.
2. Slice top off bread.
3. Scoop out soft bread from inside loaf and cut into cubes.
4. Fill bread shell with spinach filling.
5. Serve with bread cubes on the side for dipping.

8 servings

Approximate nutritional analysis per serving
Calories 393, Protein 8 g, Carbohydrates 11 g, Fat 37 g, Cholesterol 29 mg, Sodium 323 mg

◀ Approximate nutritional analysis per serving
Calories 306, Protein 33 g, Carbohydrates 8 g, Fat 16 g, Cholesterol 82 mg, Sodium 174 mg

Spinach Dip in Crusty Bread

Pita Roll-Ups

Flavored cream cheese and pita bread team up in these tasty tidbits.

INGREDIENTS

4	**9-inch (22 cm) pita breads**
1 lb	**(450 g) cream cheese, softened**
½ cup	**(125 mL) fresh basil, chopped**
1 tbsp	**(15 mL) vodka**
2 tsp	**(10 mL) lemon peel, grated**
4	**garlic cloves, minced**
⅓ cup	**(75 mL) sun-dried tomatoes, chopped**
⅓ cup	**(75 mL) sunflower seeds**
	black pepper

Step 1. Split each pita bread in half.

Step 4. Spread cream cheese mixture on pita bread halves.

Step 8. Slice each roll diagonally into 6 equal portions.

METHOD

1. Split each pita bread in half.
2. Cover pita breads with a damp cloth.
3. In a medium glass bowl, mix cream cheese, basil, vodka, lemon peel, garlic, sun-dried tomatoes and sunflower seeds. Season with pepper.
4. Spread cream cheese mixture on pita bread halves.
5. Form into tight rolls. Wrap in plastic wrap.
6. Refrigerate for 1 hour.
7. Remove plastic wrap from rolls.
8. Slice each roll diagonally into 6 equal portions.
9. Serve.

24 pieces

Approximate nutritional analysis per piece
Calories 108, Protein 3 g, Carbohydrates 7 g, Fat 8 g, Cholesterol 21 mg, Sodium 125 mg

Pita Roll-Ups

Spring Rolls

Shrimp, pork and Oriental vegetables are the filling for this satisfying snack.

INGREDIENTS

1 tbsp	**(15 mL) sesame oil**
½ cup	**(125 mL) lean raw pork, finely chopped**
¼ cup	**(50 mL) baby shrimp, chopped**
2	**green onions, finely chopped**
1 tsp	**(5 mL) ginger root, peeled and shredded**
¼ cup	**(50 mL) suey choy, shredded**
½ cup	**(125 mL) bean sprouts**
1 tbsp	**(15 mL) soy sauce**
	salt
2 tbsp	**(30 mL) all-purpose flour**
¼ cup	**(50 mL) cold water**
8	**8 x 6-inch (20 x 15 cm) spring roll wrappers**
	vegetable oil for deep frying

METHOD

1. In a skillet, heat oil over medium heat.
2. Fry pork, shrimp and green onions for 2-3 minutes.
3. Add ginger, suey choy and bean sprouts. Cook for 2 minutes, stirring occasionally.
4. Add soy sauce and salt to taste.
5. Remove from heat and allow mixture to cool.
6. In a small bowl, mix flour with water to make a smooth paste.
7. Lay out spring roll wrappers in diamond fashion.
8. Place 2 tsp (10 mL) filling in bottom corner of wrapper.
9. Fold bottom corner of wrapper over filling. Moisten edges with flour/water mixture.
10. Fold in side points and secure with flour/water mixture.
11. Roll wrapper around filling. Secure remaining point with flour/water mixture.
12. Repeat steps until all wrappers have been rolled.
13. Chill rolls in refrigerator for 30 minutes.
14. Heat oven to 400°F (205°C).
15. Place rolls on a cooling rack, seam side down, and bake for 15 minutes. Remove from oven.
16. Heat oil to 375°F (190°C).
17. Deep fry rolls for 3-4 minutes, until golden brown.
18. Remove from oil and drain on paper towels.
19. Serve spring rolls with plum sauce.

8 pieces

Step 9. Fold bottom corner of wrapper over filling. Moisten edges with flour/water mixture.

Step 10. Fold in side points and secure with flour/water mixture.

Approximate nutritional analysis per piece
Calories 83, Protein 6 g, Carbohydrates 7 g, Fat 3 g, Cholesterol 21 mg, Sodium 199 mg

Spring Rolls

Burrecks

Crêpes filled with Gruyère cheese then fried to golden perfection.

INGREDIENTS

½ cup + 1 tbsp	**(140 mL) butter**
7	**large eggs**
3½ cups	**(875 mL) milk**
1½ cups	**(375 mL) all-purpose flour**
¼ tsp	**(1 mL) salt**
¼ tsp	**(1 mL) nutmeg**
1 tbsp	**(15 mL) Worcestershire sauce**
	salt and pepper
5 cups	**(1.3 L) Gruyère cheese, grated**
1½ cups	**(375 mL) bread crumbs**
	vegetable oil for deep frying

METHOD

1. Melt 1 tbsp (15 mL) butter. Place in a medium bowl.
2. Add 4 eggs, 1½ cups (375 mL) milk, 1 cup (250 mL) flour, and salt. Mix well to form a smooth batter.
3. Cover batter with plastic wrap and refrigerate for 1 hour.
4. In a heavy saucepan, melt remaining ½ cup (125 mL) butter over medium heat.
5. Add remaining ½ cup (125 mL) flour.
6. Cook mixture, stirring constantly, for 3 minutes. Reduce heat to low.
7. Whisk in remaining 2 cups (500 mL) milk in a steady stream.
8. Add nutmeg, Worcestershire sauce, salt and pepper. Combine well.
9. Transfer filling mixture to a large bowl.
10. Cover with plastic wrap and refrigerate for 1 hour.
11. Wipe out an 8-inch (20 cm) non-stick crêpe pan with an oiled paper towel.
12. Heat crêpe pan over medium-high heat.
13. Holding pan off heat, add enough batter to coat base of pan.
14. Swirl batter to spread evenly over bottom of pan.
15. Return pan to heat. Cook until top of crêpe is dry, about 30 seconds.
16. Using a rubber or plastic spatula, flip crêpe over and cook for about 10 seconds.
17. Slide crêpe out of pan onto a dry surface. Keep warm.
18. Wipe out pan with oiled paper towel. Repeat steps until all of crêpe batter has been used.
19. Stir cheese into filling mixture.
20. Place 3 tbsp (45 mL) filling into center of each crêpe.
21. Roll edge of crêpe over filling, folding in edges to enclose filling.
22. In a small bowl, lightly beat remaining 3 eggs.
23. Heat oil to 350°F (175°C).
24. Brush outside of rolled crêpes with egg.
25. Coat crêpes with bread crumbs.
26. Deep fry for 4 minutes, until golden brown.
27. Remove from oil and drain on paper towels.
28. Serve hot.

12 servings

Approximate nutritional analysis per serving
Calories 414, Protein 22 g, Carbohydrates 19 g, Fat 28 g, Cholesterol 204 mg, Sodium 433 mg

Burrecks

Raita

A cool, refreshing dip perfect for parties.

INGREDIENTS

1 cup	**(250 mL) plain yogurt**
½ cup	**(125 mL) sour cream**
2	**medium tomatoes, diced**
1	**medium cucumber, peeled and diced**
1	**small onion, diced**
1 tsp	**(5 mL) cumin seed**
1	**garlic clove, minced**
½ tsp	**(2 mL) black pepper**
	cilantro for garnish

METHOD

1. In a medium bowl, combine yogurt and sour cream. Mix until smooth.
2. Add remaining ingredients except cilantro. Stir until well blended.
3. Cover with plastic wrap and refrigerate for 1 hour.
4. Garnish with cilantro.
5. Serve as an accompaniment to spicy dishes, such as curry.

6 servings

Approximate nutritional analysis per serving
Calories 91, Protein 3 g, Carbohydrates 8 g, Fat 6 g, Cholesterol 14 mg, Sodium 35 mg

Eggplant Hummus

Delicious and satisfying.

INGREDIENTS

1½ lbs	**(675 g) eggplant**
4	**garlic cloves**
19 oz	**(540 mL) canned chick peas (garbanzo beans), drained**
½ cup	**(125 mL) tahini (sesame seed paste)**
¼ cup	**(50 mL) fresh lemon juice**
2 tbsp	**(30 mL) hot water**
1 tsp	**(5 mL) cumin**
1 tsp	**(5 mL) salt**
1 tsp	**(5 mL) hot pepper sauce**

METHOD

1. Preheat broiler.
2. Place eggplant on a baking sheet.
3. Place baking sheet under broiler. Broil on middle rack for 6-7 minutes, turning occasionally, until eggplant skin is charred.
4. Switch oven to bake at 450°F (230°C).
5. Bake eggplant for 12-15 minutes, until very soft. Cool.
6. In a food processor, mince garlic.
7. Split eggplant in half. Scoop pulp into food processor.
8. Add chick peas, tahini, lemon juice, water, cumin, salt and hot pepper sauce to food processor. Blend until smooth.
9. Cool in refrigerator.
10. Serve with pita bread and fresh vegetable sticks.

5½ cups (1.4 L)

Approximate nutritional analysis per ½ cup (125 mL) serving
Calories 144, Protein 5 g, Carbohydrates 18 g, Fat 7 g, Cholesterol 0 mg, Sodium 346 mg

Eggplant Hummus

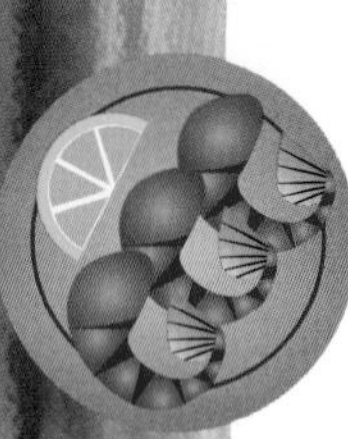

Classic Quiche

A popular choice for entertaining, this delicious hors d'oeuvre has many variations.

INGREDIENTS

3	**large eggs**
1 cup	**(250 mL) heavy cream**
1 cup	**(250 mL) milk**
	salt and white pepper
pinch	**nutmeg**
½ cup	**(125 mL) Swiss cheese, grated**
¼ cup	**(50 mL) Parmesan cheese, grated**
1	**9-inch (22 cm) pie shell, baked**

METHOD

1. Preheat oven to 375°F (190°C).
2. In a medium mixing bowl, lightly beat eggs.
3. Stir cream and milk into eggs.
4. Season egg mixture with salt, pepper and nutmeg.
5. Stir Swiss cheese and Parmesan cheese into mixture.
6. Pour into pie shell.
7. Bake for 35-40 minutes until center of quiche is set.
8. Serve hot or cold.

6 servings

Variations:

Change recipe as follows for different types of quiche:

- *Mini Quiches: Substitute unsweetened tart shells for pie shell. Fill tart shells with filling.*
- *Mushroom Quiche: Add ¾ cup (175 mL) sautéed, sliced mushrooms to filling.*
- *Quiche Lorraine: Add ½ cup (125 mL) diced, cooked ham and 1 tbsp (15 mL) chopped chives to filling.*
- *Seafood Quiche: Add ¾ cup (175 mL) cooked crab, lobster, shrimp or scallops to filling.*
- *Vegetarian Quiche: Add ¾ cup (175 mL) cooked vegetables to filling.*

Approximate nutritional analysis per serving
Calories 274, Protein 10 g, Carbohydrates 6 g, Fat 24 g, Cholesterol 179 mg, Sodium 216 mg

Classic Quiche

Salads

Papaya Seed Dressing

A versatile, peppery salad dressing.

INGREDIENTS

1½ tbsp	**(25 mL) fresh papaya seeds**
1 cup	**(250 mL) safflower oil**
½ cup	**(125 mL) tarragon vinegar**
¼ cup	**(50 mL) sugar**
2 tbsp	**(30 mL) lime juice**
1 tsp	**(5 mL) salt**
1 tsp	**(5 mL) dry mustard**
1 tsp	**(5 mL) onion, minced**
½ tsp	**(2 mL) paprika**

METHOD

1. Combine all ingredients in a food processor.
2. Blend dressing until papaya seeds are broken into small pieces.
3. Serve with fresh fruit or mixed salad greens.

1¾ cups (425 mL)

Approximate nutritional analysis per 1 tablespoon (15 mL) serving
Calories 80, Protein 0 g, Carbohydrates 2 g, Fat 8 g, Cholesterol 0 mg, Sodium 77 mg

Potato, Ham and Swiss Cheese Salad

All the fresh goodness of new potatoes.

INGREDIENTS

1½ lbs	**(675 g) new potatoes**
6	**fresh mint leaves**
2 tsp	**(10 mL) salt**
3 tbsp	**(45 mL) red wine**
2 tbsp	**(30 mL) white wine vinegar**
2 tbsp	**(30 mL) shallots, minced**
1½ tbsp	**(25 mL) Dijon mustard**
	salt and pepper
½ cup	**(125 mL) olive oil**
¼ cup	**(50 mL) fresh parsley, chopped**
12 oz	**(340 g) cooked ham, cubed**
8 oz	**(225 g) Swiss cheese, cubed**
	red cabbage or mixed salad greens for garnish

METHOD

1. Place potatoes and mint leaves in a large saucepan.
2. Cover potatoes with cold water and add salt.
3. Bring to a boil over medium-high heat. Reduce heat to medium and cook for 10-15 minutes.
4. Drain potatoes and allow to cool. Remove mint leaves and discard.
5. In a small bowl, combine wine, vinegar, shallots, mustard, salt, pepper and oil.
6. Stir parsley into dressing.
7. Cut cooled potatoes into slices and place in a medium bowl.
8. Pour two-thirds of the dressing over potatoes and toss lightly.
9. Stir in ham, cheese and remaining dressing.
10. Divide salad onto 6 plates and garnish with red cabbage or mixed salad greens.

6 servings

Approximate nutritional analysis per serving
Calories 525, Protein 23 g, Carbohydrates 20 g, Fat 39 g, Cholesterol 64 mg, Sodium 1342 mg

Potato, Ham and Swiss Cheese Salad

Ginger Dressing

Salad dressing with an Asian flair.

INGREDIENTS

3 tbsp	**(45 mL) rice wine vinegar**
2 tbsp	**(30 mL) ginger root, peeled and minced**
2 tbsp	**(30 mL) lemon juice**
2 tbsp	**(30 mL) light soy sauce**
2 tsp	**(10 mL) Dijon mustard**
	salt and pepper
6 tbsp	**(90 mL) vegetable oil**
¼ cup	**(50 mL) sesame oil**
2 tbsp	**(30 mL) fresh chives, chopped**
1	**garlic clove, minced (optional)**

METHOD

1. In a small bowl, combine vinegar, ginger, lemon juice, soy sauce, mustard, salt and pepper to taste.
2. Whisk in vegetable oil and sesame oil in a steady stream. Whisk until emulsified.
3. Add chives and garlic, whisking to combine.
4. Serve with salad greens.

1 cup (250 mL)

Approximate nutritional analysis per 1 tablespoon (15 mL) serving
Calories 83, Protein 0 g, Carbohydrates 1 g, Fat 9 g, Cholesterol 0 mg, Sodium 146 mg

Georgia Salad

A marvellous, Southern-style dish.

INGREDIENTS

½ lb	**(225 g) black-eyed peas**
1	**small bay leaf**
1	**whole clove**
1	**medium onion, diced**
1 tsp	**(5 mL) orange peel, grated**
2 tbsp	**(30 mL) orange juice**
2 tbsp	**(30 mL) red wine vinegar**
½ tsp	**(2 mL) hot pepper sauce**
1 tsp	**(5 mL) fresh cilantro, chopped**
2	**garlic cloves, crushed**
	salt and pepper
2 tsp	**(10 mL) red pepper flakes**
½ cup	**(125 mL) olive oil**
½	**English cucumber, sliced**

METHOD

1. In a large saucepan, combine black-eyed peas with 4 cups (1 L) of cold water.
2. Add bay leaf and clove.
3. Bring to a boil over medium-high heat. Reduce heat to medium.
4. Cook, stirring occasionally, for 45-50 minutes, until peas are tender. Add water if mixture becomes too dry.
5. Drain peas and rinse under cold water.
6. Remove clove and bay leaf from peas and discard.
7. Place peas in a medium bowl. Add onion and toss together.
8. In a small bowl, combine orange peel, orange juice, vinegar, hot pepper sauce, cilantro, garlic, salt, pepper and pepper flakes.
9. Whisk oil into dressing.
10. Pour dressing over peas, tossing to combine.
11. Cover salad with plastic wrap and refrigerate overnight.
12. Cut cucumber slices into quarters. Fold into salad just before serving.

4 servings

Approximate nutritional analysis per serving
Calories 325, Protein 3 g, Carbohydrates 19 g, Fat 28 g, Cholesterol 0 mg, Sodium 103 mg

Georgia Salad

Fruit Salad Dressing

A tangy complement to fresh fruit.

INGREDIENTS

⅓ cup	**(75 mL) sugar**
¼ cup	**(50 mL) cider vinegar**
1 tsp	**(5 mL) salt**
½	**small onion, diced**
1 tsp	**(5 mL) dry mustard**
1 tsp	**(5 mL) paprika**
1 tsp	**(5 mL) celery seed**
1 cup	**(250 mL) vegetable oil**

METHOD

1. In a blender, combine all ingredients except oil. Blend until mixture thickens.
2. On medium speed, add oil in a steady stream.
3. Transfer dressing to a glass bowl.
4. Cover with plastic wrap and refrigerate for 1 hour.
5. Serve with fresh fruit.

1½ cups (375 mL)

Variation:

- *Substitute balsamic, raspberry or other flavored vinegars for the cider vinegar.*

Approximate nutritional analysis per 1 tablespoon (15 mL) serving
Calories 94, Protein 0 g, Carbohydrates 3 g, Fat 9 g, Cholesterol 0 mg, Sodium 89 mg

Perfection Salad

Molded salad as pretty as a picture.

INGREDIENTS

½ cup	**(125 mL) cold water**
1 oz	**(30 g) unflavored gelatin**
3 cups	**(750 mL) boiling water**
¾ cup	**(175 mL) sugar**
1 tsp	**(5 mL) salt**
½ cup	**(125 mL) cider vinegar**
2 tbsp	**(30 mL) lemon juice**
2½ cups	**(625 mL) green cabbage, finely shredded**
¾ cup	**(175 mL) red cabbage, finely shredded**
½ cup	**(125 mL) green peppers, slivered**
½ cup	**(125 mL) red peppers, slivered**

METHOD

1. Place cold water in a large bowl.
2. Stir gelatin into water. Let mixture stand for 10 minutes to soften.
3. Add boiling water, sugar and salt to gelatin mixture.
4. Stir until mixture is clear and gelatin crystals dissolve. Allow mixture to cool.
5. Stir in vinegar and lemon juice.
6. Cover with plastic wrap and refrigerate until mixture begins to gel, but not set.
7. Fold remaining ingredients into gelatin mixture.
8. Pour mixture into 1 large or 6 individual molds.
9. Cover with plastic wrap and refrigerate for at least 2 hours.
10. To release salad from mold, run a spatula around edge of mold or dip mold in warm water for 10 seconds. Shake gently to release.
11. Serve with mayonnaise or cream dill dressing.

6 servings

Approximate nutritional analysis per serving
Calories 144, Protein 5 g, Carbohydrates 33 g, Fat 0 g, Cholesterol 0 mg, Sodium 373 mg

Perfection Salad

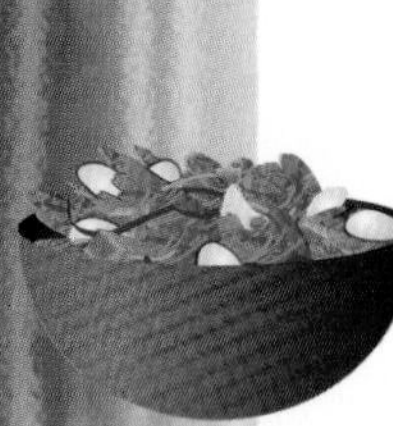

Exotic Fruit Salad

A mixture of tart and sweet tastes.

INGREDIENTS

4 tsp	**(20 mL) fresh lime juice**
pinch	**cayenne pepper**
½ cup	**(125 mL) papaya balls**
1 cup	**(250 mL) seedless red grapes, halved**
1 cup	**(250 mL) watermelon balls**
½ tsp	**(2 mL) lime peel, grated**

METHOD

1. In a small bowl, stir together lime juice and cayenne pepper.
2. In another bowl, combine papaya, grapes, watermelon and lime peel.
3. Pour dressing over salad and stir gently to combine.
4. Serve.

2 servings

◀ Approximate nutritional analysis per serving
Calories 100 Protein 1 g, Carbohydrates 25 g, Fat 1 g, Cholesterol 0 mg, Sodium 5 mg

Oriental Rice Salad

Peanuts add crunch to this rice salad.

INGREDIENTS

2 cups	**(500 mL) water**
1 tsp	**(5 mL) turmeric**
1 cup	**(250 mL) long grain converted rice, uncooked**
4 tbsp	**(60 mL) rice wine vinegar**
	salt and pepper
1 tbsp	**(15 mL) sesame oil**
½ cup	**(125 mL) salted peanuts**
⅓ cup	**(75 mL) fresh cilantro, chopped**
1 cup	**(250 mL) water chestnuts, sliced**

METHOD

1. In a medium saucepan, combine water, turmeric and rice. Bring to a boil over medium-high heat. Reduce heat to low.
2. Cover and cook for 15-20 minutes.
3. Remove rice from heat and allow to cool.
4. Stir in vinegar, salt and pepper.
5. Add oil, peanuts, cilantro and water chestnuts. Stir to combine thoroughly.
6. Cover tightly and chill in the refrigerator for at least 2 hours.
7. Serve cold.

4 servings

Approximate nutritional analysis per serving
Calories 326, Protein 8 g, Carbohydrates 45 g, Fat 13 g, Cholesterol 0 mg, Sodium 106 mg

Oriental Rice Salad

Molded Salmon Salad

Salmon, sour cream and dill are the stars in this masterpiece.

INGREDIENTS

15 oz	**(425 g) canned pink salmon, drained**
2 tbsp	**(30 mL) lemon juice**
2 tbsp	**(30 mL) ketchup**
1 tbsp	**(15 mL) tomato paste**
1 cup	**(250 mL) sour cream**
2 tbsp	**(30 mL) fresh dill, chopped**
2 tbsp	**(30 mL) onion, grated**
1 tbsp	**(15 mL) cider vinegar**
2	**envelopes unflavored gelatin**
1 cup	**(250 mL) whipping cream**
	salt and white pepper

Step 11. Pour salmon mixture into 1 large or 6 individual molds.

Step 13. To release salad from mold, run a spatula gently around edge of mold.

Step 14. Dip mold in warm water for 10 seconds.

METHOD

1. Remove bones and skin from salmon. Break salmon into pieces with a fork.
2. In a food processor, blend salmon and lemon juice.
3. Add ketchup and tomato paste to food processor. Purée until smooth. Transfer mixture to a medium bowl.
4. Fold sour cream, dill and onions into salmon mixture.
5. In a small bowl, combine vinegar with ½ cup (125 mL) of cold water.
6. Sprinkle gelatin over vinegar mixture. Let stand for 5 minutes to soften.
7. Place gelatin mixture over a pan of boiling water to dissolve all gelatin crystals.
8. Stir dissolved gelatin into salmon mixture.
9. In a medium bowl, beat whipping cream until it holds soft peaks.
10. Fold whipped cream into salmon mixture. Season with salt and pepper to taste.
11. Pour salmon mixture into 1 large or 6 individual molds.
12. Cover with plastic wrap and refrigerate for at least 2 hours.
13. To release salad from mold, run a spatula gently around edge of mold.
14. Dip mold in warm water for 10 seconds.
15. Shake mold gently to release salad onto a serving platter.

6 servings

Approximate nutritional analysis per serving
Calories 343, Protein 19 g, Carbohydrates 6 g, Fat 27 g, Cholesterol 113 mg, Sodium 245 mg

Molded Salmon Salad

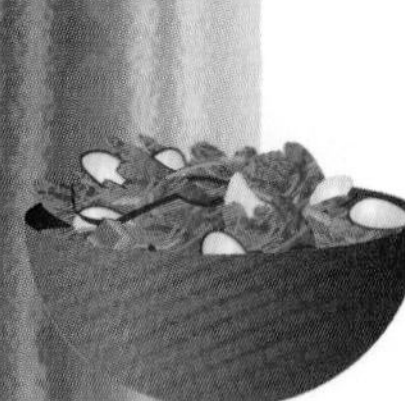

Artichoke and Watercress Salad

A light and delicious salad in minutes.

INGREDIENTS

1	**bunch watercress, washed thoroughly and drained**
6 oz	**(170 mL) marinated artichoke hearts, drained, marinade reserved**
2 tbsp	**(30 mL) capers**
½ cup	**(125 mL) red bell peppers, diced**

METHOD

1. Divide watercress onto 2 serving plates.
2. Arrange artichoke hearts on watercress.
3. Garnish with capers and peppers.
4. Dress with reserved artichoke marinade and serve.

2 servings

◀ Approximate nutritional analysis per serving
Calories 94, Protein 3 g, Carbohydrates 9 g, Fat 7 g, Cholesterol 0 mg, Sodium 774 mg

Shrimp and Carnation Salad

A sparkling blend of flavors in each bite.

INGREDIENTS

1 lb	**(450 g) cooked shrimp**
10 oz	**(284 mL) canned Mandarin orange segments, drained**
¼ cup	**(50 mL) red onions, diced**
¼ cup	**(50 mL) toasted, sliced almonds**
2 tbsp	**(30 mL) fresh lemon juice**
2 tbsp	**(30 mL) honey**
1 tsp	**(5 mL) toasted sesame seeds**
½ tsp	**(2 mL) ginger root, peeled and grated**
2	**carnations for garnish**
	mixed salad greens

METHOD

1. In a medium bowl, combine all ingredients except carnations and salad greens.
2. Divide shrimp mixture onto 4 serving plates.
3. Garnish with carnations and mixed salad greens. Serve.

4 servings

Variation:

- *Instead of using salad greens as a garnish, toss with shrimp mixture just before serving.*

Approximate nutritional analysis per serving
Calories 223, Protein 26 g, Carbohydrates 20 g, Fat 5 g, Cholesterol 221 mg, Sodium 270 mg

Shrimp and Carnation Salad

Coleslaw Vinaigrette

A refreshing, ever-popular favorite.

INGREDIENTS

4 cups	**(1 L) green cabbage, shredded**
2 cups	**(500 mL) red cabbage, shredded**
1	**large carrot, peeled and shredded**
1	**medium green pepper, cut into thin strips**
3	**scallions, chopped**
1 cup	**(250 mL) vegetable oil**
⅓ cup	**(75 mL) cider vinegar**
1 tsp	**(5 mL) Worcestershire sauce**
¼ tsp	**(1 mL) salt**
¼ tsp	**(1 mL) white pepper**
¼ tsp	**(1 mL) sugar**

METHOD

1. In a large bowl, toss together green cabbage, red cabbage, carrots, peppers and scallions.
2. In a small bowl, combine oil, vinegar, Worcestershire sauce, salt, pepper, and sugar.
3. Pour dressing over salad and toss lightly.
4. Serve immediately.

4 servings

Five Bean Salad

The perfect salad for your next picnic.

INGREDIENTS

10 oz	**(284 mL) canned kidney beans, drained**
10 oz	**(284 mL) canned chick peas, drained**
8 oz	**(225 g) yellow wax beans, cooked**
8 oz	**(225 g) cut green beans, cooked**
10 oz	**(284 mL) canned lima beans, drained**
1	**large red onion, diced**
1	**large red pepper, diced**
4	**celery stalks, small diced**
	salt and pepper
2 cups	**(500 mL) vegetable oil**
⅔ cup	**(150 mL) white wine vinegar**
2 tbsp	**(30 mL) grain mustard**

METHOD

1. In a large bowl, combine first eight ingredients. Season with salt and pepper to taste.
2. In a medium bowl, stir together oil, vinegar and mustard.
3. Pour dressing over salad. Combine gently.
4. Cover with plastic wrap and marinate in the refrigerator for 2 hours before serving.

10 servings

Approximate nutritional analysis per serving
Calories 498, Protein 6 g, Carbohydrates 21 g, Fat 45 g, Cholesterol 0 mg, Sodium 394 mg

◀ Approximate nutritional analysis per serving
Calories 535, Protein 2 g, Carbohydrates 13 g, Fat 55 g, Cholesterol 0 mg, Sodium 142 mg

Five Bean Salad

Grilled Scallops with Orange and Grapefruit

Delicate scallops and juicy citrus fruits complemented by a warm orange sauce.

INGREDIENTS

1 tsp	**(5 mL) garlic, minced**
1 tsp	**(5 mL) Dijon mustard**
1 tbsp	**(15 mL) white wine vinegar**
	salt and pepper
¼ cup	**(50 mL) olive oil**
2 tbsp	**(30 mL) butter**
4	**shallots, minced**
½ cup	**(125 mL) white wine**
⅓ cup	**(75 mL) orange juice**
1	**orange peel, blanched and julienned**
⅔ cup	**(150 mL) heavy cream**
12	**large scallops**
¼ cup	**(50 mL) flour, seasoned with salt and white pepper**
1 tbsp	**(15 mL) vegetable oil**
8 cups	**(2 L) mixed salad greens**
1	**orange, peeled and segmented**
1	**grapefruit, peeled and segmented**

METHOD

1. Preheat broiler.
2. In a small bowl, whisk together garlic, mustard, vinegar, salt and pepper.
3. Add olive oil and whisk dressing until emulsified.
4. In a saucepan, heat butter over medium heat.
5. Add shallots and cook for 2 minutes until soft.
6. Add wine, orange juice and half the orange peel. Boil mixture, stirring constantly, until reduced to ½ cup (125 mL).
7. Reduce heat to low. Add cream and reduce to 1 cup (250 mL).
8. Remove from heat. Cover sauce with a lid and keep warm.
9. Dust scallops with seasoned flour.
10. Brush scallops with oil. Place on a baking sheet.
11. Broil scallops for 4-5 minutes until just firm. Do not overcook.
12. Toss salad greens with dressing and arrange on 4 plates.
13. Place scallops on salad greens. Pour warm orange sauce on top of scallops.
14. Garnish with orange and grapefruit segments.
15. Sprinkle with remaining orange peel and serve.

4 servings

Approximate nutritional analysis per serving
Calories 489, Protein 10 g, Carbohydrates 25 g, Fat 38 g, Cholesterol 81 mg, Sodium 176 mg

Grilled Scallops with Orange and Grapefruit

Vegetable Medley in Watercress Dressing

A light and tangy summer salad.

INGREDIENTS

Watercress Dressing

3 tbsp	**(45 mL) olive oil**
1½ tsp	**(7 mL) fresh lemon juice**
1 tsp	**(5 mL) tarragon vinegar**
½ tsp	**(2 mL) Dijon mustard**
pinch	**tarragon**
¼ cup	**(50 mL) watercress leaves, minced**
	salt and black pepper
½ cup	**(125 mL) zucchini, julienned**
½ cup	**(125 mL) carrots, peeled and julienned**
½ cup	**(125 mL) radishes, julienned**

METHOD

1. In a small bowl, whisk together all dressing ingredients.
2. Place zucchini, carrots and radishes in a medium bowl.
3. Add dressing to vegetables and toss together.
4. Refrigerate for 1 hour.
5. Place on 4 plates and serve.

4 servings

Baby Shrimp with Vegetable Julienne

An elegant dish your guests will love.

INGREDIENTS

½ cup	**(125 mL) dry white wine**
1	**medium leek, thinly sliced**
4 oz	**(115 g) cooked baby shrimp**
½	**celery root, peeled and cut into thin strips**
8	**medium, white mushroom caps, thinly sliced**
1 tbsp	**(15 mL) lemon juice**
14 oz	**(398 mL) canned, marinated artichoke hearts, drained**
1	**medium red pepper, thinly sliced**
	fresh chives, chopped
	fresh tarragon, chopped

METHOD

1. Place wine and leeks in a medium saucepan.
2. Poach leeks over medium heat for 5-6 minutes, until leeks are soft. Remove leeks with a slotted spoon and reserve.
3. Bring cooking liquid to a boil. Remove saucepan from heat.
4. Stir shrimp into saucepan. Allow to cool in cooking liquid.
5. In a medium bowl, toss together celery root, mushrooms and lemon juice.
6. Add artichokes, peppers and reserved leeks.
7. Remove shrimp from liquid and add to salad. Combine well.
8. Divide salad onto 4 plates.
9. Garnish with chives and tarragon. Serve.

4 servings

Approximate nutritional analysis per serving
Calories 201, Protein 11 g, Carbohydrates 19 g, Fat 9 g, Cholesterol 49 mg, Sodium 598 mg

◀ Approximate nutritional analysis per serving
Calories 103, Protein 1 g, Carbohydrates 3 g, Fat 10 g, Cholesterol 0 mg, Sodium 26 mg

Baby Shrimp with Vegetable Julienne

Southern Pork Salad

A meal in itself, this combination of yams, pork and apples is hard to resist.

INGREDIENTS

3 tbsp	**(45 mL) Dijon mustard**
3 tbsp	**(45 mL) molasses**
3 tbsp	**(45 mL) bourbon**
¼ tsp	**(1 mL) hot pepper sauce**
1½ lbs	**(675 g) boneless pork chops**
2	**medium yams, peeled and sliced**
½ cup	**(125 mL) lime juice**
1 tbsp	**(15 mL) shallots, minced**
1 tbsp	**(15 mL) fresh parsley, chopped**
	salt and black pepper
½ cup	**(125 mL) vegetable oil**
1	**small romaine lettuce head**
2 cups	**(500 mL) red cabbage, shredded**
2	**small apples, peeled, cored, and cut into cubes or wedges**

METHOD

1. In a medium glass bowl, combine 1½ tbsp (25 mL) mustard, 1½ tbsp (25 mL) molasses, 1½ tbsp (25 mL) bourbon and ⅛ tsp (0.5 mL) hot pepper sauce.
2. Add pork chops and yams, tossing to coat with marinade.
3. Cover with plastic wrap and refrigerate for 2 hours.
4. Heat grill.
5. Drain marinade from pork chops and yams. Discard marinade.
6. Grill pork chops and yams until cooked, about 7-8 minutes per side. Cool.
7. In a small, glass bowl, combine remaining mustard, molasses, bourbon and hot pepper sauce with lime juice, shallots, parsley, salt and pepper to make a dressing.
8. Slowly whisk oil into dressing.
9. Cut pork chops into thin strips and place in a large bowl.
10. Add yams and dressing, tossing to combine.
11. Cut lettuce into bite-sized pieces. Add to salad.
12. Add cabbage and apples, tossing gently to combine.
13. Serve immediately.

6 servings

Tip:

- *This salad may be prepared the night before, but do not add the romaine lettuce until just before serving.*

Approximate nutritional analysis per serving
Calories 554, Protein 35 g, Carbohydrates 34 g, Fat 30 g, Cholesterol 90 mg, Sodium 624 mg

Southern Pork Salad

Carrot, Radish and Chive Salad

Serve this at your next family barbecue.

INGREDIENTS

1 lb	**(450 g) carrots, peeled and grated**
12 oz	**(340 g) radishes, grated**
3 tbsp	**(45 mL) fresh lemon juice**
1 tsp	**(5 mL) sugar**
	salt and pepper
½ cup	**(125 mL) olive oil**
4 tbsp	**(60 mL) fresh chives, chopped**

METHOD

1. In a medium bowl, toss together carrots and radishes.
2. In a small bowl, whisk together lemon juice, sugar, salt and pepper to taste.
3. Continuing to whisk dressing, add oil in a stream. Whisk until emulsified.
4. Stir chives into dressing.
5. Pour dressing over salad. Toss together and serve.

6 servings

Tip:

- *This salad may be marinated in the refrigerator for 2 hours before serving.*

◀ Approximate nutritional analysis per serving
Calories 48, Protein 1 g, Carbohydrates 11 g, Fat 1 g, Cholesterol 0 mg, Sodium 106 mg

Sweet Potato and Parsley Salad

A satisfying blend of flavors.

INGREDIENTS

6	**sweet potatoes**
⅓ cup	**(75 mL) olive oil**
½ cup	**(125 mL) fresh parsley, chopped**
2 tbsp	**(30 mL) lemon juice**
1 tbsp	**(15 mL) light soy sauce**
1 tbsp	**(15 mL) fresh chives, chopped**
	salt and pepper
1	**medium onion, small diced**
2	**celery stalks, small diced**
½ cup	**(125 mL) roasted cashew nuts**

METHOD

1. Place sweet potatoes in a large saucepan. Cover with cold water.
2. Bring to a boil over medium-high heat. Reduce heat to medium.
3. Cook sweet potatoes until they are just tender, about 30-40 minutes.
4. Drain sweet potatoes and allow to cool.
5. Peel sweet potatoes and slice or dice. Place in a serving dish.
6. In a small bowl, combine oil, parsley, lemon juice, soy sauce, chives, salt and pepper.
7. Add onions and celery to sweet potatoes.
8. Pour dressing over vegetables and toss together.
9. Garnish with cashew nuts and serve.

6 servings

Approximate nutritional analysis per serving
Calories 301, Protein 4 g, Carbohydrates 34 g, Fat 17 g, Cholesterol 0 mg, Sodium 177 mg

Sweet Potato and Parsley Salad

Roma Tomato Dijon Salad

Fresh tasting and simple to prepare.

INGREDIENTS

¼ cup	**(50 mL) vegetable oil**
1 tbsp	**(15 mL) cider vinegar**
2 tsp	**(10 mL) dark brown sugar**
1½ tsp	**(7 mL) Dijon mustard**
	salt and pepper
4	**large Roma tomatoes**
4	**scallions, chopped**

METHOD

1. In a small bowl, whisk together oil, vinegar, brown sugar and mustard.
2. Season with salt and pepper to taste.
3. Slice tomatoes and arrange on a serving plate.
4. Pour dressing over tomatoes.
5. Garnish with scallions and serve.

4 servings

◀ Approximate nutritional analysis per serving
Calories 150, Protein 1 g, Carbohydrates 6 g, Fat 14 g, Cholesterol 0 mg, Sodium 152 mg

Minted Squash and Apple Salad

Mint adds a special touch to this salad.

INGREDIENTS

¼ cup	**(50 mL) currants**
2 tbsp	**(30 mL) Madeira wine**
1½ lbs	**(675 g) Granny Smith apples**
½ lb	**(225 g) zucchini**
½ lb	**(225 g) chayote squash**
2 tbsp	**(30 mL) lemon juice**
1 lb	**(450 g) Swiss cheese, cut into ¼-inch (0.6 cm) strips**
2	**medium red onions, thinly sliced**
¼ cup	**(50 mL) virgin olive oil**
¼ cup	**(50 mL) red wine vinegar**
	salt and pepper
¼ cup	**(50 mL) fresh mint leaves, minced**

METHOD

1. Place currants and Madeira in a small bowl. Cover with plastic wrap and refrigerate overnight.
2. Remove cores from apples, and peel, if desired.
3. Dice apples, zucchini and squash or cut into baton shapes. Place in a medium bowl.
4. Add lemon juice and toss together.
5. Add cheese and onions to apple mixture. Combine well.
6. In a medium bowl, whisk together oil, vinegar, salt and pepper.
7. Drain currants and discard marinade.
8. Stir currants and mint into dressing. Pour dressing over salad and toss gently.
9. Serve at room temperature.

6 servings

Approximate nutritional analysis per serving
Calories 480, Protein 24 g, Carbohydrates 30 g, Fat 30 g, Cholesterol 69 mg, Sodium 208 mg

Minted Squash and Apple Salad

Rose Petal Salad

A unique, dramatic luncheon salad.

INGREDIENTS

¼ cup	**(50 mL) rose water**
¼ cup	**(50 mL) honey**
¼ cup	**(50 mL) lemon juice**
6	**roses, different colors**
½ cup	**(125 mL) walnuts, chopped**
3	**celery stalks, thinly sliced**

METHOD

1. In a small bowl, combine rose water, honey and lemon juice.
2. Remove petals from 3 roses. Cut each petal into 3 pieces.
3. In a medium bowl, toss cut petals, walnuts and celery with dressing.
4. Divide mixture onto 4 plates.
5. Remove petals from remaining 3 roses.
6. Sprinkle petals on edges and tops of salads. Serve.

4 servings

Tip:

- *Rose water is available at most pharmacies.*

Zesty Potato Salad

Red peppers add color to this favorite.

INGREDIENTS

¼ cup	**(50 mL) vegetable oil**
2 tbsp	**(30 mL) white wine vinegar**
2 cups	**(500 mL) cooked potatoes, diced**
2	**hard-boiled eggs, chopped**
1 tbsp	**(15 mL) green onions, chopped**
1 tbsp	**(15 mL) fresh parsley, chopped**
1 tbsp	**(15 mL) red peppers, chopped**
1 tsp	**(5 mL) salt**
1 tsp	**(5 mL) white pepper**

METHOD

1. In a medium bowl, combine oil and vinegar.
2. Stir in potatoes and eggs. Cover with plastic wrap and refrigerate for 1 hour.
3. Stir in remaining ingredients with a wooden spoon.
4. Garnish with chopped parsley, diced pickles, sliced hard-boiled eggs or red peppers.
5. Serve cold.

4 servings

Approximate nutritional analysis per serving
Calories 207, Protein 4 g, Carbohydrates 11 g, Fat 16 g, Cholesterol 106 mg, Sodium 749 mg

◀ Approximate nutritional analysis per serving
Calories 166, Protein 2 g, Carbohydrates 22 g, Fat 9 g, Cholesterol 0 mg, Sodium 19 mg

Zesty Potato Salad

Fresh and Sun-Dried Tomatoes with Squash

A lovely marinated tomato salad.

INGREDIENTS

1 lb	**(450 g) fresh Roma tomatoes, cut into wedges**
½ lb	**(225 g) baby butternut squash, cut into rounds**
6	**sun-dried tomato halves**
2 tbsp	**(30 mL) olive oil**
2 tsp	**(10 mL) balsamic vinegar**
½ tsp	**(2 mL) salt**
¼ tsp	**(1 mL) black pepper**

METHOD

1. Toss all ingredients together in a medium bowl.
2. Marinate at room temperature for 1 hour.
3. Divide mixture onto 4 plates and serve.

4 servings

Mosaic Chicken Salad

A delightful salad for any occasion.

INGREDIENTS

4 cups	**(1 L) cooked chicken, diced**
1 cup	**(250 mL) celery, sliced**
⅓ cup	**(75 mL) mayonnaise**
2 tbsp	**(30 mL) lemon juice**
2 tsp	**(10 mL) onions, grated**
1 tsp	**(5 mL) salt**
1	**romaine or butter lettuce head**
1 cup	**(250 mL) cantaloupe balls**
1 cup	**(250 mL) seedless grapes**
¼ cup	**(50 mL) toasted, slivered almonds**

METHOD

1. In a large bowl, combine chicken, celery, mayonnaise, lemon juice, onions and salt. Mix gently.
2. Cover with plastic wrap and refrigerate for 1 hour.
3. Separate lettuce leaves. Wash, dry and refrigerate leaves for 1 hour.
4. Divide lettuce onto 6 plates.
5. Arrange chicken mixture on top of lettuce.
6. Garnish with cantaloupe and grapes.
7. Sprinkle almonds on top and serve.

6 servings

Approximate nutritional analysis per serving
Calories 263, Protein 24 g, Carbohydrates 11 g, Fat 14 g, Cholesterol 62 mg, Sodium 511 mg

◀ Approximate nutritional analysis per serving
Calories 136, Protein 4 g, Carbohydrates 17 g, Fat 8 g, Cholesterol 0 mg, Sodium 593 mg

Mosaic Chicken Salad

Radish Sesame Salad

Sesame seeds add sparkle to this salad.

INGREDIENTS

6 oz	**(170 g) radishes, grated**
2 tbsp	**(30 mL) cider vinegar**
2 tsp	**(10 mL) sugar**
2 tbsp	**(30 mL) light soy sauce**
1 tsp	**(5 mL) sesame oil**
2 tbsp	**(30 mL) toasted sesame seeds**

METHOD

1. In a plastic container with a lid, combine radishes, vinegar, sugar, soy sauce and oil.
2. Place lid on container and shake ingredients together.
3. Refrigerate overnight.
4. Place salad on a serving plate.
5. Sprinkle with sesame seeds and serve.

4 servings

Lentil, Rice and Bean Sprout Salad

Wholesome goodness in every bite.

INGREDIENTS

⅔ cup	**(150 mL) red lentils**
⅓ cup	**(75 mL) olive oil**
¼ cup	**(50 mL) malt vinegar**
	salt and pepper
⅔ cup	**(150 mL) long grain converted rice, uncooked**
3 cups	**(750 mL) bean sprouts**
3 tbsp	**(45 mL) fresh parsley, chopped**
2 tbsp	**(30 mL) fresh dill, chopped**
1 tbsp	**(15 mL) lemon juice**

METHOD

1. In a medium saucepan, combine lentils with 1½ cups (375 mL) of water.
2. Cook lentils for 20-30 minutes over medium-low heat, until lentils are tender. Do not overcook.
3. Drain lentils and transfer to a medium bowl.
4. Add oil and vinegar to lentils. Season to taste with salt and pepper.
5. Cover lentil mixture with plastic wrap and refrigerate for 1 hour.
6. Cook rice according to package directions. Drain and cool for about 20 minutes.
7. Transfer rice to a medium bowl. Separate rice grains with a fork.
8. Add lentil mixture to rice.
9. Stir remaining ingredients into rice and lentil mixture, combining well.
10. Season with salt and pepper to taste. Serve.

4 servings

Approximate nutritional analysis per serving
Calories 407, Protein 14 g, Carbohydrates 48 g, Fat 19 g, Cholesterol 0 mg, Sodium 113 mg

◄ Approximate nutritional analysis per serving
Calories 60, Protein 2 g, Carbohydrates 6 g, Fat 4 g, Cholesterol 0 mg, Sodium 263 mg

Lentil, Rice and Bean Sprout Salad

Tomatillo Rice Salad

Papaya, mint and tomatillos are the colorful ingredients in this tasty rice salad.

INGREDIENTS

4	**fresh tomatillos**
3 cups	**(750 mL) long grain converted rice, cooked**
	salt and black pepper
1	**large papaya, peeled and diced**
1 tbsp	**(15 mL) fresh mint leaves, chopped**
2	**garlic cloves, unpeeled**
1 tbsp	**(15 mL) ginger root, peeled and grated**
1 tbsp	**(15 mL) sugar**
3 tbsp	**(45 mL) lime juice**
1 tsp	**(5 mL) sesame oil**
1 tsp	**(5 mL) light soy sauce**

Step 1. Remove husks from tomatillos.

Step 3. Pierce tomatillos once or twice with a sharp, pointed knife.

Step 7. Using a melon baller, remove white cores from tomatillos and discard.

METHOD

1. Remove husks from tomatillos.
2. Rinse tomatillos under cold water to remove sticky coating. Dry thoroughly.
3. Pierce tomatillos once or twice with a sharp, pointed knife.
4. Line a heavy skillet with aluminum foil. Place tomatillos in skillet.
5. Cook over medium-high heat until tomatillos are blackened in spots, about 6-8 minutes. Remove from heat.
6. Cut tomatillos in half.
7. Using a melon baller, remove white cores from tomatillos and discard.
8. Dice tomatillos and place in a large bowl.
9. Add rice, salt, pepper, papaya and mint, stirring to combine.
10. Cut garlic cloves in half and place in skillet.
11. Roast garlic over medium heat for 3-4 minutes, turning frequently.
12. When garlic is soft, remove from heat and peel.
13. In a food processor, blend garlic, ginger and sugar. Pureé until smooth.
14. Add lime juice, oil and soy sauce. Process until dressing is well blended.
15. Add dressing to rice mixture, tossing to combine.
16. Cover with plastic wrap and refrigerate for 1 hour before serving.

6 servings

Approximate nutritional analysis per serving
Calories 185, Protein 4 g, Carbohydrates 39 g, Fat 1 g, Cholesterol 0 mg, Sodium 104 mg

Tomatillo Rice Salad

Soups

Ham and Lentil Soup

A wholesome and hearty soup. Perfect on a winter evening.

INGREDIENTS

1	**medium red pepper, chopped**
4	**orange peel strips**
1 tbsp	**(15 mL) olive oil**
2	**garlic cloves, chopped**
1	**large onion, chopped**
1 lb	**(450 g) smoked ham or smoked pork jowl**
3 cups	**(750 mL) chicken broth**
4 cups	**(1 L) water**
½ lb	**(225 g) lentils, rinsed**
¼ cup	**(50 mL) fresh parsley, chopped**
2 tsp	**(10 mL) salt**
1 tsp	**(5 mL) black pepper**
½ cup	**(125 mL) plain yogurt or sour cream**
4 oz	**(115 g) smoked ham, diced, for garnish**

Sachet

1	**bay leaf**
1	**fresh thyme sprig**
4	**fresh parsley stems**
2	**whole cloves**

METHOD

1. Reserve 4 tsp (20 mL) peppers and 1 orange peel strip for garnish.
2. In a heavy saucepan, heat oil over medium heat. Reduce heat to low.
3. Cook remaining peppers, garlic and onions for 5 minutes, until soft.
4. Place sachet ingredients in a cheesecloth. Tie with string.
5. Add sachet, ham and remaining orange peel to saucepan.
6. Stir in chicken broth, water and lentils.
7. Bring mixture to a boil. Reduce heat to low.
8. Cook for 1 hour, until lentils are very soft.
9. Using a slotted spoon, remove ham from soup and discard.
10. Remove sachet.
11. Pour soup into a food processor. Purée soup until it has a smooth texture, adding more chicken broth if soup is too thick.
12. Return soup to saucepan. Cook over medium heat until soup is heated through.
13. Stir in parsley and season with salt and pepper.
14. Cut reserved orange peel into thin strips.
15. Blanch orange peel in boiling water for 30 seconds.
16. Cut reserved peppers into strips.
17. Ladle soup into serving bowls.
18. Garnish with yogurt, orange peel strips, red peppers and ham.

8 servings

Approximate nutritional analysis per serving
Calories 283, Protein 29 g, Carbohydrates 21 g, Fat 9 g, Cholesterol 43 mg, Sodium 1771 mg

Ham and Lentil Soup

Chilled Melon Soup

Cool, refreshing and so smooth.

INGREDIENTS

1	**medium, ripe honeydew or casaba melon**
2 tbsp	**(30 mL) lemon juice**
¼ tsp	**(1 mL) salt**
¼ tsp	**(1 mL) freshly ground pepper**
¼ tsp	**(1 mL) nutmeg, grated**
½ cup	**(125 mL) apple or orange juice**

METHOD

1. Peel melon and remove seeds.
2. Cut melon into 1-inch (2.5 cm) chunks.
3. In a food processor, purée melon, lemon juice, salt, pepper and nutmeg.
4. If soup appears too thick, add apple juice to adjust consistency.
5. Transfer soup to a medium bowl. Refrigerate for 2 hours.
6. Serve soup chilled.

4 servings

Variation:

- *Add 1 oz (30 mL) cognac to purée just before refrigeration.*

Hearty Corn Soup

A tasty meal in itself.

INGREDIENTS

2 tbsp	**(30 mL) vegetable oil**
1	**carrot, peeled and chopped**
1	**celery stalk, chopped**
1	**medium onion, chopped**
1	**garlic clove, minced**
1	**small bay leaf**
pinch	**saffron threads**
12 oz	**(341 mL) canned whole kernel corn, drained**
4 cups	**(1 L) chicken broth**
1 tsp	**(5 mL) salt**
¼ tsp	**(1 mL) white pepper**
¼ tsp	**(1 mL) cayenne pepper**
¼ cup	**(50 mL) fresh parsley, chopped**

METHOD

1. In a large saucepan, heat oil over medium heat.
2. Place carrots, celery, onions, garlic, bay leaf and saffron in saucepan. Cook for 10 minutes, until vegetables are soft.
3. Stir in corn and chicken broth. Bring to a boil. Reduce heat to low.
4. Simmer soup for 5 minutes, until corn is very tender.
5. Remove bay leaf from soup.
6. Place soup in a food processor and purée.
7. Return soup to saucepan. Cook over medium heat until soup is heated through.
8. Add salt, pepper and cayenne pepper to taste.
9. Stir parsley into soup.
10. Serve hot with bread sticks.

6 servings

Approximate nutritional analysis per serving
Calories 149, Protein 9 g, Carbohydrates 15 g, Fat 7 g, Cholesterol 2 mg, Sodium 1497 mg

◄ Approximate nutritional analysis per serving
Calories 124, Protein 4 g, Carbohydrates 30 g, Fat 1 g, Cholesterol 0 mg, Sodium 185 mg

Hearty Corn Soup

Carrot Orange Soup

A picture perfect combination of colors and flavors.

INGREDIENTS

¼ cup	**(50 mL) butter**
2 cups	**(500 mL) onions, chopped**
1½ lbs	**(675 g) carrots, peeled and diced**
4 cups	**(1 L) chicken broth**
1 cup	**(250 mL) orange juice**
1 tbsp	**(15 mL) orange liqueur**
1 tsp	**(5 mL) salt**
½ tsp	**(2 mL) pepper**
½ cup	**(125 mL) whipping cream, lightly beaten**

Step 15. Draw the back edge of a small knife through cream.

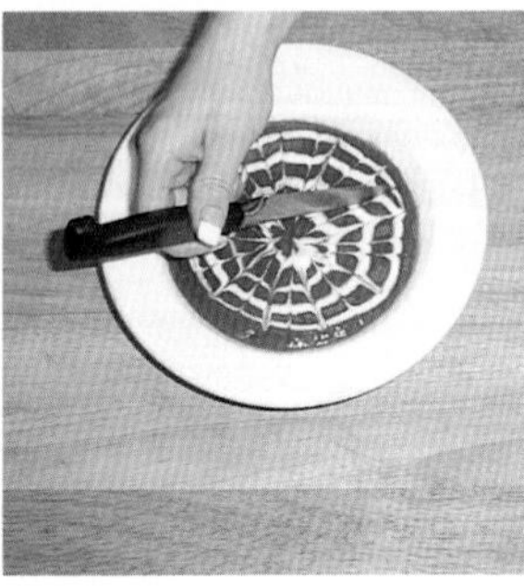

Step 16. Continue drawing with the knife until desired pattern has been created.

METHOD

1. In a large saucepan, heat butter over medium heat.
2. Add onions to saucepan. Reduce heat to low.
3. Simmer onions for 15 minutes, until soft and golden in color.
4. Add carrots and chicken broth. Bring to a boil.
5. Cover and reduce heat to low.
6. Simmer for 30 minutes, until carrots are tender.
7. Drain vegetables, reserving cooking liquid.
8. In a food processor, purée vegetables along with 2 cups (500 mL) of the cooking liquid.
9. Return pureé to saucepan. Stir in remaining cooking liquid.
10. Stir in orange juice, orange liqueur, salt and pepper.
11. Cook over medium heat, until heated through.
12. Pour soup into serving bowls.
13. Place whipped cream into a piping bag with a small tube tip.
14. Pipe a decorative pattern on top of each bowl of soup.
15. Draw the back edge of a small knife through cream.
16. Continue drawing with the knife until desired pattern has been created.
17. Serve hot with baking powder biscuits or corn bread thins.

6 servings

Approximate nutritional analysis per serving
Calories 288, Protein 9 g, Carbohydrates 24 g, Fat 17 g, Cholesterol 49 mg, Sodium 1352 mg

Carrot Orange Soup

Cold Cucumber Mint Soup

The perfect soup for a hot summer day.

INGREDIENTS

4	**small English cucumbers**
1 cup	**(250 mL) buttermilk**
½ cup	**(125 mL) plain yogurt**
2 tsp	**(10 mL) fresh lemon juice**
1 tbsp	**(15 mL) fresh mint leaves, minced**
2 tsp	**(10 mL) red peppers, chopped**

METHOD

1. Peel, seed and coarsely chop 3 cucumbers.
2. Place chopped cucumbers in a food processor. Purée until smooth.
3. Add buttermilk and yogurt. Purée mixture for 20 more seconds.
4. Stir in lemon juice.
5. Transfer soup to a medium bowl.
6. Peel, seed, and finely dice remaining cucumber.
7. Add diced cucumbers and mint to purée. Stir to combine.
8. Cover with plastic wrap and refrigerate for 2 hours, until soup is well chilled.
9. Ladle soup into chilled serving bowls.
10. Garnish with red peppers and serve.

6 servings

Spring Vegetable Soup

Tender vegetables with a hint of curry.

INGREDIENTS

4 cups	**(1 L) chicken broth**
1	**small leek**
½ cup	**(125 mL) carrots, peeled and thinly sliced**
4 oz	**(115 g) spinach leaves**
¾ cup	**(175 mL) frozen peas**
½ cup	**(125 mL) whipping cream**
2	**large egg yolks**
½ tsp	**(2 mL) curry powder**
¼ tsp	**(1 mL) allspice**
1 tsp	**(5 mL) salt**
1 tsp	**(5 mL) black pepper**

METHOD

1. Place chicken broth in a large saucepan. Bring to a boil.
2. Trim root and leaves from leek, leaving only white stalk.
3. Chop stalk into thin slices.
4. Add carrots and leeks to chicken broth. Reduce heat to medium.
5. Cook for 7-8 minutes, until vegetables are tender.
6. Roll spinach leaves together into a cigar shape. Slice thinly.
7. Add spinach and peas to broth.
8. Cook for 2 minutes. Remove from heat.
9. In a small bowl, combine cream, egg yolks, curry, allspice, salt and pepper.
10. Stir cream mixture into soup.
11. Return saucepan to heat. Cook gently over low heat to heat through. Do not boil.
12. Adjust seasoning to taste.
13. Serve with fresh, warm bread.

6 servings

Approximate nutritional analysis per serving
Calories 173, Protein 10 g, Carbohydrates 10 g, Fat 11 g, Cholesterol 100 mg, Sodium 1355 mg

◀ Approximate nutritional analysis per serving
Calories 64, Protein 4 g, Carbohydrates 10 g, Fat 1 g, Cholesterol 4 mg, Sodium 65 mg

Spring Vegetable Soup

Southwest Salsa Cream Soup

Captures the warmth of the sun.

INGREDIENTS

3 tbsp	**(45 mL) butter**
1	**red onion, chopped**
2	**garlic cloves, minced**
1 tsp	**(5 mL) cumin**
1 tsp	**(5 mL) black pepper**
2 cups	**(500 mL) medium hot salsa**
3 cups	**(750 mL) half and half cream**
¼ cup	**(50 mL) Cheddar cheese, grated**

METHOD

1. In a skillet, melt butter over medium heat.
2. Add onions and garlic. Cook until onions are soft, about 5 minutes.
3. Stir in cumin and pepper. Remove from heat.
4. Place salsa in a large saucepan. Heat over medium heat. Do not boil.
5. Add onion mixture to salsa, stirring to combine.
6. In a saucepan, heat cream over medium heat. Do not allow cream to boil.
7. Stir cream into salsa mixture.
8. Pour soup into serving bowls.
9. Garnish with cheese and serve.

4 servings

Minted Pea Soup

The perfect start to a memorable meal.

INGREDIENTS

3 tbsp	**(45 mL) butter**
1	**medium onion, chopped**
3½ cups	**(875 mL) chicken broth**
1	**large potato, chopped**
3½ cups	**(875 mL) frozen peas**
3 tbsp	**(45 mL) fresh parsley, chopped**
3 tbsp	**(45 mL) fresh mint leaves, chopped**
1 cup	**(250 mL) water**
½ tsp	**(2 mL) black pepper**
¼ cup	**(50 mL) whipping cream, lightly beaten**

METHOD

1. In a large saucepan, melt butter over medium heat.
2. Cook onions for 3 minutes, until just softened.
3. Add chicken broth and potatoes. Bring to a boil.
4. Cover and reduce heat to low. Cook for 10 minutes, until potatoes are cooked.
5. Add peas. Simmer, uncovered, for 3 minutes, until peas are tender.
6. Stir in parsley and mint.
7. Transfer soup to a food processor, and purée.
8. Return soup to saucepan. Stir in water and season with pepper.
9. Cook over medium heat for 3 minutes to blend flavors.
10. Garnish with cream and serve.

4 servings

Approximate nutritional analysis per serving
Calories 359, Protein 19 g, Carbohydrates 34 g, Fat 17 g, Cholesterol 46 mg, Sodium 1506 mg

◄ Approximate nutritional analysis per serving
Calories 423, Protein 4 g, Carbohydrates 14 g, Fat 39 g, Cholesterol 130 mg, Sodium 845 mg

Minted Pea Soup

Cheddar Cheese Vegetable Chowder

Savor the creamy goodness of this chowder by the fire-side.

INGREDIENTS

¼ cup	**(50 mL) vegetable oil**
1	**large onion, chopped**
1	**large red pepper, small diced**
1 lb	**(450 g) potatoes, peeled and diced into ¼-inch (0.6 cm) cubes**
1 lb	**(450 g) zucchini, diced**
10 oz	**(285 g) whole kernel corn, drained**
⅓ cup	**(75 mL) all-purpose flour**
4 cups	**(1 L) chicken broth**
2 cups	**(500 mL) milk**
¼ tsp	**(1 mL) cayenne pepper**
1 tsp	**(5 mL) Worcestershire sauce**
2½ cups	**(625 mL) extra old Cheddar cheese, grated**

METHOD

1. In a large saucepan, heat oil over medium heat.
2. Cook onions for 8-10 minutes, stirring frequently, until onions are soft.
3. Add peppers and continue cooking for 4 minutes, stirring occasionally.
4. Add potatoes, zucchini and corn. Cook for an additional 6 minutes.
5. Stir in flour. Cook for 4 minutes, stirring frequently.
6. Add chicken broth, milk, cayenne pepper and Worcestershire sauce, stirring to combine.
7. Bring chowder to a boil over medium-high heat. Reduce heat to low.
8. Add cheese in small amounts, melting cheese after each addition. Do not boil soup or cheese will separate.
9. Serve hot with biscuits or bread.

10 servings

Approximate nutritional analysis per serving
Calories 301, Protein 15 g, Carbohydrates 21 g, Fat 18 g, Cholesterol 37 mg, Sodium 985 mg

Cheddar Cheese Vegetable Chowder

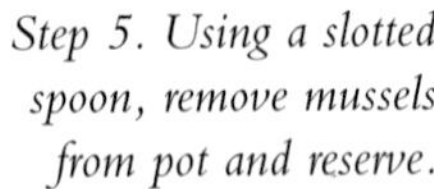

Salmon Mussel Chowder

A delicate blend of flavors makes this velvety-smooth chowder unforgettable.

INGREDIENTS

2 tbsp	**(30 mL) butter**
1	**leek, julienned**
1 tsp	**(5 mL) salt**
2 lbs	**(900 g) mussels, scrubbed and bearded**
1 cup	**(250 mL) dry white wine**
1	**potato, peeled and diced into ¼-inch (0.6 cm) pieces**
2 cups	**(500 mL) heavy cream**
2 cups	**(500 mL) milk**
2 tbsp	**(30 mL) fresh basil, minced**
¼ tsp	**(1 mL) saffron threads**
½ lb	**(225 g) salmon fillets, diced into ¼-inch (0.6 cm) pieces**
1 tsp	**(5 mL) black pepper**

METHOD

1. In a large saucepan, melt butter over medium heat.
2. Add leeks and salt. Cook for 10 minutes, until leeks are soft.
3. Place mussels and wine in a large stockpot. Cover.
4. Bring to a boil over medium-high heat. Steam mussels for 4 minutes, until shells are barely open.
5. Using a slotted spoon, remove mussels from pot and reserve.
6. Strain cooking liquid through several layers of cheesecloth. Reserve liquid.
7. Add potatoes and strained broth to leek mixture. Simmer over low heat for 15 minutes.
8. Stir in cream, milk, basil and saffron. Simmer chowder for an additional 10 minutes.
9. Remove mussels from their shells.
10. Add mussels and salmon to chowder. Cook gently for 5 minutes.
11. Season to taste with pepper.
12. Serve hot with bread.

8 servings

Step 5. Using a slotted spoon, remove mussels from pot and reserve.

Step 6. Strain cooking liquid through several layers of cheesecloth. Reserve liquid.

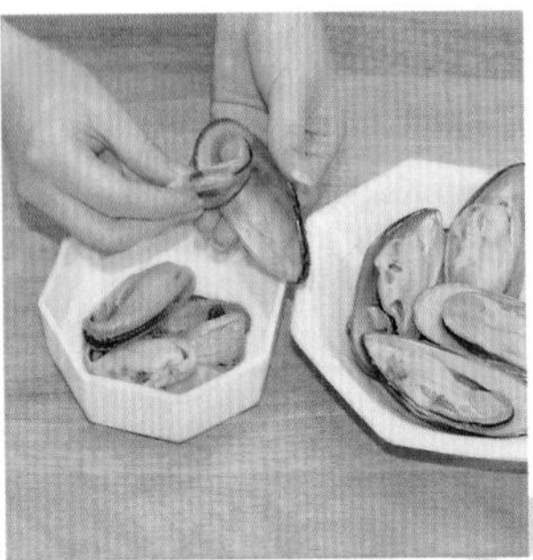

Step 9. Remove mussels from their shells.

Approximate nutritional analysis per serving
Calories 453, Protein 23 g, Carbohydrates 15 g, Fat 31 g, Cholesterol 145 mg, Sodium 661 mg

Salmon Mussel Chowder

Island-Style Fish Soup

Cool avocado slices are an enticing addition to this Caribbean soup.

INGREDIENTS

3 tbsp	**(45 mL) vegetable oil**
2	**garlic cloves, crushed**
1	**medium onion, sliced**
1	**small red pepper, sliced**
1	**small green pepper, sliced**
2 cups	**(500 mL) canned fish stock**
1 lb	**(450 g) red snapper fillets**
¼ cup	**(50 mL) fresh lime juice**
2 tbsp	**(30 mL) all-purpose flour**
¾ cup	**(175 mL) water**
	salt and black pepper
1	**avocado, not overripe, chilled**
1	**lime, cut into wedges**
	hot pepper sauce

METHOD

1. In a saucepan, heat oil over medium heat.
2. Add garlic, onions, red peppers and green peppers.
3. Cook for 5 minutes, until vegetables are soft.
4. Add fish stock to saucepan. Simmer gently for 5 minutes.
5. Cut red snapper into 1-inch (2.5 cm) cubes.
6. Place red snapper in saucepan. Cook for 3 minutes, until fish is opaque.
7. Add lime juice, stirring gently to blend flavors.
8. In a small bowl, combine flour with water to form a smooth paste.
9. Add flour mixture to soup. Stirring gently, bring to a simmer.
10. Cook soup for 2 minutes.
11. Season to taste with salt and pepper.
12. Peel avocado and slice into quarters.
13. Pour soup into serving bowls.
14. Place 1 slice of cold avocado in each bowl.
15. Serve soup with lime wedges and hot pepper sauce.

4 servings

Approximate nutritional analysis per serving
Calories 500, Protein 21 g, Carbohydrates 18 g, Fat 40 g, Cholesterol 99 mg, Sodium 815 mg

Island-Style Fish Soup

Wonton Soup

A light, seasoned broth full of homemade wontons — what a treat!

INGREDIENTS

3 oz	**(85 g) ground pork**
1 tsp	**(5 mL) cornstarch**
1	**garlic clove, crushed**
1 tsp	**(5 mL) fresh ginger root, peeled and grated**
	salt and pepper
16	**wonton wrappers**
1 oz	**(30 g) cellophane noodles, uncooked**
20 oz	**(568 mL) beef consommé**
4 oz	**(115 g) leeks, julienned and blanched**
1	**small red pepper, julienned and blanched**
3 oz	**(85 g) oyster mushrooms, sliced**
3 oz	**(85 g) morel mushrooms, sliced**
3	**green onions, chopped**

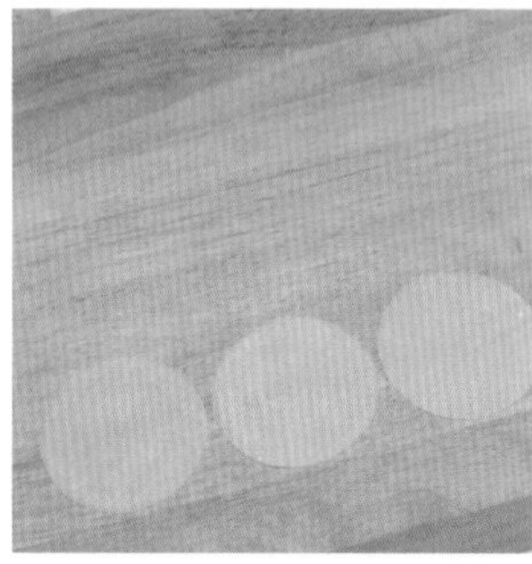

Step 3. Lay out wonton wrappers on a flat surface.

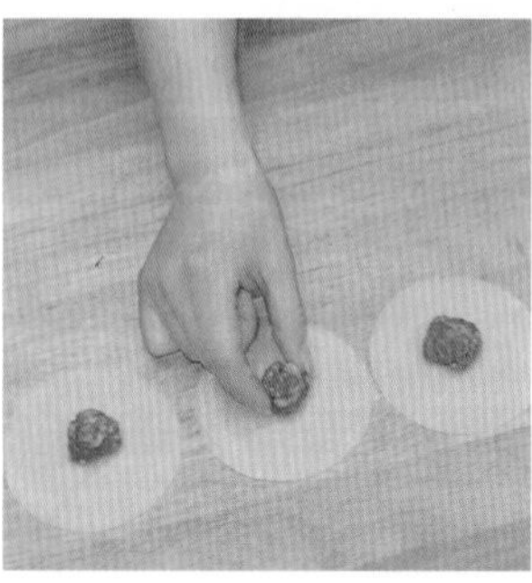

Step 4. Place 1 pork ball in center of each wrapper.

Step 5. Pinch edges of each wrapper around pork mixture to seal.

METHOD

1. In a medium bowl, combine ground pork, cornstarch, garlic, ginger, salt and pepper.
2. Form pork mixture into 16 small balls.
3. Lay out wonton wrappers on a flat surface.
4. Place 1 pork ball in center of each wrapper.
5. Pinch edges of each wrapper around pork mixture to seal.
6. Poach wontons in simmering water for 8-10 minutes. Remove with a slotted spoon.
7. Cook noodles according to package directions.
8. In a small saucepan, heat consommé over medium heat.
9. Divide wontons, leeks, peppers and noodles into serving bowls.
10. Add oyster and morel mushrooms to bowls. Pour hot consommé over top.
11. Garnish with green onions and serve.

4 servings

Approximate nutritional analysis per serving
Calories 268, Protein 19 g, Carbohydrates 35 g, Fat 6 g, Cholesterol 23 mg, Sodium 949 mg

Wonton Soup

Poultry

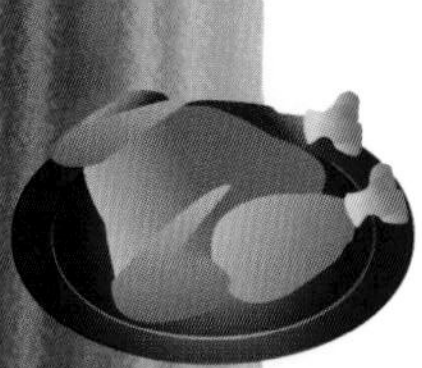

Tarragon Rhubarb Sauce

Fabulous sauce for barbecued chicken.

INGREDIENTS

2 lbs	**(900 g) fresh rhubarb or frozen rhubarb, thawed**
⅔ cup	**(150 mL) sugar**
1 cup	**(250 mL) water**
2 tsp	**(10 mL) fresh tarragon, minced**

METHOD

1. Slice enough of the rhubarb into ¼-inch (0.6 cm) slices to measure 2½ cups (625 mL). Set aside.
2. Slice the rest of the rhubarb into 1-inch (2.5 cm) pieces. Place in a stainless steel saucepan.
3. Add sugar and water to saucepan. Bring to a boil over high heat.
4. Reduce heat to medium. Cook, stirring occasionally, for 10 minutes, until rhubarb pieces dissolve and mixture thickens.
5. Press rhubarb mixture through a strainer or food mill. Discard stringy pieces of rhubarb.
6. Return rhubarb purée to saucepan. Stir in reserved rhubarb.
7. Bring mixture to a boil over high heat. Cook for 1-3 minutes, until rhubarb is softened but retains its shape.
8. Stir in tarragon. Remove from heat.
9. Serve hot or cold as an accompaniment to roasted or grilled poultry.

4 cups (1 L)

Tip:

- *This sauce may be kept covered in the refrigerator for up to 2 weeks.*

Approximate nutritional analysis per 1 tablespoon (15 mL) serving
Calories 11, Protein 0 g, Carbohydrates 3 g, Fat 0 g, Cholesterol 0 mg, Sodium 1 mg

Tomato Ginger Preserve

A spicy taste for your favorite dishes.

INGREDIENTS

2 lbs	**(900 g) ripe tomatoes, blanched, peeled, seeded and diced**
2 oz	**(55 g) fresh ginger root, peeled and diced into ¼-inch (0.6 cm) pieces**
pinch	**salt**
1½ cups	**(375 mL) sugar**
¼ cup	**(50 mL) fresh lemon juice**

METHOD

1. In a glass bowl, toss together tomatoes, ginger and salt.
2. Cover with plastic wrap and refrigerate overnight.
3. Strain all the liquid from the tomatoes into a stainless steel saucepan. Reserve tomatoes.
4. Stir sugar into saucepan.
5. Bring to a boil over medium-high heat, stirring constantly.
6. Cook for 8 minutes, until thick and syrupy.
7. Stir in reserved tomatoes and lemon juice.
8. Continue cooking for 10 minutes, until mixture is the consistency of jam. Remove from heat.
9. Allow mixture to cool.
10. Serve as an accompaniment to roasted or grilled poultry, pork or lamb.

2 cups (500 mL)

Tip:

- *This preserve may be kept covered in the refrigerator for up to 3 months.*

Approximate nutritional analysis per 1 tablespoon (15 mL) serving
Calories 44, Protein 0 g, Carbohydrates 11 g, Fat 0 g, Cholesterol 0 mg, Sodium 4 mg

Savory Rice Stuffing

A fantastic, all-purpose stuffing for poultry, meat or fish.

INGREDIENTS

½ cup	**(125 mL) wild rice, uncooked**
½ cup	**(125 mL) long grain rice, uncooked**
3 cups	**(750 mL) chicken broth**
6 tbsp	**(90 mL) butter**
1 tbsp	**(15 mL) lemon juice**
1 tsp	**(5 mL) tarragon**
½ lb	**(225 g) mushrooms, chopped**
1	**large onion, minced**
1	**red pepper, chopped**
1 tsp	**(5 mL) hot pepper sauce**
¼ cup	**(50 mL) dry sherry**
¼ cup	**(50 mL) fresh parsley, chopped**
¼ cup	**(50 mL) pine nuts (optional)**
½ tsp	**(2 mL) salt**
½ tsp	**(2 mL) pepper**

METHOD

1. In a medium saucepan, combine wild and long grain rice, chicken broth and 2 tbsp (30 mL) butter.
2. Bring to a boil over medium-high heat. Cover and reduce heat to low.
3. Simmer rice gently for 20 minutes.
4. Remove cover and cook until all of the broth has been absorbed.
5. Stir in lemon juice and tarragon. Remove from heat.
6. In a large skillet, melt remaining butter over medium heat.
7. Sauté mushrooms, onions and peppers for 5 minutes, until soft.
8. Stir in hot pepper sauce and sherry. Cook for another 2 minutes.
9. Add rice to skillet and combine with vegetables.
10. Toss in parsley and pine nuts.
11. Season with salt and pepper.
12. Use as a stuffing or serve as a rice pilaf.

3 cups (750 mL)

Approximate nutritional analysis per ½ cup (125 mL) serving
Calories 281 Protein 9 g, Carbohydrates 31 g, Fat 13 g, Cholesterol 32 mg, Sodium 1012 mg

Coconut Mango Chicken

Tropical flavors are captured in this easy-to-prepare recipe.

INGREDIENTS

4	**chicken breasts, boned and skinned**
2 tsp	**(10 mL) black pepper**
1	**large mango, peeled and sliced**
14 oz	**(398 mL) canned coconut milk**
2 tbsp	**(30 mL) curry paste**
2 tbsp	**(30 mL) lemon grass, minced**
2 tbsp	**(30 mL) lime peel, grated**
2 tbsp	**(30 mL) fresh lime juice**
2 tbsp	**(30 mL) vegetable oil**

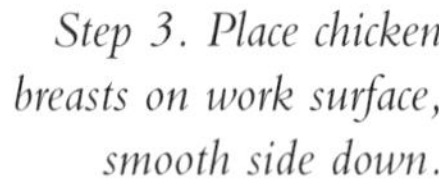

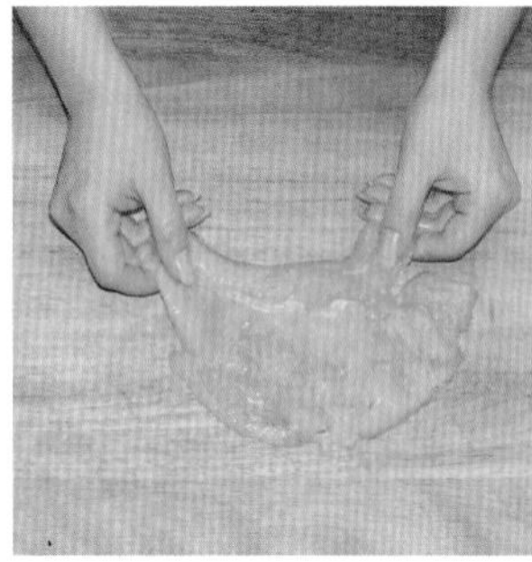

Step 3. Place chicken breasts on work surface, smooth side down.

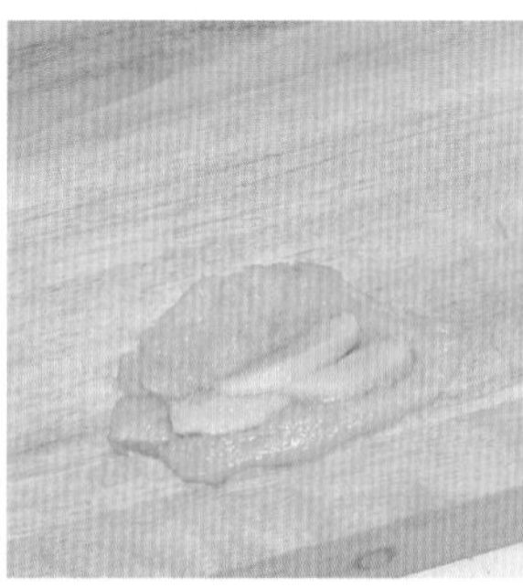

Step 5. Place mango slices on top of chicken breasts.

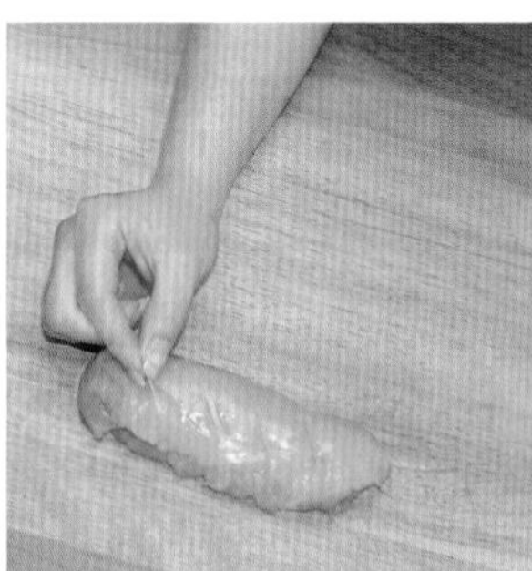

Step 6. Roll chicken breasts around mango slices. Secure with wooden picks.

METHOD

1. Place chicken breasts between 2 sheets of plastic wrap. Flatten slightly with the flat edge of a meat mallet.
2. Remove plastic wrap.
3. Place chicken breasts on work surface, smooth side down.
4. Season chicken breasts with pepper.
5. Place mango slices on top of chicken breasts.
6. Roll chicken breasts around mango slices. Secure with wooden picks.
7. Combine coconut milk, curry paste, lemon grass, lime peel and lime juice in a shallow bowl.
8. Add chicken to bowl, and coat with marinade.
9. Cover with plastic wrap and refrigerate overnight.
10. Heat broiler.
11. Remove chicken from marinade and place on a baking sheet. Reserve marinade.
12. Brush chicken with oil.
13. Broil on top oven rack for 10 minutes, until chicken is lightly browned. Brush frequently with oil.
14. Pour reserved marinade into a skillet.
15. Over medium-high heat, boil for 5 minutes, stirring occasionally.
16. Strain sauce and return to skillet. Keep warm.
17. Serve chicken accompanied by sauce.

4 servings

Approximate nutritional analysis per serving
Calories 451, Protein 30 g, Carbohydrates 19 g, Fat 30 g, Cholesterol 68 mg, Sodium 93 mg

Coconut Mango Chicken

Sautéed Chicken with Raisins and Olives

A magical blend of sweet and sour flavors.

INGREDIENTS

¼ cup	**(50 mL) raisins**
½ cup	**(125 mL) dry sherry**
2	**garlic cloves, chopped**
1 tbsp	**(15 mL) fresh parsley, chopped**
¼ cup	**(50 mL) orange juice**
4	**chicken breasts, boned and skinned**
½ cup	**(125 mL) all-purpose flour**
2 tsp	**(10 mL) salt**
1 tsp	**(5 mL) white pepper**
½ cup	**(125 mL) olive oil**
¼ cup	**(50 mL) butter**
½ cup	**(125 mL) pitted green olives, drained**
¼ cup	**(50 mL) blanched almonds, sliced**

METHOD

1. Place raisins and sherry in a small bowl.
2. Cover with plastic wrap and refrigerate for 2 hours.
3. Combine garlic, parsley and orange juice in a blender.
4. Place orange juice mixture and chicken breasts in a medium bowl. Coat chicken with marinade.
5. Cover chicken with plastic wrap and marinate in the refrigerator for 1 hour.
6. Combine flour, salt and pepper in a medium bowl.
7. Remove chicken from marinade and dredge with seasoned flour.
8. In a large skillet, heat oil over medium heat.
9. Cook chicken breasts on both sides, until golden brown.
10. Remove chicken from skillet. Drain oil from skillet.
11. Drain raisins, reserving sherry.
12. Using the same skillet, heat butter and reserved sherry over medium heat.
13. Cook for 1 minute, stirring frequently.
14. Add raisins, olives, almonds and chicken breasts. Reduce heat to low.
15. Simmer for 10 minutes, turning chicken breasts occasionally.
16. Serve hot.

4 servings

Approximate nutritional analysis per serving
Calories 647, Protein 31 g, Carbohydrates 25 g, Fat 46 g, Cholesterol 100 mg, Sodium 1733 mg

Sautéed Chicken with Raisins and Olives

Chicken Mexicana

A mild, mouth-watering combination of orange and pine nuts.

INGREDIENTS

3 tbsp	**(45 mL) butter**
1 tbsp	**(15 mL) olive oil**
4	**chicken breasts, boned and skinned**
½ tsp	**(2 mL) salt**
1 tsp	**(5 mL) pepper**
⅓ cup	**(75 mL) brandy**
2	**garlic cloves, thinly sliced**
6 tbsp	**(90 mL) green chili peppers, chopped**
dash	**hot pepper sauce**
¼ cup	**(50 mL) orange juice concentrate**
¼ cup	**(50 mL) pine nuts, toasted**
4	**orange slices**

METHOD

1. In a large skillet, heat butter and oil over medium heat.
2. Sauté chicken breasts until browned.
3. Season with salt and pepper.
4. Add brandy to skillet and carefully set aflame.
5. When the flames die down, add garlic, peppers, and hot pepper sauce.
6. Stir in orange juice concentrate. Reduce heat to low.
7. Simmer for 25 minutes, until chicken is tender and cooked through.
8. Remove chicken breasts from skillet and place on a serving platter.
9. Pour sauce over chicken breasts.
10. Garnish with pine nuts and orange slices.

4 servings

Tip:

- *How To Toast Pine Nuts: Place pine nuts on a baking sheet and bake in a 325°F (160°C) oven for 5 minutes.*

Approximate nutritional analysis per serving
Calories 359, Protein 30 g, Carbohydrates 12 g, Fat 17 g, Cholesterol 92 mg, Sodium 435 mg

Chicken Mexicana

Ballottines of Chicken

A delectable and economical chicken recipe enhanced by savory rice stuffing.

INGREDIENTS

4	**chicken legs, thigh attached**	**1 cup**	**(250 mL) white rice, cooked**
3	**small bacon slices, diced**	**1 cup**	**(250 mL) wild rice, cooked**
1	**medium onion, diced**	**½ tsp**	**(2 mL) salt**
2	**celery stalks, diced**	**½ tsp**	**(2 mL) pepper**
1	**garlic clove, chopped**	**1 tbsp**	**(15 mL) vegetable oil**

METHOD

1. Preheat oven to 350°F (175°C).

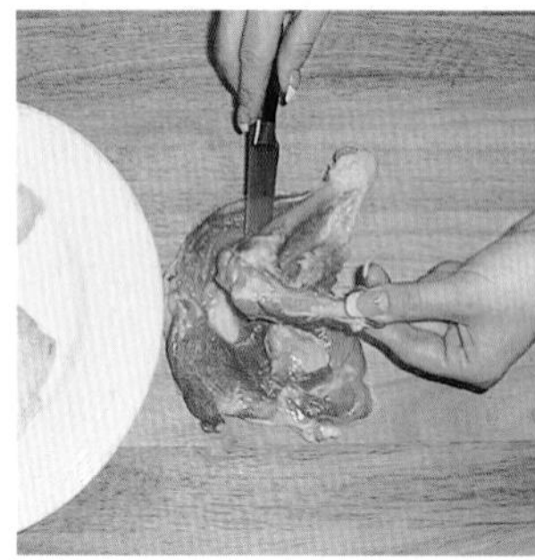

Step 2. Position chicken pieces skin side down. Bone each chicken leg and thigh, leaving skin intact.

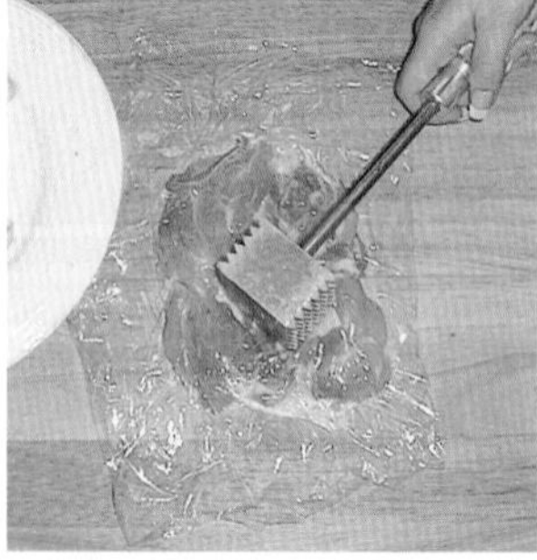

Step 3. Place chicken pieces between 2 sheets of plastic wrap. Flatten with the flat edge of a meat mallet.

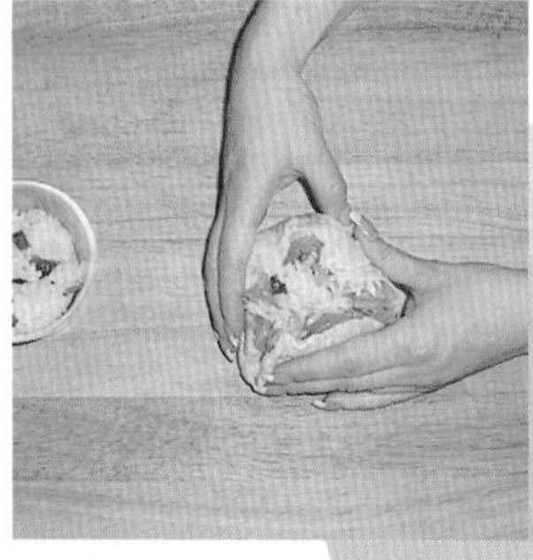

Step 10. Mold chicken around rice mixture to form a ball.

2. Position chicken pieces skin side down. Bone each chicken leg and thigh, leaving skin intact.
3. Place chicken pieces between 2 sheets of plastic wrap. Flatten with the flat edge of a meat mallet.
4. Remove plastic wrap.
5. Place bacon, onions, celery and garlic in a skillet. Cook over medium heat for 5 minutes, until vegetables are soft. Remove from heat.
6. In a medium bowl, combine white rice, wild rice and bacon mixture.
7. Season with salt and pepper.
8. Place chicken skin side down.
9. Divide rice mixture onto each piece of chicken.
10. Mold chicken around rice mixture to form a ball.
11. Turn pieces upside down to seal the edges.
12. Place on a baking sheet and brush tops with oil.
13. Cut four 18 x 1-inch (45 x 2.5 cm) strips of aluminum foil.
14. Fold each strip of foil into thirds lengthwise.
15. Rub foil strips with oil, and wrap one strip around each chicken ballottine. Secure with wooden picks.
16. Bake for 30 minutes.
17. Cool for 5 minutes. Remove foil strips.
18. Serve hot.

4 servings

Approximate nutritional analysis per serving
Calories 498, Protein 36 g, Carbohydrates 27 g, Fat 27 g, Cholesterol 142 mg, Sodium 494 mg

Ballottines of Chicken

Chicken with Rhubarb Sauce

Tangy and tantalizing — a truly memorable recipe.

INGREDIENTS

4	**chicken breasts, boned and skinned**
½ cup	**(125 mL) all-purpose flour**
2 tsp	**(10 mL) salt**
1 tsp	**(5 mL) white pepper**
2	**large eggs**
3 tbsp	**(45 mL) butter**
4	**rhubarb stalks, chopped**
½ cup	**(125 mL) water**
3 tbsp	**(45 mL) honey**
1 tbsp	**(15 mL) cornstarch**
1½ tbsp	**(25 mL) cold water**
2 tbsp	**(30 mL) orange liqueur**
1 tbsp	**(15 mL) lime juice**

METHOD

1. Place chicken breasts between 2 sheets of plastic wrap. Flatten with the flat edge of a meat mallet.
2. Remove plastic wrap.
3. In a medium bowl, combine flour, salt and pepper.
4. Place eggs in a bowl and beat lightly.
5. Dredge chicken breasts in seasoned flour, then dip in beaten eggs.
6. In a large skillet, melt butter over medium heat.
7. Sauté chicken breasts for 4-5 minutes per side, until golden brown.
8. While chicken is cooking, place rhubarb and water in a stainless steel pot.
9. Cook over medium heat for 5 minutes.
10. Stir honey into rhubarb.
11. In a small bowl, dissolve cornstarch in cold water.
12. Stir cornstarch mixture into rhubarb. Cook for 1 minute.
13. Add orange liqueur and lime juice, stirring sauce to combine.
14. Place chicken breasts on a platter and serve with sauce.

4 servings

Approximate nutritional analysis per serving
Calories 382, Protein 33 g, Carbohydrates 29 g, Fat 13 g, Cholesterol 198 mg, Sodium 1265 mg

Chicken with Rhubarb Sauce

Coconut Chicken in Bamboo Leaves

These tasty, wrapped packages contain the delicious flavors of the Orient.

INGREDIENTS

10	**bamboo leaves or ½ lb (225 g) frozen banana leaves, thawed**
4	**chicken breasts, boned and skinned**
2 tbsp	**(30 mL) fresh ginger root, peeled and grated**
2 tbsp	**(30 mL) lemon grass, chopped**
1¾ cups	**(425 mL) coconut milk**

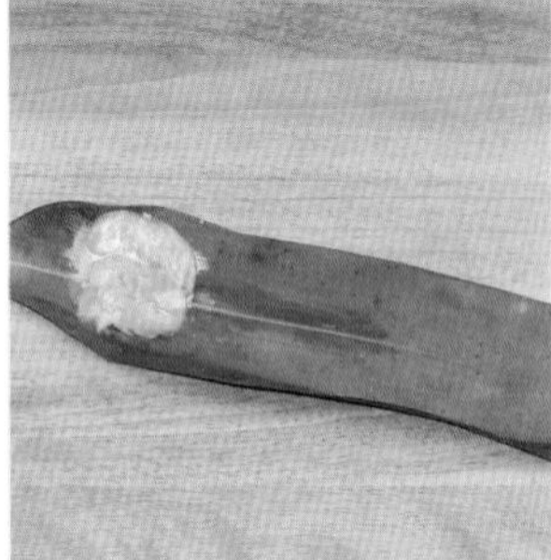

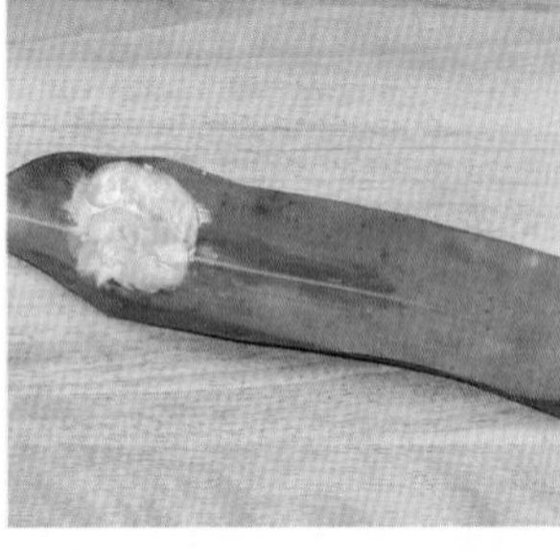

Step 6. Place 2 pieces of chicken on each uncut bamboo leaf.

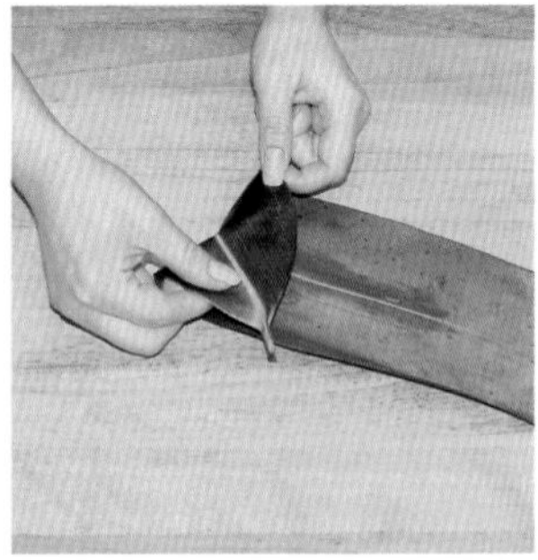

Step 7. Fold bamboo leaves around chicken to form packets.

Step 8. Tie each packet with a bamboo leaf strip.

METHOD

1. Soak bamboo leaves in water overnight to soften them. Banana leaves will be pliable enough to use from the package.
2. Cut chicken breasts into 2 x ½-inch (5 x 1.3 cm) pieces.
3. Place chicken in a ceramic bowl. Stir in ginger, lemon grass and coconut milk.
4. Cover with plastic wrap and marinate in the refrigerator overnight.
5. Cut 2 bamboo leaves into 1-inch (2.5 cm) wide strips.
6. Place 2 pieces of chicken on each uncut bamboo leaf.
7. Fold bamboo leaves around chicken to form packets.
8. Tie each packet with a bamboo leaf strip.
9. Place packets in a bamboo steam basket. Steam for 30 minutes over a pot of boiling water.
10. Serve the chicken in the leaves with mango chutney, peanut sauce, scented rice or soy sauce.

4 servings

Tip:

- *Bamboo and banana leaves are available at most Oriental supermarkets.*

Approximate nutritional analysis per serving
Calories 330, Protein 29 g, Carbohydrates 4 g, Fat 23 g, Cholesterol 68 mg, Sodium 90 mg

Coconut Chicken in Bamboo Leaves

Baked Parmesan Chicken

Herbs and cheese make this dish special.

INGREDIENTS

⅓ cup	**(75 mL) vegetable oil**
4	**chicken thighs**
4	**chicken legs**
1 tsp	**(5 mL) oregano**
½ tsp	**(2 mL) thyme**
1 tsp	**(5 mL) black pepper**
1 tsp	**(5 mL) paprika**
3 tbsp	**(45 mL) Parmesan cheese, freshly grated**

METHOD

1. Preheat oven to 425°F (220°C).
2. Line a shallow baking pan with aluminum foil.
3. Pour oil into pan. Place in the oven to heat for about 5 minutes.
4. Remove skin from chicken pieces, if desired.
5. Place chicken pieces in heated baking pan.
6. Reduce oven temperature to 350°F (175°C).
7. Combine remaining ingredients in a small bowl.
8. Sprinkle chicken pieces with half of the Parmesan cheese mixture.
9. Bake for 30 minutes.
10. Turn chicken pieces and sprinkle with remaining Parmesan cheese mixture.
11. Bake for 10 more minutes.
12. Serve hot.

4 servings

Chicken Provençale

French, country-style fare.

INGREDIENTS

4	**chicken thighs**
4	**chicken legs or 4 chicken breasts, boned**
1 tbsp	**(15 mL) seasoning salt**
½ tsp	**(2 mL) black pepper**
½ tsp	**(2 mL) paprika**
¼ cup	**(50 mL) olive oil**
1	**medium onion, thinly sliced**
½ lb	**(225 g) mushrooms, sliced**
½ cup	**(125 mL) white wine**
2	**tomatoes, blanched, peeled, seeded and coarsely chopped**
2 tbsp	**(30 mL) fresh parsley, chopped**

METHOD

1. Sprinkle chicken pieces with seasoning salt, pepper and paprika.
2. In a large skillet, heat oil over medium heat.
3. Cook chicken pieces for 10–15 minutes, until browned. Remove from skillet and keep hot.
4. Place onions in skillet and cook for 5 minutes, until soft.
5. Add mushrooms and cook for 2 minutes.
6. Return chicken pieces to skillet.
7. Add wine and bring to a boil. Cover and reduce heat to low.
8. Cook gently for another 10–15 minutes.
9. Sprinkle with tomatoes and parsley. Serve.

4 servings

Approximate nutritional analysis per serving
Calories 443, Protein 31 g, Carbohydrates 7 g, Fat 31 g, Cholesterol 127 mg, Sodium 1175 mg

◀ Approximate nutritional analysis per serving
Calories 506, Protein 33 g, Carbohydrates 2 g, Fat 41 g, Cholesterol 144 mg, Sodium 229 mg

Chicken Provençale

Curry-Glazed Chicken Breasts

A rare mixture of flavors beautifully balanced in this simple recipe.

INGREDIENTS

½ cup + 1 tbsp	**(140 mL) all-purpose flour**
2 tsp	**(10 mL) salt**
1 tsp	**(5 mL) white pepper**
4	**chicken breasts, boned and skinned**
3 tbsp	**(45 mL) butter**
⅓ cup	**(75 mL) olive oil**
½ cup	**(125 mL) onions, chopped**
1½ tsp	**(7 mL) curry powder or curry paste**
1 cup	**(250 mL) chicken broth**
½ cup	**(125 mL) orange marmalade**
2 tbsp	**(30 mL) ketchup**
1 tbsp	**(15 mL) lemon juice**

METHOD

1. Preheat oven to 400°F (205°C).
2. In a medium bowl, combine ½ cup (125 mL) flour with salt and pepper.
3. Dredge chicken breasts in seasoned flour.
4. In a large skillet, heat butter over medium heat.
5. Brown chicken breasts on both sides. Transfer to an ovenproof casserole dish.
6. Bake for 15 minutes.
7. While chicken bakes, heat oil in a saucepan over medium heat.
8. Sauté onions for 5 minutes, until soft.
9. Stir in remaining flour and cook for 3 minutes.
10. Add remaining ingredients, stirring to combine.
11. Bring mixture to a boil. Reduce heat to medium-low.
12. Simmer for 15 minutes to make a glaze.
13. Spoon some of the glaze over the chicken breasts.
14. Return chicken to oven and cook for an additional 5 minutes.
15. Serve chicken with remaining glaze as an accompaniment.

4 servings

Approximate nutritional analysis per serving
Calories 565, Protein 32 g, Carbohydrates 46 g, Fat 29 g, Cholesterol 92 mg, Sodium 1700 mg

Curry-Glazed Chicken Breasts

Chicken with Leeks and Mushrooms

A recipe you will want to prepare time and time again.

INGREDIENTS

½ lb	**(225 g) oyster mushrooms**	**¼ cup**	**(50 mL) chicken broth**
2 tbsp	**(30 mL) butter**	**½ cup**	**(125 mL) heavy cream**
4	**chicken thighs**	**1 tsp**	**(5 mL) salt**
2	**small leeks, julienned**	**1 tsp**	**(5 mL) pepper**
½ cup	**(125 mL) white wine**	**pinch**	**nutmeg**

METHOD

1. Remove tough stems from mushrooms. Slice mushrooms.
2. In a large skillet, heat butter over medium heat.
3. Sauté chicken thighs, skin side down, until golden brown.
4. Turn chicken thighs and cook other side until browned.
5. Add leeks and cook for 3 minutes, until leeks are soft.
6. Stir in wine and chicken broth. Bring to a simmer. Cover and reduce heat to low.
7. Simmer gently for 10-15 minutes.
8. Remove chicken and keep warm.
9. Add mushrooms to skillet. Cook over medium-high heat, until sauce has thickened slightly.
10. Reduce heat to low. Stir in cream and simmer gently for 1 minute.
11. Season with salt, pepper and nutmeg.
12. Spoon sauce over chicken and serve.

4 servings

Tip:

- *Julienned, deep-fried leeks are a nice garnish for this dish.*

Approximate nutritional analysis per serving
Calories 420, Protein 20 g, Carbohydrates 10 g, Fat 32 g, Cholesterol 136 mg, Sodium 863 mg

Chicken with Leeks and Mushrooms

Chicken and Melon Stir-Fry

Mild, sweet melon adds sparkle to this popular favorite.

INGREDIENTS

1 tbsp	**(15 mL) oyster sauce**
2 tsp	**(10 mL) dry white wine**
1 tsp	**(5 mL) light soy sauce**
1 tsp	**(5 mL) sesame oil**
1 tsp	**(5 mL) fresh ginger root, peeled and grated**
2 tsp	**(10 mL) cornstarch**
1 tsp	**(5 mL) sugar**
	salt and pepper
1 lb	**(450 g) chicken fillets**
3 tbsp	**(45 mL) peanut oil**
3 oz	**(85 g) snow peas, sliced diagonally**
4	**green onions, cut into ½-inch (1.3 cm) pieces**
½	**small honeydew melon, peeled and cut into small cubes**
½	**small cantaloupe, peeled and cut into small cubes**
1 tbsp	**(15 mL) garlic, minced**

METHOD

1. In a medium bowl, combine oyster sauce, wine, soy sauce, sesame oil, ginger, cornstarch, sugar, salt and pepper.
2. Place chicken in bowl, stirring to coat with marinade.
3. Cover with plastic wrap and refrigerate for 1 hour.
4. Heat a wok or large skillet over high heat for 1 minute.
5. Place 1 tbsp (15 mL) peanut oil in wok, moving oil in wok to coat sides.
6. When the oil begins to smoke, add snow peas and green onions.
7. Cook, stirring constantly, until snow peas are bright green.
8. Add honeydew and cantaloupe to wok. Cook until melon is hot.
9. Transfer contents of wok to a bowl and set aside.
10. Carefully rinse wok with hot water. Wipe dry.
11. Reheat wok over high heat.
12. Add remaining oil, heating until smoking point is reached.
13. Place garlic in wok, cooking until light brown.
14. Add a small amount of chicken to wok. Cook for 1 minute. Remove chicken from wok.
15. Cook remaining chicken in small batches.
16. Return vegetables and melons to wok. Cook just until hot.
17. Add chicken to wok, cooking to heat through.
18. Serve hot.

4 servings

Approximate nutritional analysis per serving
Calories 273, Protein 28 g, Carbohydrates 10 g, Fat 13 g, Cholesterol 66 mg, Sodium 824 mg

Chicken and Melon Stir-Fry

Tagine

A timeless combination of chicken, ginger and olives.

INGREDIENTS

2 tbsp	**(30 mL) butter**
2 tbsp	**(30 mL) vegetable oil**
6	**chicken breasts, boned and skinned**
4	**medium onions, sliced**
1½ tsp	**(7 mL) ginger**
1 tsp	**(5 mL) paprika**
1 cup	**(250 mL) water**
	salt and black pepper
1 cup	**(250 mL) pimiento-stuffed green olives, drained and sliced**
¼ cup	**(50 mL) fresh parsley, chopped**
2 tbsp	**(30 mL) lemon juice**

METHOD

1. In a large skillet, heat butter and oil over medium heat.
2. Brown chicken pieces on all sides. Remove from skillet.
3. Stir in onions, ginger, paprika, water, salt and pepper.
4. Return chicken to skillet, basting well with liquid.
5. Cover. Reduce heat to low.
6. Cook for 15 minutes, until chicken is tender.
7. Remove chicken from skillet and keep warm.
8. Skim any fat from skillet.
9. Stir in olives, parsley and lemon juice.
10. Pour sauce over chicken pieces.
11. Serve hot with couscous.

6 servings

Variation:

- *2 small frying chickens, cut up, may be substituted for the chicken breasts. Cooking time will increase from 15 minutes to 25 minutes.*

Approximate nutritional analysis per serving
Calories 263, Protein 29 g, Carbohydrates 5 g, Fat 14 g, Cholesterol 79 mg, Sodium 1079 mg

Tagine

Chicken Livers Forestière

Rich and sensational, this recipe brims with French flair.

INGREDIENTS

2 lbs	**(900 g) chicken livers, washed and trimmed**
1 cup	**(250 mL) all-purpose flour**
1 tsp	**(5 mL) paprika**
6 tbsp	**(90 mL) vegetable oil**
2 tbsp	**(30 mL) butter**
12	**large mushrooms, sliced**
¾ cup	**(175 mL) onions, finely diced**
1	**garlic clove, crushed**
2 tbsp	**(30 mL) olive oil**
½ cup	**(125 mL) dry white wine**
½ tsp	**(2 mL) fennel seeds**
1	**large tomato, blanched, peeled, seeded and chopped**
	salt and freshly ground pepper

METHOD

1. Dry chicken livers with paper towels.
2. Dust with flour and paprika.
3. In a large skillet, heat 3 tbsp (45 mL) vegetable oil and 1 tbsp (15 mL) butter over medium-high heat.
4. Sauté mushrooms for 1 minute. Remove mushrooms from skillet with a slotted spoon.
5. Return skillet to heat and add remaining vegetable oil and butter.
6. Add onions and garlic to skillet. Sauté for 2 minutes over medium heat. Remove onion mixture with a slotted spoon.
7. Heat olive oil in skillet over medium-high heat.
8. Add chicken livers to skillet. Cook for 4-5 minutes, turning occasionally, until evenly browned.
9. Remove livers from skillet and keep warm.
10. Stir wine and fennel into skillet. Simmer over medium heat for 4-5 minutes.
11. Return onion mixture, mushrooms and chicken livers to skillet. Add tomatoes and heat through.
12. Season with salt and pepper. Serve.

4 servings

Approximate nutritional analysis per serving
Calories 811, Protein 60 g, Carbohydrates 33 g, Fat 46 g, Cholesterol 1435 mg, Sodium 186 mg

Chicken Livers Forestière

Chicken Chow Mein

A classic stir-fry so easy to prepare.

INGREDIENTS

2½ tbsp	**(40 mL) light soy sauce**
1 tsp	**(5 mL) brown sugar**
1 tsp	**(5 mL) salt**
1 lb	**(450 g) chicken, boned and cut into strips**
2 tbsp	**(30 mL) vegetable oil**
1	**large onion, sliced**
2½ cups	**(625 mL) bean sprouts**
2 tsp	**(10 mL) sesame oil**
8 oz	**(250 mL) canned baby corn, drained**
1 tbsp	**(15 mL) cornstarch**
1 cup	**(250 mL) chicken broth**

METHOD

1. In a medium bowl, combine soy sauce, brown sugar and salt.
2. Add chicken to bowl, tossing to coat with marinade.
3. Cover with plastic wrap and refrigerate for 30 minutes.
4. Drain marinade from chicken.
5. Place vegetable oil in a wok or large skillet. Over high heat, bring oil to smoking point.
6. Sauté chicken for 2-3 minutes, stirring constantly. Remove chicken from wok.
7. Place onions in wok and sauté for 1 minute.
8. Add bean sprouts and sauté for an additional 2-3 minutes, stirring frequently.
9. Return chicken to wok, along with sesame oil and corn. Cook for 1 minute to heat through and blend flavors.
10. In a small bowl, combine cornstarch and chicken broth.
11. Stir cornstarch mixture into wok.
12. Cook for 2-3 minutes, stirring frequently, until sauce thickens.
13. Serve over rice or noodles.

4 servings

Approximate nutritional analysis per serving
Calories 290, Protein 33 g, Carbohydrates 14 g, Fat 12 g, Cholesterol 66 mg, Sodium 1291 mg

Chicken Chow Mein

Arroz Con Pollo

This flavorful chicken and rice dish is a Spanish specialty.

INGREDIENTS

¼ cup	**(50 mL) olive oil**
1	**3-lb (1.4 kg) frying chicken, cut into 8 pieces**
1	**large onion, chopped**
1	**medium red pepper, diced**
1	**medium green pepper, diced**
2	**garlic cloves, crushed**
1 cup	**(250 mL) long grain rice, uncooked**
2 cups	**(500 mL) chicken broth**
8 oz	**(250 mL) canned tomatoes, crushed, undrained**
2 cups	**(500 mL) mushrooms, sliced**
2 tbsp	**(30 mL) fresh parsley, chopped**
2 tbsp	**(30 mL) tomato paste**
2	**saffron threads, crushed**
1 tsp	**(5 mL) salt**
1 tsp	**(5 mL) pepper**

METHOD

1. Preheat oven to 350°F (175°C).
2. In an ovenproof skillet, heat oil over medium heat.
3. Brown chicken on all sides. Remove from skillet and keep warm.
4. Sauté onions, red peppers, green peppers and garlic for 6-7 minutes, until soft.
5. Add rice and chicken broth to skillet. Cook for 2 minutes.
6. Stir in tomatoes with their juice, mushrooms, parsley and tomato paste.
7. Add saffron, stirring to combine.
8. Return chicken to skillet. Season with salt and pepper. Cover.
9. Bake for 35-40 minutes, until chicken and rice are tender.
10. Serve hot with fresh bread.

4 servings

Approximate nutritional analysis per serving
Calories 782, Protein 84 g, Carbohydrates 50 g, Fat 26 g, Cholesterol 239 mg, Sodium 1669 mg

Arroz Con Pollo

Three Pepper Chicken with Rosemary

A simple recipe your family will love.

INGREDIENTS

2 tbsp	**(30 mL) lemon juice**
2 tbsp	**(30 mL) olive oil**
1 tsp	**(5 mL) fresh rosemary, crushed**
¼ tsp	**(1 mL) red pepper flakes, crushed**
¼ tsp	**(1 mL) paprika**
1 tsp	**(5 mL) black pepper**
4	**garlic cloves, crushed**
1 tsp	**(5 mL) salt**
4	**chicken breasts, boned and skinned**
2 tsp	**(10 mL) vegetable oil**

METHOD

1. In a glass bowl, combine lemon juice, olive oil, rosemary, pepper flakes, paprika, pepper, garlic and salt.
2. Place chicken breasts in bowl, turning to coat with marinade.
3. Cover with plastic wrap and refrigerate for 1 hour, turning once or twice.
4. In a large skillet, heat oil over medium heat.
5. Remove chicken breasts from marinade and place in skillet, smooth side down.
6. Sauté chicken breasts for 4-5 minutes per side, until lightly browned and cooked through.
7. Serve hot.

4 servings

Almond Chicken Bites

Tender chicken with a nutty coating.

INGREDIENTS

4	**chicken breasts, boned and skinned**
3 tbsp	**(45 mL) Marsala wine**
2 tbsp	**(30 mL) cornstarch**
1 tbsp	**(15 mL) soy sauce**
½ tsp	**(2 mL) sugar**
¾ cup	**(175 mL) ground almonds**
1	**large egg**
	vegetable oil for deep frying

METHOD

1. Cut chicken breasts into 3 x 1-inch (7 x 2.5 cm) pieces.
2. In a medium bowl, combine Marsala, 1 tbsp (15 mL) cornstarch, soy sauce and sugar.
3. Place chicken pieces in bowl, tossing to coat with marinade.
4. Cover with plastic wrap and refrigerate for 1 hour.
5. Heat oil to 375°F (190°C).
6. In a bowl, combine remaining cornstarch and almonds.
7. Place egg in a bowl, and beat lightly with a whisk.
8. Dip chicken pieces in egg and then into almond mixture.
9. Deep fry chicken pieces for 3 minutes, until golden brown.
10. Remove from oil and drain on paper towels.
11. Serve hot with sweet and sour sauce or plum sauce.

4 servings

Approximate nutritional analysis per serving
Calories 441, Protein 38 g, Carbohydrates 14 g, Fat 24 g, Cholesterol 122 mg, Sodium 351 mg

◀Approximate nutritional analysis per serving
Calories 221, Protein 28 g, Carbohydrates 3 g, Fat 11 g, Cholesterol 68 mg, Sodium 615 mg

Almond Chicken Bites

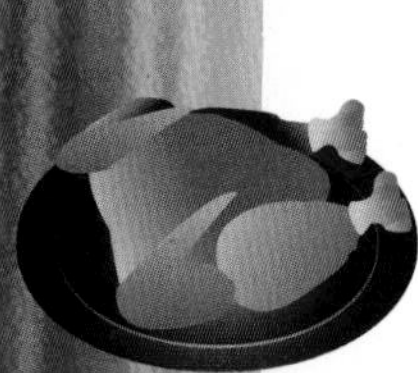

Stuffed Turkey with Berries and Apples

Savory bread stuffing and a delicious fruit sauce make this recipe extra special.

INGREDIENTS

6 tbsp	**(90 mL) butter**
6	**white or brown bread slices, small diced**
½ tsp	**(2 mL) sage**
½ tsp	**(2 mL) thyme**
2	**small McIntosh apples**
1	**celery stalk, small diced**
1	**garlic clove, minced**
1	**small onion, small diced**
1½ cups	**(375 mL) chicken broth**
1½ lbs	**(675 g) turkey fillets, boned**
2 cups	**(500 mL) apple cider**
2 tbsp	**(30 mL) cornstarch**
¼ cup	**(50 mL) cold water**
1 cup	**(250 mL) frozen pearl onions, thawed and drained**
¼ cup	**(50 mL) cranberries or Saskatoons**
1 tbsp	**(15 mL) fresh parsley, chopped**

METHOD

1. Preheat oven to 350°F (175°C).
2. Melt 2 tbsp (30 mL) butter. Place in an ovenproof casserole dish.
3. Add bread, sage and thyme to casserole dish. Toss mixture together.
4. Bake for 10 minutes.
5. Peel, core and finely chop one of the apples.
6. In a medium skillet, heat 2 tbsp (30 mL) butter over medium heat.
7. Sauté celery, garlic, chopped apples and onions for 5 minutes, until vegetables are soft.
8. Stir in ½ cup (125 mL) chicken broth. Bring to a boil.
9. Stir in bread mixture until combined. Remove stuffing from heat.
10. Place turkey between 2 sheets of plastic wrap. Flatten with the flat edge of a meat mallet.
11. Remove plastic wrap.
12. Divide stuffing onto flattened turkey.
13. Pin edges of turkey around stuffing with wooden skewers.
14. In a large skillet, heat remaining butter over medium heat.
15. Sauté turkey until lightly browned on all sides.
16. Add cider and bring to a boil.
17. Cover and reduce heat to low. Simmer for 15 minutes, until turkey is tender.
18. Transfer turkey to a serving platter and keep warm. Remove skewers.
19. In a small bowl, dissolve cornstarch in water.
20. Peel, core and slice remaining apple.
21. Place remaining chicken broth in skillet. Bring to a boil over medium heat.
22. Add cornstarch mixture to skillet, stirring sauce as it thickens.
23. Stir in pearl onions, apples, and berries. Cook until fruit is heated through.
24. Spoon sauce around turkey.
25. Garnish with parsley and serve.

6 servings

Approximate nutritional analysis per serving
Calories 445, Protein 40 g, Carbohydrates 38 g, Fat 15 g, Cholesterol 127 mg, Sodium 717 mg

Stuffed Turkey with Berries and Apples

Favorite Roast Turkey with Dressing

Roast turkey makes any day a special occasion.

INGREDIENTS

Turkey

1	**7-lb (3.2 kg) turkey**
	salt and pepper
2 tbsp	**(30 mL) vegetable oil**

Turkey Dressing

¼ cup	**(50 mL) butter**
2 cups	**(500 mL) onions, small diced**
1 cup	**(250 mL) celery, small diced**
16	**stale white bread slices**
2 tbsp	**(30 mL) fresh parsley, chopped**
2 tsp	**(10 mL) thyme**
2 tsp	**(10 mL) sage**
2 tsp	**(10 mL) poultry seasoning**
½ cup	**(125 mL) chicken broth**
	salt and pepper

METHOD

Turkey

1. Preheat oven to 350°F (175°C).
2. Remove giblets from turkey cavity. Rinse cavity with cold, running water.
3. Place turkey in a roasting pan, breast side up.
4. Twist wing tips underneath back of turkey.
5. Season turkey cavity with salt and pepper.
6. Rub oil on turkey skin and season with salt and pepper.
7. Roast for 3 hours on bottom oven rack, basting regularly. Turkey is cooked when a meat thermometer inserted into thickest part of thigh reads 180°F (80°C).
8. Remove turkey from roasting pan. Let stand in a warm place for 15 minutes before carving.

Dressing

9. Heat oven to 325°F (160°C).
10. In a small skillet, heat butter over medium heat.
11. Sauté onions and celery for 5 minutes. Remove from heat and cool.
12. Slice bread into small cubes.
13. In a medium bowl, combine cooled onion mixture and bread cubes.
14. Add parsley, thyme, sage, poultry seasoning, salt and pepper. Mix well.
15. Add chicken broth in small amounts until dressing is moist, but not wet.
16. Place dressing in a baking dish. Cover.
17. Bake for 30 minutes, until center of dressing is hot.

10 servings

Tip:

- *Dressing may be precooked and refrigerated. Reheat in oven or microwave until hot.*

Approximate nutritional analysis per serving
Calories 771, Protein 99 g, Carbohydrates 31 g, Fat 25 g, Cholesterol 255 mg, Sodium 933 mg

Favorite Roast Turkey with Dressing

Lime Game Hens

Game hens marinated in citrus juices, then broiled to tender perfection.

INGREDIENTS

1	**lime, cut in half**
1	**orange, cut in half**
1 cup	**(250 mL) water**
1 cup	**(250 mL) sugar**
4	**Cornish game hens**
1	**medium red onion, sliced**
¾ cup	**(175 mL) light soy sauce**
½ cup	**(125 mL) green onions, chopped**
½ cup	**(125 mL) orange juice**
½ cup	**(125 mL) chicken broth**
⅓ cup	**(75 mL) lime juice**
1 tbsp	**(15 mL) fresh ginger root, peeled and minced**
3 tbsp	**(45 mL) fresh cilantro, chopped**

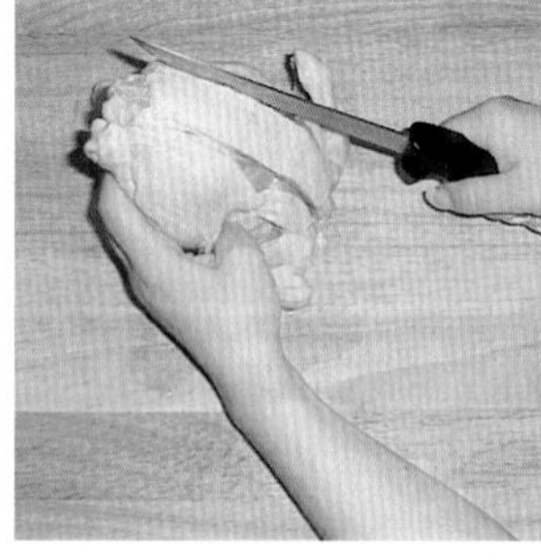

Step 6. Sitting each game hen in an upright position, split back of hen on each side of the backbone.

Step 8. Make a small slit in the skin below each drumstick. Tuck the legs into the slits.

METHOD

1. Remove peels from one lime half and one orange half. Cut peel into fine strips.
2. Blanch lime and orange peel strips in boiling water for 1 minute. Drain.
3. In a saucepan, combine water and sugar over medium heat. Bring mixture to a boil.
4. Add lime and orange peel strips. Boil until liquid has evaporated.
5. Remove fruit peel strips from saucepan and reserve.
6. Sitting each game hen in an upright position, split back of hen on each side of the backbone.
7. Remove backbone from each game hen. Lay game hens flat, breast sides up.
8. Make a small slit in the skin below each drumstick. Tuck the legs into the slits.
9. Tuck the wings underneath the breast.
10. In a large glass bowl, combine onions, soy sauce, green onions, orange juice, chicken broth, lime juice, ginger and 1 tbsp (15 mL) cilantro.
11. Place game hens in bowl and coat with marinade.
12. Cover with plastic wrap and refrigerate overnight.
13. Heat broiler.
14. Remove game hens from marinade and place on a wire rack on a baking sheet. Reserve marinade.
15. Broil game hens on middle oven rack for 10-12 minutes per side. Turn occasionally and brush with marinade.
16. Slice remaining lime and orange halves.
17. Garnish game hens with lime and orange slices, remaining cilantro and reserved fruit peel strips.

4 servings

Approximate nutritional analysis per serving
Calories 1036, Protein 91 g, Carbohydrates 72 g, Fat 42 g, Cholesterol 268 mg, Sodium 2715 mg

Lime Game Hens

Roasted Herb Game Hens

Fresh herbs add rich flavor to this delightful recipe.

INGREDIENTS

¼ cup	**(50 mL) butter, softened**
4	**garlic cloves, finely chopped**
2 cups	**(500 mL) fresh herbs, chopped**
4	**Cornish game hens**
	salt and black pepper

Step 4. Spread some of the herb butter under the skin on the breast of each game hen.

Step 6. Rub remaining herb butter over the game hens.

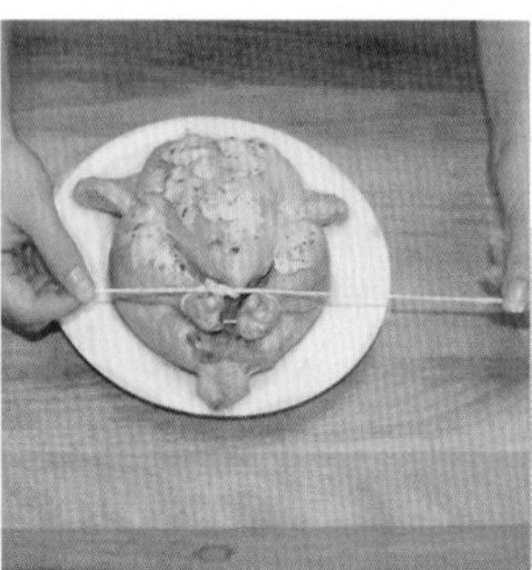

Step 7. Tie the legs of each hen together with string.

METHOD

1. Preheat oven to 375°F (190°C).
2. In a medium bowl, combine butter, garlic and herbs into a coarse paste.
3. Loosen the skin on the breast portion of each game hen by running a spoon between the skin and breast.
4. Spread some of the herb butter under the skin on the breast of each game hen.
5. Season with salt and pepper.
6. Rub remaining herb butter over the game hens.
7. Tie the legs of each hen together with string.
8. Tuck the wings of each hen underneath the back.
9. Place game hens in a roasting pan, breast side up.
10. Roast for 1 hour, basting regularly with pan juices.
11. Test game hens for doneness with a meat thermometer or by pricking with a fork. Meat is cooked once thermometer reads 170°F (75°C), or when juices run clear when thigh is pricked.
12. Serve hot.

4 servings

Tip:

- *Suitable herbs for this recipe include tarragon, thyme, sage, parsley and oregano.*

Approximate nutritional analysis per serving
Calories 835, Protein 83 g, Carbohydrates 1 g, Fat 53 g, Cholesterol 299 mg, Sodium 1075 mg

Roasted Herb Game Hens

Beef

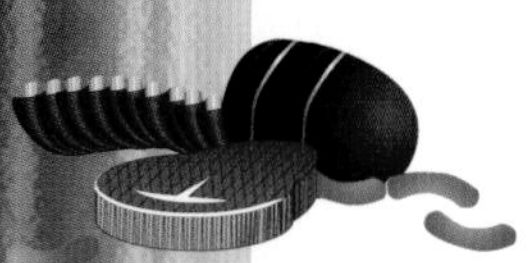

Lemon Beef Kebabs

Grill these delicious kebabs on the barbecue for a flavor bonus.

INGREDIENTS

Marinade

½ cup	**(125 mL) fresh parsley, chopped**
2	**garlic cloves**
1	**medium onion, quartered**
1 cup	**(250 mL) vegetable oil**
⅓ cup	**(75 mL) fresh lemon juice**
1 tsp	**(5 mL) dried oregano**
1 tsp	**(5 mL) beef bouillon powder**
1 tsp	**(5 mL) salt**
	black pepper

Kebabs

4 lbs	**(1.8 kg) sirloin tip beef, cut into 1-inch (2.5 cm) cubes**
3	**large bell peppers, cut into 1-inch (2.5 cm) pieces**
32	**mushrooms**
3	**small lemons**

METHOD

1. In a food processor, combine parsley and garlic by pulsing.
2. Add onions to parsley mixture, and pulse for a few more seconds.
3. Add remaining marinade ingredients. Pulse to combine.
4. Place beef and peppers in a large bowl.
5. Pour marinade over beef and peppers, tossing to coat with marinade.
6. Cover with plastic wrap and refrigerate overnight.
7. Gently remove mushroom stems, reserving caps.
8. Add mushroom caps to marinade 2 hours before cooking.
9. Heat broiler.
10. Cut each lemon into 8 wedges.
11. Thread pieces on skewers, alternating mushrooms, lemons, beef and peppers.
12. Place kebabs on a baking sheet.
13. Broil for 10-12 minutes, brushing occasionally with marinade.
14. Serve hot.

10 servings

Variation:

- *Orange Beef Kebabs: Substitute 3 small oranges for the lemons.*

Step 7. Gently remove mushroom stems, reserving caps.

Step 11. Thread pieces on skewers, alternating mushrooms, lemons, beef and peppers.

Approximate nutritional analysis per serving
Calories 591, Protein 57 g, Carbohydrates 6 g, Fat 37 g, Cholesterol 162 mg, Sodium 580 mg

Lemon Beef Kebabs

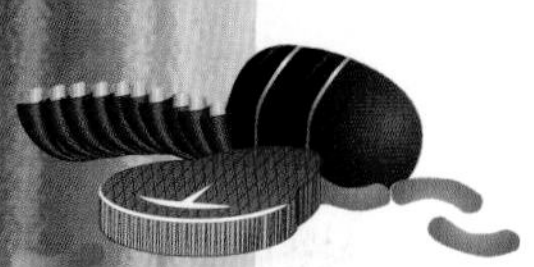

Traditional Beef Pot Roast

This familiar stand-by is both economical and irresistible.

INGREDIENTS

3 lbs	**(1.4 kg) beef bottom round roast, well trimmed of fat**
2 tbsp	**(30 mL) vegetable oil**
1	**medium onion, diced**
2	**medium celery stalks, diced**
1	**medium carrot, peeled and diced**
2 tbsp	**(30 mL) tomato sauce**
½ cup	**(125 mL) canned tomatoes, drained**
3½ cups	**(875 mL) beef broth**
5 tbsp	**(75 mL) all-purpose flour**
½ cup	**(125 mL) cold water**
	salt and pepper

Sachet

1	**small bay leaf**
1	**fresh thyme sprig**
4	**fresh parsley stems**
2	**peppercorns**
1	**garlic clove**

METHOD

1. Preheat oven to 300°F (150°C).
2. Pat roast dry with paper towels.
3. In a large, ovenproof pot, heat oil over high heat.
4. When the oil begins to smoke, place roast in pot. Brown on all sides.
5. Remove roast from pot. Reduce heat to medium-high.
6. Place onions, celery and carrots in pot.
7. Cook vegetables for 2 minutes, until browned.
8. Add tomato sauce, tomatoes and beef broth to vegetables. Stir to combine.
9. Cook until mixture begins to simmer, stirring occasionally.
10. Place sachet ingredients in a cheesecloth and tie with string.

Step 10. Place sachet ingredients in a cheesecloth and tie with string.

11. Place sachet in pot. Return roast to pot and bring to a boil. Remove from heat.
12. Cover pot and place in the oven.
13. Check roast after 20 minutes. Increase or decrease oven temperature to keep liquid at a simmer.
14. Braise roast for 2-3 hours, until tender.
15. Remove roast from pot and keep warm. Discard sachet.
16. Skim any fat from braising liquid.
17. In a small bowl, mix flour and water to make a smooth paste.
18. Bring braising liquid to a boil over medium heat.
19. Stir flour mixture into braising liquid.
20. Reduce heat to low. Simmer sauce for 10 minutes, stirring occasionally.
21. Strain sauce using a sieve.
22. Season sauce to taste with salt and pepper.
23. Place roast on a platter.
24. Using a sharp knife, slice roast across the grain.
25. Serve pot roast accompanied by sauce and roasted vegetables.

8 servings

Approximate nutritional analysis per serving
Calories 440, Protein 57 g, Carbohydrates 10 g, Fat 18 g, Cholesterol 163 mg, Sodium 765 mg

Traditional Beef Pot Roast

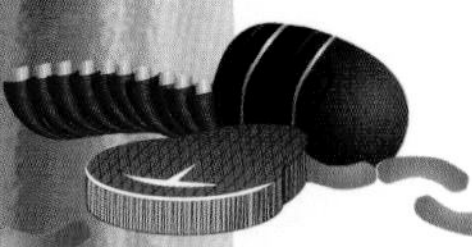

Home-Style Baked Meat Loaf

Comfort food at its finest.

INGREDIENTS

1½ lbs	**(675 g) ground beef**
1 cup	**(250 mL) fresh bread crumbs**
2	**large eggs, beaten**
1 cup	**(250 mL) tomato sauce**
1	**medium onion, finely chopped**
2 tbsp	**(30 mL) green pepper, chopped**
3 tbsp	**(45 mL) Parmesan cheese, grated**
1 tsp	**(5 mL) dried thyme leaves**
	salt and pepper

METHOD

1. Preheat oven to 350°F (175°C).
2. Combine all ingredients in a large bowl. Mix well.
3. Form mixture into a loaf and place in a shallow baking pan.
4. Bake for 1 hour, until a meat thermometer inserted into center of meat loaf reaches 165°F (74°C).
5. Serve hot.

6 servings

Approximate nutritional analysis per serving
Calories 268, Protein 28 g, Carbohydrates 8 g, Fat 13 g, Cholesterol 115 mg, Sodium 467 mg

Beef and Broccoli Stir-Fry

A fabulous meal in minutes.

INGREDIENTS

¼ cup	**(50 mL) peanut oil**
1 lb	**(450 g) beef tenderloin, cut into 3 x 1-inch (7 x 2.5 cm) strips**
4	**garlic cloves, chopped**
1 cup	**(250 mL) onions, sliced**
1 tbsp	**(15 mL) ginger root, peeled and grated**
2 lbs	**(900 g) broccoli, cut into flowerets and blanched**
6 oz	**(170 g) snow peas, blanched**
1¼ cups	**(300 mL) beef broth**
2 tbsp	**(30 mL) soy sauce**
	salt and pepper
1 tbsp	**(15 mL) cornstarch**
3 tbsp	**(45 mL) water**

METHOD

1. Place oil in a wok or large skillet.
2. Over high heat, bring oil to smoking point.
3. Add beef to wok. Sauté for 2 minutes, stirring constantly.
4. Add garlic, onions and ginger, stirring to combine.
5. Still sautéeing over high heat, stir in broccoli and snow peas.
6. Add beef broth, soy sauce, salt and pepper.
7. In a small bowl, dissolve cornstarch in water.
8. Stir cornstarch mixture into wok.
9. Cook for 30 seconds, until sauce has thickened.
10. Serve immediately over rice or noodles.

8 servings

Approximate nutritional analysis per serving
Calories 233, Protein 23 g, Carbohydrates 11 g, Fat 12 g, Cholesterol 51 mg, Sodium 717 mg

Beef and Broccoli Stir-Fry

Marinated Flank Steak

Flank steak is a rare treat when cooked over a very hot flame.

INGREDIENTS

1 lb	**(450 g) beef flank steak**
	black pepper
¼ cup	**(50 mL) olive oil**
3 tbsp	**(45 mL) fresh lemon juice**
2 tbsp	**(30 mL) light soy sauce**
2	**garlic cloves, minced**
1 tbsp	**(15 mL) brown sugar**

Step 1. Rub both sides of steak with pepper.

Step 4. Pour marinade over steak. Turn steak to coat well with marinade.

Step 10. Slice steak against the grain, holding knife at a 45° angle.

METHOD

1. Rub both sides of steak with pepper.
2. In a small bowl, whisk together oil, lemon juice, soy sauce, garlic and brown sugar.
3. Place steak in a flat pan.
4. Pour marinade over steak. Turn steak to coat well with marinade.
5. Marinate steak in the refrigerator for 2-3 hours, turning steak occasionally.
6. Oil grilling rack with vegetable oil. Heat grill.
7. Cook steak over a hot flame for 5-6 minutes, brushing occasionally with marinade.
8. Turn steak over and grill for another 5-6 minutes. Brush with marinade.
9. Remove steak from grill and let stand for 10 minutes.
10. Slice steak against the grain, holding knife at a 45° angle.
11. Serve with baked potatoes or rice.

2 servings

Tip:

- *Do not overcook flank steak as it will become very dry.*

Approximate nutritional analysis per serving
Calories 749, Protein 63 g, Carbohydrates 9 g, Fat 50 g, Cholesterol 153 mg, Sodium 700 mg

Marinated Flank Steak

Classic Roast Beef Au Jus

A timeless recipe for entertaining family and friends.

INGREDIENTS

2½ lbs	**(1.2 kg) beef rib roast**
	salt and pepper
2 cups	**(500 mL) beef broth**

METHOD

1. Preheat oven to 350°F (175°C).
2. Place roast, fat side up, in a roasting pan.
3. Season with salt and pepper.
4. Place in oven and cook for 1-1½ hours, basting occasionally with pan juices.
5. Remove roast once desired degree of doneness is reached. Meat thermometer readings for doneness:
   Rare: 125°F (52°C)
   Medium: 160°F (71°C)
   Well Done: 170°F (77°C)
6. Remove roast from pan.
7. Skim excess fat from pan drippings.
8. Add beef broth to pan.
9. Cook over medium heat for 3-4 minutes, stirring occasionally.
10. Strain au jus with a sieve.
11. Cut roast toward ribs into slices.
12. Serve beef slices accompanied by au jus.

6 servings

Variations:

- *Season beef with 2 tsp (10 mL) garlic powder or onion powder before roasting.*
- *2 sprigs of fresh herbs, such as rosemary, or 2 tsp (10 mL) dried herbs may be rubbed into roast before cooking.*

Approximate nutritional analysis per serving
Calories 459, Protein 54 g, Carbohydrates 1 g, Fat 25 g, Cholesterol 155 mg, Sodium 4350 mg

Classic Roast Beef Au Jus

New England Boiled Dinner

This tasty meal in itself is traditionally accompanied by cooked beets.

INGREDIENTS

3 lbs	**(1.4 kg) corned beef brisket, trimmed of excess fat**
1	**small rutabaga or turnip, trimmed, peeled and cut into 1-inch (2.5 cm) pieces**
4	**medium carrots, peeled and cut into 1-inch (2.5 cm) pieces**
4	**small white onions, cut into wedges**
1	**small green cabbage head, cut into wedges**

METHOD

1. Place brisket in a stockpot.
2. Add enough cold water to cover brisket.
3. Bring to a boil. Reduce heat to low.
4. Simmer brisket for 2-3 hours, until tender.
5. Slice brisket across grain into thin slices. Reserve cooking liquid.
6. Place sliced brisket, covered with ½ cup (125 mL) cooking liquid, in a warm place.
7. Place remaining cooking liquid, rutabaga and carrots in a large skillet.
8. Over medium heat, cook vegetables for 7-8 minutes.
9. Add onions to vegetable mixture and cook for 4-5 minutes.
10. Add cabbage and cook for an additional 5 minutes.
11. Drain cooking liquid from vegetables.
12. Serve vegetables with warm brisket slices.

6 servings

Tip:

- *Corned beef may also be served cold. Serve sliced with pickles and potato salad or use for sandwiches.*

Approximate nutritional analysis per serving
Calories 668, Protein 45 g, Carbohydrates 24 g, Fat 44 g, Cholesterol 222 mg, Sodium 2675 mg

New England Boiled Dinner

Meatballs in Pasta Nests

Mouth-watering meatballs nestled on perfect beds of pasta.

INGREDIENTS

2 tbsp	**(30 mL) vegetable oil**
⅔ cup	**(175 mL) onion, finely chopped**
½ cup	**(125 mL) white bread crumbs**
1 cup	**(250 mL) milk**
2	**medium eggs, beaten**
1½ lbs	**(675 g) ground beef**
6½ oz	**(185 g) ground pork**
½ tsp	**(2 mL) dill weed**
¼ tsp	**(1 mL) nutmeg**
¼ tsp	**(1 mL) allspice**
	salt and pepper
6	**pasta nests**

Step 6. Add onions and bread crumb mixture to ground meat. Mix well.

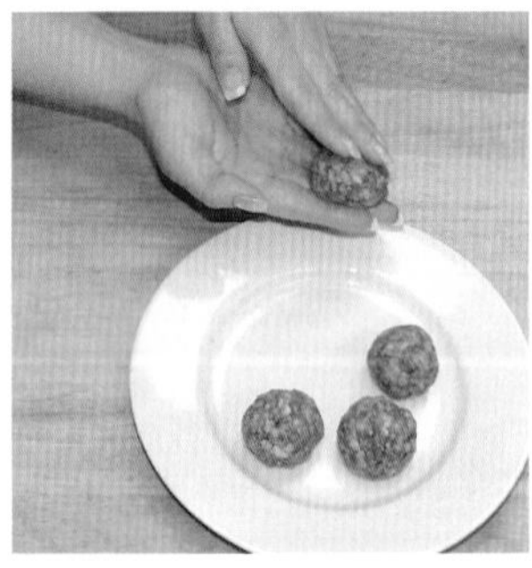

Step 10. Form meat mixture into 1-inch (2.5 cm) balls.

Step 13. Place 3 meatballs in each pasta nest.

METHOD

1. In a small skillet, heat oil over medium heat.
2. Sauté onions for 4-5 minutes, until tender.
3. Remove from heat and cool.
4. In a medium bowl, combine bread crumbs, milk and eggs. Let stand for 15 minutes.
5. In a large bowl, combine ground beef and pork.
6. Add onions and bread crumb mixture to ground meat. Mix well.
7. Add dill, nutmeg, allspice, salt and pepper. Combine thoroughly.
8. Cover with plastic wrap and refrigerate for 1 hour.
9. Heat oven to 350°F (175°C).
10. Form meat mixture into 1-inch (2.5 cm) balls.
11. Place meatballs on a baking sheet and bake for 10 minutes.
12. While the meatballs are baking, cook pasta nests according to package directions.
13. Place 3 meatballs in each pasta nest.
14. Serve hot with a cream or tomato sauce and grated Parmesan cheese.

6 servings

Tip:

- *Pasta nests are noodles formed into nest shapes. They are available in the pasta section of most supermarkets.*

Approximate nutritional analysis per serving
Calories 520, Protein 40 g, Carbohydrates 31 g, Fat 25 g, Cholesterol 164 mg, Sodium 264 mg

Meatballs in Pasta Nests

Beef Ragout with Rosemary

A rich, flavorful stew brimming with good taste.

INGREDIENTS

½ cup	**(125 mL) all-purpose flour**
2 tsp	**(10 mL) salt**
1 tsp	**(5 mL) white pepper**
5 tbsp	**(75 mL) olive oil**
1 lb	**(450 g) stew beef, cut into 1-inch (2.5 cm) cubes**
4 cups	**(1 L) dry red wine**
16 oz	**(500 mL) canned tomatoes, undrained**
3	**garlic cloves, crushed**
3	**fresh rosemary sprigs**
1	**large red onion, chopped**
1	**medium carrot, peeled and chopped**
1	**celery stalk, chopped**
	salt and pepper

Bouquet Garni

6	**fresh parsley stems**
3	**fresh rosemary sprigs**
1	**whole clove**
6	**peppercorns**

METHOD

1. In a medium bowl, combine flour, salt and pepper.
2. Dredge stew beef in seasoned flour. Shake off excess.
3. In a large skillet, heat 3 tbsp (45 mL) oil over high heat.
4. Brown stew beef, turning cubes until they are evenly browned.
5. Stir in red wine and bring to a boil. Reduce heat to low.
6. Cover and simmer for 1 hour.
7. Add tomatoes with their juice, garlic, and rosemary.
8. Simmer ragout, uncovered, for 1 hour, stirring occasionally.
9. In a skillet, heat remaining oil over medium heat.
10. Add onions, carrots and celery to skillet.
11. Sauté vegetables for 7-8 minutes, until they are partially cooked.
12. Add vegetable mixture to ragout.
13. Cook, uncovered, for 40-45 minutes, stirring occasionally.
14. Place bouquet garni ingredients in a cheesecloth and tie with a string.
15. Add bouquet garni to ragout.
16. Season ragout to taste with salt and pepper.
17. Simmer for 15-20 minutes.
18. Remove bouquet garni and rosemary sprigs.
19. Serve hot with bread.

6 servings

Approximate nutritional analysis per serving
Calories 466, Protein 26 g, Carbohydrates 19 g, Fat 20 g, Cholesterol 77 mg, Sodium 724 mg

Beef Ragout with Rosemary

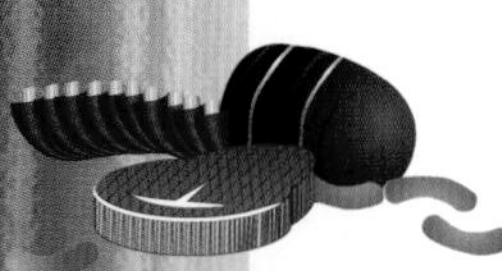

Island Beef Stew

A hearty, satisfying recipe. Your guests will want seconds!

INGREDIENTS

1½ lbs	**(675 g) stew beef, cut into 1-inch (2.5 cm) cubes**
3 tbsp	**(45 mL) vegetable oil**
3 tbsp	**(45 mL) all-purpose flour**
14 oz	**(398 mL) canned tomatoes, undrained**
2	**medium onions, sliced**
1 tsp	**(5 mL) celery salt**
¼ tsp	**(1 mL) black pepper**
⅓ cup	**(75 mL) cider vinegar**
⅓ cup	**(75 mL) molasses**
1 cup	**(250 mL) beef broth**
3	**medium carrots, peeled and chopped**
½ cup	**(125 mL) raisins**
½ tsp	**(2 mL) ginger root, peeled and grated**

METHOD

1. Preheat oven to 350°F (175°C).
2. Pat beef dry with paper towels.
3. In an ovenproof skillet, heat oil over high heat.
4. Brown beef, turning cubes until they are evenly browned.
5. Add flour to skillet. Cook, stirring constantly, for 1 minute.
6. Reduce heat to medium.
7. Add tomatoes with their juice, onions, celery salt and pepper. Stir to combine.
8. In a small bowl, combine vinegar, molasses and beef broth.
9. Add vinegar mixture to stew. Stir well and bring to a boil.
10. Cover skillet and place in the oven.
11. Bake for 2 hours, until beef is tender.
12. Stir in carrots, raisins and ginger.
13. Continue baking until carrots are tender, about 20 minutes.
14. Serve hot with rice and biscuits.

6 servings

Approximate nutritional analysis per serving
Calories 436, Protein 39 g, Carbohydrates 37 g, Fat 15 g, Cholesterol 110 mg, Sodium 822 mg

Island Beef Stew

Chili Cheese Burritos

Cheddar cheese, sour cream and salsa add zest to this family favorite.

INGREDIENTS

1 tbsp	**(15 mL) vegetable oil**
1	**medium onion, sliced**
2	**garlic cloves, minced**
1 lb	**(450 g) ground beef**
1½ cups	**(375 mL) chunky salsa**
2 tbsp	**(30 mL) chili powder**
1 cup	**(250 mL) canned kidney beans, drained**
4	**10-inch (25 cm) soft tortilla shells**
1¼ cups	**(300 mL) Cheddar cheese, grated**
4 tbsp	**(60 mL) sour cream**
¼	**lettuce head, shredded**
2	**tomatoes, chopped**

METHOD

1. In a large skillet, heat oil over medium-high heat.
2. Add onions and garlic. Sauté for 2 minutes, until soft.
3. Add ground beef to skillet and cook until browned. Drain off fat.
4. Stir in salsa and chili powder. Bring to a simmer.
5. Reduce heat to medium. Cover and simmer for 1 hour.
6. Add kidney beans and continue cooking for 10-15 minutes.
7. Place tortilla shells on a flat surface.
8. Spoon ground beef mixture evenly onto one side of each tortilla shell.
9. Place ¼ cup (50 mL) cheese, 1 tbsp (15 mL) sour cream, lettuce and tomatoes on top of ground beef.
10. Fold shell over filling.
11. Fold in sides of shells and finish rolling the rest of the way around filling.
12. Garnish burritos with remaining cheese.
13. Serve with chili sauce.

4 servings

Step 8. Spoon ground beef mixture evenly onto one side of each tortilla shell.

Step 10. Fold shell over filling.

Step 11. Fold in sides of shells and finish rolling the rest of the way around filling.

Approximate nutritional analysis per serving
Calories 601, Protein 41 g, Carbohydrates 41 g, Fat 31 g, Cholesterol 85 mg, Sodium 1131 mg

Chili Cheese Burritos

Mazatlan Tacos

An easy recipe full of Mexican flavor.

INGREDIENTS

1½ lbs	**(675 g) ground beef**
1	**medium onion, chopped**
1	**garlic clove, minced**
1 tsp	**(5 mL) chili powder**
½ tsp	**(2 mL) cumin**
	salt and pepper
½ cup	**(125 mL) tomato sauce**
6	**hard taco shells**

METHOD

1. Place ground beef in a heavy skillet.
2. Cook over medium heat, stirring to break beef into small pieces. Remove from heat when ground beef is well-browned and crumbly.
3. Pour off any excess fat.
4. Return skillet to heat. Add onions and garlic.
5. Cook for 5 minutes over medium heat, stirring occasionally, until onions are soft.
6. Stir in chili powder, cumin, salt, pepper and tomato sauce.
7. Continue cooking over medium heat for 10-15 minutes.
8. Spoon ground beef mixture into taco shells.
9. Serve with grated Cheddar cheese, shredded lettuce, chopped tomatoes and sour cream.

6 servings

Texas Chili

Perfect for an informal get-together.

INGREDIENTS

¼ cup	**(50 mL) vegetable oil**
1	**large onion, finely chopped**
1	**green pepper, chopped**
½ cup	**(125 mL) celery, finely chopped**
1 lb	**(450 g) lean ground beef**
½ tsp	**(2 mL) paprika**
1 tsp	**(5 mL) chili powder**
2½ cups	**(625 mL) canned, chopped tomatoes, undrained**
2½ cups	**(625 mL) red kidney beans, drained**

METHOD

1. In a heavy skillet, heat oil over medium-high heat.
2. Cook onions, green peppers and celery in skillet until browned. Remove from skillet.
3. Still over medium-high heat, cook ground beef until browned.
4. Drain excess fat from ground beef.
5. Return vegetables to skillet.
6. Add paprika, chili powder and tomatoes with their juice. Stir to mix well.
7. Reduce heat to low.
8. Cover and simmer for 1 hour.
9. Stir in kidney beans. Cook for 5 minutes.
10. Serve hot with fresh or toasted bread.

6 servings

Tip:

- *1 oz (30 g) dark, unsweetened chocolate added to this recipe imparts a wonderful color and flavor to the chili.*

Approximate nutritional analysis per serving
Calories 336, Protein 23 g, Carbohydrates 25 g, Fat 17 g, Cholesterol 28 mg, Sodium 595 mg

◀ Approximate nutritional analysis per serving
Calories 415, Protein 29 g, Carbohydrates 18 g, Fat 25 g, Cholesterol 89 mg, Sodium 257 mg

Texas Chili

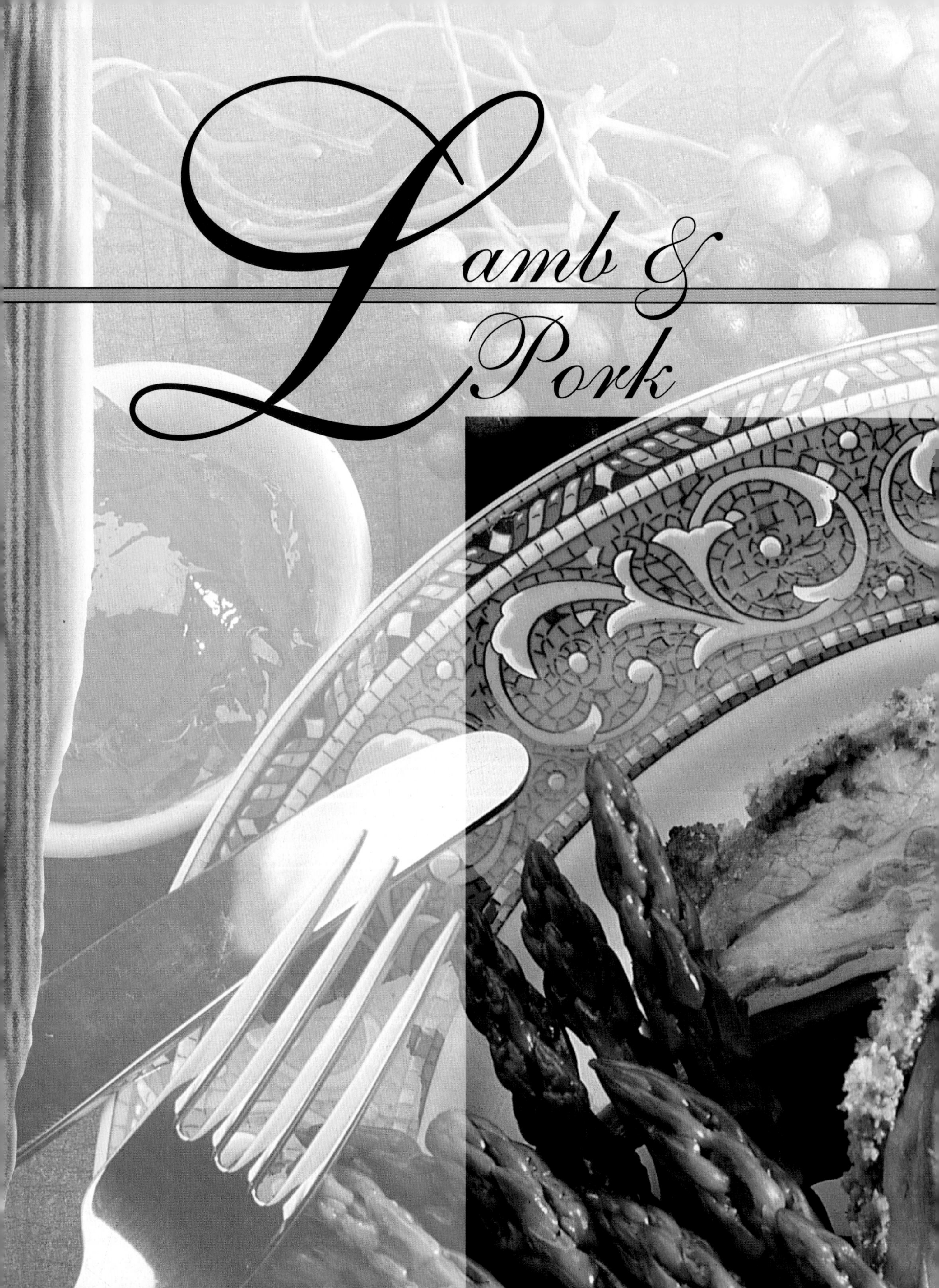
Lamb &
Pork

Onion, Apricot and Raisin Relish

A tasty relish for your favorite meat.

INGREDIENTS

⅓ cup **(75 mL) dried apricots, chopped**
⅓ cup **(75 mL) golden raisins**
½ cup **(125 mL) Madeira wine**
6 tbsp **(90 mL) butter**
1½ cups **(375 mL) red onion, finely diced**
2 tbsp **(30 mL) sugar**
⅓ cup **(75 mL) white wine vinegar**
½ cup **(125 mL) dry white wine**
1 tsp **(5 mL) cinnamon (optional)**

METHOD

1. Place apricots, raisins and Madeira in a small bowl.
2. Cover with plastic wrap and marinate in refrigerator for at least 2 hours.
3. In a saucepan, melt butter over medium heat.
4. Add onions and sugar to saucepan.
5. Cover. Cook for 15 minutes, stirring occasionally.
6. Stir in vinegar and wine.
7. Cook mixture, uncovered, for 20 minutes, until liquid is reduced by two-thirds.
8. Add apricot mixture and cinnamon. Cook, stirring constantly, until mixture is thick.
9. Serve as an accompaniment to pork, lamb or chicken.

1½ cups (375 mL)

Tip:

- *This relish may be refrigerated for up to 3 months.*

Approximate nutritional analysis per 1 tablespoon (15 mL) serving
Calories 56, Protein 0 g, Carbohydrates 6 g, Fat 3 g, Cholesterol 8 mg, Sodium 2 mg

Cranberry Pork Tenderloin

Simple, quick and delicious.

INGREDIENTS

1½ lbs **(675 g) pork tenderloin**
1 tsp **(5 mL) salt**
1 tsp **(5 mL) pepper**
2 tbsp **(30 mL) vegetable oil**
1 cup **(250 mL) cranberries**
½ cup **(125 mL) honey**
¼ tsp **(1 mL) cloves**
¼ tsp **(1 mL) nutmeg**

METHOD

1. Cut pork tenderloin into 2-inch (5 cm) thick slices.
2. Place pork between 2 pieces of plastic wrap.
3. Gently flatten pork with a small rolling pin.
4. Season pork with salt and pepper.
5. In a heavy skillet, heat oil over medium heat.
6. Brown pork slices. Remove from skillet and keep warm.
7. Add remaining ingredients to skillet.
8. Cook over medium heat for 4-5 minutes, until cranberries are soft.
9. Return pork to skillet. Cook for an additional 3 minutes.
10. Serve hot with vegetables and rice or potatoes.

4 servings

Approximate nutritional analysis per serving
Calories 482, Protein 48 g, Carbohydrates 38 g, Fat 15 g, Cholesterol 134 mg, Sodium 631 mg

Cranberry Pork Tenderloin

Pork Loin Braised in Ale

A special recipe full of rich flavors.

INGREDIENTS

4 lbs	**(1.8 kg) boneless pork loin**
1 tbsp	**(15 mL) salt**
½ tsp	**(2 mL) dried thyme**
¼ tsp	**(1 mL) ground bay leaf**
¼ tsp	**(1 mL) dried marjoram**
3 tbsp	**(45 mL) vegetable oil**
2	**large onions, chopped**
1	**garlic clove, chopped**
2 cups	**(500 mL) dark ale**
1 tbsp	**(15 mL) dark brown sugar**
¼ cup	**(50 mL) butter, softened**
6 tbsp	**(90 mL) all-purpose flour**

METHOD

1. Preheat oven to 300°F (150°C).
2. Trim excess fat from pork. Tie pork loin with string.
3. In a small bowl, combine salt, thyme, bay leaf, and marjoram.
4. Rub seasoning mixture over pork.
5. Place pork in a shallow pan. Cover with plastic wrap and refrigerate for 2 hours.
6. In a heavy skillet, heat oil over medium heat.
7. Cook pork loin until browned on all sides. Transfer to an ovenproof casserole dish.
8. Place onions and garlic in skillet. Cook for 5 minutes, until browned.
9. Stir in ale and brown sugar. Bring mixture to a boil.
10. Pour onion mixture over pork loin.
11. Bake for 1½-2 hours, until juices run clear when pork is pricked with a fork.
12. Remove pork loin from casserole dish and place on a platter.
13. In a small bowl, combine butter and flour to form a smooth paste (beurre manié).
14. Heat casserole dish over medium heat. Bring cooking liquid to a boil.
15. Using a whisk, slowly add just enough beurre manié to thicken sauce. Reduce heat to low.
16. Simmer sauce for 3 minutes.
17. Cut pork loin into slices.
18. Pour sauce over pork slices and serve.

8 servings

Tip:

- *Any remaining beurre manié may be stored in a plastic bag in the refrigerator for up to 3 months.*

Approximate nutritional analysis per serving
Calories 701, Protein 63 g, Carbohydrates 11 g, Fat 42 g, Cholesterol 197 mg, Sodium 971 mg

Pork Loin Braised in Ale

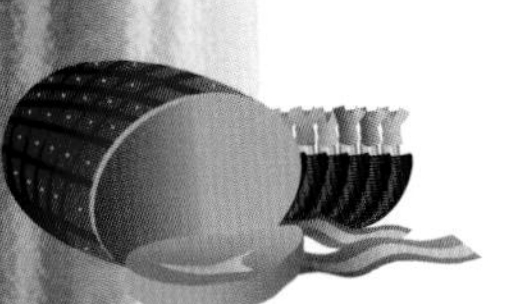

Pork Chops with Glazed Onions

A delectable blend of tangy and sweet flavors.

INGREDIENTS

¼ cup	**(50 mL) all-purpose flour**
1 tsp	**(5 mL) salt**
½ tsp	**(2 mL) white pepper**
4	**6-oz (170 g) center cut pork chops**
3 tbsp	**(45 mL) olive oil**
2	**medium red onions, sliced**
2 cups	**(500 mL) whole, stewed tomatoes, undrained**
1 cup	**(250 mL) red wine**
1 cup	**(250 mL) sweet pickled onions, drained**
1 tbsp	**(15 mL) cider vinegar**
½ tsp	**(2 mL) fresh thyme, chopped**
	salt and black pepper
1 tbsp	**(15 mL) brown sugar**

METHOD

1. Preheat oven to 350°F (175°C).
2. In a medium bowl, combine flour with salt and pepper.
3. Dredge pork chops with seasoned flour.
4. In a heavy skillet, heat 2 tbsp (30 mL) oil over medium heat.
5. Cook pork chops in skillet until browned on both sides.
6. Transfer pork chops to an ovenproof casserole dish.
7. Using the same skillet, heat remaining oil over medium heat.
8. Sauté onions for 5 minutes, until soft.
9. In a medium bowl, crush tomatoes and their juice with a fork.
10. Add tomatoes and wine to skillet. Simmer for 5 minutes.
11. Add pickled onions and vinegar. Cook for an additional 3 minutes.
12. Stir in thyme and season with salt and pepper.
13. Pour mixture over pork chops. Sprinkle with brown sugar.
14. Cover and bake for 1 hour, until pork chops are tender.
15. Serve hot.

4 servings

Approximate nutritional analysis per serving
Calories 851, Protein 49 g, Carbohydrates 25 g, Fat 58 g, Cholesterol 119 mg, Sodium 950 mg

Pork Chops with Glazed Onions

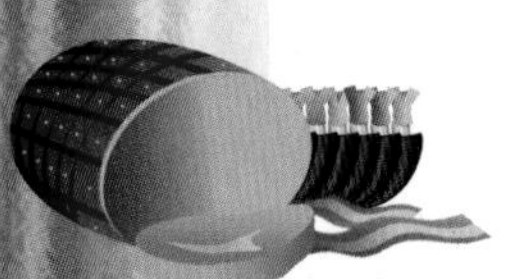

Caribbean Pork Tenderloin

Coconut adds a delicious, subtle flavor to this colorful dish.

INGREDIENTS

2 lbs	**(900 g) pork tenderloin**
1¼ cups	**(300 mL) coconut milk**
4 tbsp	**(60 mL) vegetable oil**
1	**medium green pepper, diced**
1	**medium yellow pepper, diced**
1	**medium red pepper, diced**
1 tbsp	**(15 mL) cornstarch**
3 tbsp	**(45 mL) cold water**
1 tbsp	**(15 mL) sugar**
1¼ cups	**(300 mL) unsweetened coconut, shredded**
1	**lime, cut into wedges**

METHOD

1. Place pork tenderloin and half the coconut milk in a shallow pan.
2. Cover with plastic wrap and marinate in refrigerator for 3 hours.
3. Heat oven to 375°F (190°C).
4. In a heavy skillet, heat 3 tbsp (45 mL) oil over medium heat.
5. Remove pork from marinade and place in skillet.
6. Brown pork on all sides. Transfer to a roasting pan.
7. Bake for 20-25 minutes.
8. Using the same skillet, heat remaining oil over medium heat.
9. Sauté peppers for 5 minutes, until soft.
10. In a small bowl, dissolve cornstarch in water.
11. Stir remaining coconut milk into skillet.
12. Add sugar, stirring to combine.
13. Bring sauce to a boil. Stir in cornstarch mixture.
14. Cook, stirring constantly, until sauce thickens.
15. Remove sauce from heat and stir in coconut.
16. Slice pork and arrange on 4 serving plates.
17. Pour sauce over pork slices.
18. Garnish pork with lime wedges.
19. Serve with sliced melon or fried bananas.

4 servings

Approximate nutritional analysis per serving
Calories 874, Protein 72 g, Carbohydrates 28 g, Fat 53 g, Cholesterol 213 mg, Sodium 233 mg

Caribbean Pork Tenderloin

Marinated Pork with Clams

A fresh loaf of bread is the perfect accompaniment to this tasty recipe.

INGREDIENTS

1½ cups	**(375 mL) dry white wine**
4 tsp	**(20 mL) paprika**
1	**bay leaf**
	salt and pepper
6	**garlic cloves, crushed**
2 lbs	**(900 g) boneless pork loin, cut into 1-inch (2.5 cm) cubes**
2 tbsp	**(30 mL) vegetable oil**
2	**medium onions, sliced**
1	**medium red pepper, sliced**
16 oz	**(500 mL) canned tomatoes, drained and chopped**
1 tbsp	**(15 mL) hot pepper sauce**
24	**small, hard-shell clams**
¼ cup	**(50 mL) fresh parsley, chopped**

METHOD

1. In a large bowl, combine wine, paprika, bay leaf, salt, pepper and garlic.
2. Add pork, tossing well to coat with marinade.
3. Cover with plastic wrap and refrigerate for 4 hours, turning pork occasionally.
4. Drain pork and reserve marinade.
5. Remove bay leaf and garlic from marinade.
6. Pat pork dry with paper towels.
7. In a heavy skillet, heat oil over medium-high heat.
8. Cook pork in small batches until browned.
9. Remove pork with a slotted spoon and place in a bowl. Reduce heat to medium.
10. Add onions and peppers to skillet. Cook for 5 minutes, until onions are soft.
11. Stir reserved marinade and tomatoes into skillet.
12. Add salt, pepper and hot pepper sauce, stirring to combine.
13. Place clams in skillet and cover.
14. Cook for 5 minutes, until clams are open.
15. Return pork to skillet and heat through. Season with salt and pepper to taste.
16. Sprinkle with parsley and serve.

4 servings

Tip:

- *How To Select Clams: When purchasing clams, select only those with tightly-closed shells. Clams with open shells are dead or dying, and should be passed up.*

Approximate nutritional analysis per serving
Calories 668, Protein 55 g, Carbohydrates 14 g, Fat 37 g, Cholesterol 170 mg, Sodium 458 mg

Marinated Pork with Clams

Pork Chops with Sour Berries

Just a hint of tart fruit flavor.

INGREDIENTS

4	**7-oz (200 g) center cut pork chops**
	salt and black pepper
2 tbsp	**(30 mL) vegetable oil**
1 cup	**(250 mL) long grain rice, uncooked**
¾ cup	**(175 mL) sour berries, such as cranberries, sour cherries or Saskatoons**
2 cups	**(500 mL) orange juice**
¼ tsp	**(1 mL) cinnamon**
2 tsp	**(10 mL) lemon peel, grated**

METHOD

1. Preheat oven to 350°F (175°C).
2. Season pork chops with salt and pepper.
3. In a large skillet, heat oil over medium heat.
4. Brown pork chops on both sides.
5. Place rice in an ovenproof casserole dish.
6. Add berries to rice, stirring to combine.
7. In a medium bowl, combine orange juice, cinnamon and lemon peel. Pour over rice mixture.
8. Arrange pork chops on top of rice.
9. Cover and bake for 1 hour, until rice is cooked.
10. Serve hot.

4 servings

Glazed Ham with Sweet Mustard Sauce

A taste sensation for any occasion.

INGREDIENTS

3	**10-oz (285 g) boneless cooked ham slices, cut ½-inch (1.3 cm) thick**
¼ cup	**(50 mL) butter, melted**
½ cup	**(125 mL) maple syrup**
¼ cup	**(50 mL) country-style Dijon mustard**
1 cup	**(250 mL) sugar**
4 tbsp	**(60 mL) dry mustard**
2 tbsp	**(30 mL) cornstarch**
6	**medium eggs**
1 cup	**(250 mL) white vinegar**

METHOD

1. Preheat broiler.
2. Place ham slices in a broiling pan. Brush with butter and maple syrup.
3. Broil on top oven rack for 5 minutes.
4. Turn ham slices. Brush with butter, maple syrup and Dijon mustard and broil for another 3 minutes, until ham is heated through.
5. In a medium bowl, combine sugar, dry mustard and cornstarch.
6. In another medium bowl, whisk eggs.
7. Add eggs to sugar mixture, stirring sauce to combine.
8. Stir in vinegar. Transfer sauce to a double boiler.
9. Cook over medium heat for 10 minutes, stirring constantly.
10. Place ham slices on a cutting board. Cut into quarters.
11. Arrange ham on a platter. Serve hot with sauce.

6 servings

Approximate nutritional analysis per serving
Calories 644, Protein 32 g, Carbohydrates 89 g, Fat 19 g, Cholesterol 237 mg, Sodium 2043 mg

◀ Approximate nutritional analysis per serving
Calories 1180, Protein 61 g, Carbohydrates 94 g, Fat 63 g, Cholesterol 139 mg, Sodium 621 mg

Glazed Ham with Sweet Mustard Sauce

Ratatouille with Sausage

This French classic may be served hot or cold.

INGREDIENTS

1	**large eggplant, cut into 1-inch (2.5 cm) cubes**
4	**medium zucchini, sliced**
¼ cup	**(50 mL) all-purpose flour**
5 tbsp	**(75 mL) olive oil**
3	**small onions, sliced**
3	**garlic cloves, minced**
3	**green peppers, seeded and diced**
4	**tomatoes, blanched, peeled, seeded and chopped**
½ cup	**(125 mL) fresh parsley, chopped**
1 tsp	**(5 mL) oregano**
1 tsp	**(5 mL) thyme**
1 tsp	**(5 mL) basil**
1 tsp	**(5 mL) salt**
1 tsp	**(5 mL) black pepper**
6	**chorizo sausages, sliced ¼-inch (0.6 cm) thick**

METHOD

1. Preheat oven to 350°F (175°C).
2. Dredge eggplant and zucchini with flour.
3. In a heavy skillet, heat 3 tbsp (45 mL) oil over medium heat.
4. Sauté eggplant and zucchini in batches for 3 minutes. Drain on paper towels.
5. Place eggplant and zucchini in a large, ovenproof casserole dish.
6. Using the same skillet, heat remaining oil over medium heat.
7. Sauté onions, garlic and green peppers for 5 minutes, until soft.
8. Place onion mixture on top of eggplant and zucchini in casserole dish.
9. Layer tomatoes and parsley on top of onion mixture.
10. Sprinkle oregano, thyme, basil, salt and pepper on top of casserole.
11. Cover and bake for 35 minutes.
12. While casserole is baking, heat skillet over medium heat.
13. Sauté sausage slices for 2-3 minutes per side, until browned. Add more oil if required.
14. Drain sausage slices on paper towels.
15. Place sausage slices in casserole dish, pushing some of the slices down into vegetable mixture.
16. Bake for 20 more minutes.
17. Garnish with parsley and serve with Italian bread and a green salad.

6 servings

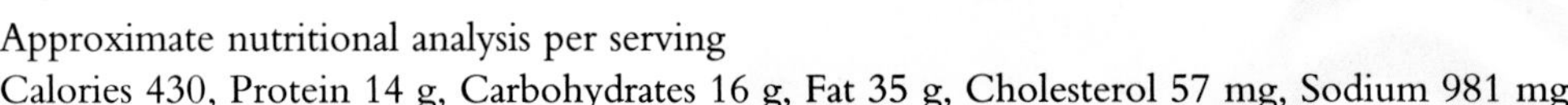

Approximate nutritional analysis per serving
Calories 430, Protein 14 g, Carbohydrates 16 g, Fat 35 g, Cholesterol 57 mg, Sodium 981 mg

Ratatouille with Sausage

Roasted Souchong Spareribs

These mouth-watering ribs are a blend of smoky, sweet and spicy tastes.

INGREDIENTS

2½ tbsp	**(40 mL) Lapsang Souchong tea leaves**
2 cups	**(500 mL) boiling water**
⅓ cup	**(75 mL) dark soy sauce**
4	**garlic cloves, crushed**
3	**whole cloves**
1	**star anise pod**
¼ cup	**(50 mL) brown sugar**
3 lbs	**(1.4 kg) lean pork spareribs, cut between ribs**
¼ cup	**(50 mL) butter**
2	**large onions, thinly sliced**

METHOD

1. Place tea leaves in a medium bowl.
2. Pour water over tea leaves and steep for 5 minutes.
3. Strain tea into a large bowl.
4. Stir in soy sauce, garlic, cloves, anise and 2 tbsp (30 mL) brown sugar. Allow marinade to cool.
5. Place ribs in a large saucepan. Cover with water and bring to a boil.
6. Reduce heat to low and simmer for 20 minutes.
7. Drain ribs and rinse under warm water.
8. Place ribs in tea marinade, tossing to coat.
9. Cover with plastic wrap and refrigerate for 4 hours, turning ribs frequently.
10. Heat oven to 350°F (175°C).
11. Remove ribs from marinade and place on a baking sheet.
12. Brush ribs with marinade.
13. Bake for 40-45 minutes, basting frequently with marinade, until ribs are tender.
14. In a heavy skillet, melt butter over medium heat.
15. Cook onions for 5 minutes, until translucent.
16. Sprinkle remaining brown sugar over onions. Increase heat to medium-high.
17. Cook onions, stirring constantly, until they are deep brown in color.
18. Add ⅔ cup (150 mL) marinade to onions. Reduce heat to low.
19. Simmer for 4 minutes.
20. Transfer onion mixture to a food processor. Purée sauce until smooth.
21. Remove ribs from oven and brush with sauce.
22. Bake ribs for an additional 5 minutes.
23. Serve ribs accompanied by remaining sauce.

4 servings

Tip:

- *Lapsang Souchong is a type of black tea, characterized by a distinctive, smoky flavor. It is available in the tea section of most supermarkets.*

Approximate nutritional analysis per serving
Calories 974, Protein 91 g, Carbohydrates 17 g, Fat 58 g, Cholesterol 323 mg, Sodium 1695 mg

Roasted Souchong Spareribs

Special Glazed Spareribs

Tender, glazed ribs so irresistible your guests will want the recipe!

INGREDIENTS

Marinade

1	**medium onion, sliced**
1 cup	**(250 mL) soy sauce**
1 cup	**(250 mL) red wine**
3	**garlic cloves, minced**
2 tbsp	**(30 mL) prepared horseradish**
1 tbsp	**(15 mL) fresh ginger root, peeled and grated**
1 tsp	**(5 mL) lemon peel, grated**

5 lbs	**(2.3 kg) lean pork spareribs**

Glaze

1½ tsp	**(7 mL) cornstarch**
½ cup	**(125 mL) brown sugar**
½ cup	**(125 mL) apple juice**
¼ cup	**(50 mL) ketchup**
¼ tsp	**(1 mL) cloves**
¼ tsp	**(1 mL) nutmeg, grated**

METHOD

1. In a medium bowl, combine all marinade ingredients.
2. Cut spareribs into serving size pieces.
3. Place ribs in a stockpot. Cover with water and bring to a boil.
4. Reduce heat to low and simmer for 15 minutes.
5. Drain ribs and rinse under cold, running water.
6. Place ribs in a shallow pan. Pour marinade over ribs, tossing to coat with marinade.
7. Cover with plastic wrap and refrigerate overnight.
8. Heat grill.
9. In a small saucepan, combine all glaze ingredients.
10. Bring glaze mixture to a boil over medium-high heat, stirring constantly. Remove from heat.
11. Remove ribs from marinade.
12. Brush ribs with glaze and place on grill.
13. Grill ribs, turning and basting occasionally with glaze. Cook for 15-20 minutes, until tender.
14. Serve with corn salad or cobs of corn.

6 servings

Approximate nutritional analysis per serving
Calories 1019, Protein 101 g, Carbohydrates 25 g, Fat 52 g, Cholesterol 324 mg, Sodium 3114 mg

Special Glazed Spareribs

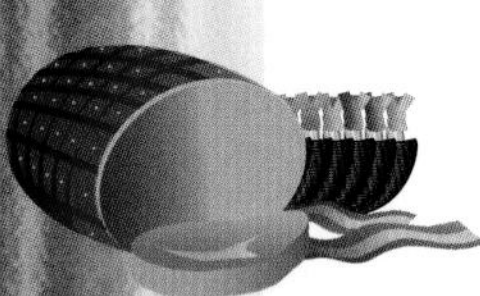

Seasoned Sausage Patties

The wonderful taste of fresh herbs.

INGREDIENTS

1½ lbs	**(675 g) ground pork**
1½ tbsp	**(25 mL) fresh thyme, minced**
1 tbsp	**(15 mL) fresh sage, minced**
½ cup	**(125 mL) fresh parsley, chopped**
½ tsp	**(2 mL) salt**
½ tsp	**(2 mL) black pepper**
2 tbsp	**(30 mL) vegetable oil**

METHOD

1. In a medium bowl, combine all ingredients except oil.
2. Form mixture into patties and place on a plate.
3. Cover with plastic wrap and refrigerate overnight.
4. In a large skillet, heat oil over medium heat.
5. Cook patties for 4-5 minutes per side, until no traces of pink remain.
6. Drain patties on paper towels.
7. Serve with applesauce.

4 servings

Kielbasas in Ale

A unique, new way to prepare sausages.

INGREDIENTS

4	**smoked kielbasa sausages**
2 cups	**(500 mL) water**
1 tbsp	**(15 mL) butter**
1	**medium onion, sliced**
1	**bay leaf**
½ tsp	**(2 mL) fennel seeds**
3	**whole peppercorns**
1½ cups	**(300 mL) ale**

METHOD

1. Prick sausages with a fork.
2. Place sausages and water in a large skillet.
3. Bring to a boil over medium-high heat. Cover.
4. Reduce heat to medium and simmer for 3-4 minutes.
5. Drain sausages and return to heat. Increase heat to medium-high.
6. Add butter to skillet. Cook sausages until browned.
7. Add remaining ingredients to skillet.
8. Simmer, uncovered, for 5 minutes until sausages are heated through. Turn sausages occasionally.
9. Serve hot with braised cabbage.

4 servings

Approximate nutritional analysis per serving
Calories 459, Protein 16 g, Carbohydrates 9 g, Fat 37 g, Cholesterol 88 mg, Sodium 1109 mg

◀ Approximate nutritional analysis per serving
Calories 576, Protein 44 g, Carbohydrates 2 g, Fat 43 g, Cholesterol 161 mg, Sodium 396 mg

Kielbasas in Ale

Sausage-Stuffed Apples

This dish is an excellent accompaniment to roast turkey.

INGREDIENTS

8	**large McIntosh apples**
1 tbsp	**(15 mL) lemon juice**
3 tbsp	**(45 mL) butter**
1¼ cups	**(300 mL) onion, minced**
½ lb	**(225 g) pork sausage meat**
½ cup	**(125 mL) fresh bread crumbs**
1½ tsp	**(7 mL) dried sage**
1 tsp	**(5 mL) lemon peel, grated**
½ tsp	**(2 mL) nutmeg, grated**
1 tsp	**(5 mL) salt**
1 tsp	**(5 mL) pepper**
1½ cups	**(375 mL) chicken broth**
1 tbsp	**(15 mL) cornstarch**
3 tbsp	**(45 mL) water**

METHOD

1. Preheat oven to 400°F (205°C).
2. Cut apples in half lengthwise.
3. Remove apple cores and brush cut edges with lemon juice.
4. In a skillet, melt butter over medium heat.
5. Sauté onions for 5 minutes, until soft. Transfer onions to a bowl.
6. In the same skillet, sauté sausage meat for 5-7 minutes, breaking meat apart as it cooks.
7. Using a slotted spoon, place sausage meat in bowl with onions.
8. Add bread crumbs, sage, lemon peel, nutmeg, salt and pepper to bowl. Combine well.
9. Stuff apples with sausage mixture.
10. Set stuffed apples in an ovenproof casserole dish. Add chicken broth.
11. Cover and bake for 35-40 minutes.
12. Remove apples from casserole dish and keep warm. Pour cooking liquid into a small skillet.
13. Heat cooking liquid over medium heat for 3 minutes.
14. In a small bowl, dissolve cornstarch in water.
15. Add cornstarch mixture to skillet. Cook until sauce has thickened.
16. Serve sauce with stuffed apples.

8 servings

Approximate nutritional analysis per serving
Calories 285, Protein 10 g, Carbohydrates 38 g, Fat 12 g, Cholesterol 39 mg, Sodium 613 mg

Sausage-Stuffed Apples

Scotch Eggs

Serve with salad for a complete meal.

INGREDIENTS

4	**hard-boiled eggs**
2 lbs	**(900 g) pork sausage meat**
3	**medium eggs**
1 tsp	**(5 mL) salt**
1 tsp	**(5 mL) pepper**
3 cups	**(750 mL) fresh bread crumbs**
	vegetable oil for deep frying

METHOD

1. Preheat oven to 350°F (175°C).
2. Remove shells from hard-boiled eggs.
3. In a medium bowl, combine sausage meat with 1 egg. Mix well.
4. Season sausage mixture with salt and pepper.
5. In a small bowl, lightly beat remaining eggs.
6. Heat oil to 300°F (150°C).
7. Pat a thick layer of sausage meat onto each hard-boiled egg.
8. Dip each sausage-covered egg in beaten egg and then into bread crumbs.
9. Deep fry for 2 minutes, until golden brown.
10. Drain eggs on paper towels and place on a baking sheet.
11. Bake for 8-10 minutes.
12. Serve hot or cold.

4 servings

Lamb in Marmalade Sauce

So simple and delicious.

INGREDIENTS

2 lbs	**(900 g) boneless, lean lamb, cut into 1-inch (2.5 cm) cubes**
3 tbsp	**(45 mL) vegetable oil**
2	**medium onions, diced**
2	**garlic cloves, crushed**
2 cups	**(500 mL) three-peel marmalade**
3 tbsp	**(45 mL) cider vinegar**
2 tbsp	**(30 mL) fresh mint leaves, chopped**
1 tsp	**(5 mL) salt**
½ tsp	**(2 mL) pepper**
½ tsp	**(2 mL) cayenne pepper**

METHOD

1. Pat lamb cubes dry with paper towels.
2. In a large skillet, heat oil over medium heat.
3. Sauté onions and garlic for 5 minutes, until golden brown.
4. Remove onion mixture from skillet and keep warm.
5. Increase heat to medium-high.
6. Place lamb in skillet, and cook until browned.
7. Add marmalade, vinegar, mint and onion mixture. Stir to combine.
8. Season with salt, pepper and cayenne pepper. Reduce heat to medium.
9. Cover. Cook for 20 minutes, stirring occasionally, until lamb is thoroughly cooked and tender.
10. Serve with rice, couscous or potatoes.

6 servings

Approximate nutritional analysis per serving
Calories 641, Protein 45 g, Carbohydrates 79 g, Fat 18 g, Cholesterol 136 mg, Sodium 548 mg

◀ Approximate nutritional analysis per serving
Calories 892, Protein 72 g, Carbohydrates 18 g, Fat 57 g, Cholesterol 567 mg, Sodium 973 mg

Lamb in Marmalade Sauce

Apricot-Stuffed Lamb Chops

Lamb with a hint of herbs and the sweet flavor of apricots.

INGREDIENTS

16	**dried apricot halves**
4	**8-oz (225 g) lamb chops, double thick**
1 cup	**(250 mL) onions, sliced**
½ cup	**(125 mL) fresh parsley sprigs**
1 tbsp	**(15 mL) olive oil**
1 tsp	**(5 mL) dried thyme leaves**
1 tsp	**(5 mL) dried basil**
2	**garlic cloves**
3 tbsp	**(45 mL) lemon juice**
1 tsp	**(5 mL) lemon peel, grated**
¼ tsp	**(1 mL) salt**
½ tsp	**(2 mL) black pepper**

Step 2. Cut each lamb chop horizontally through to center bone to form a pocket.

Step 3. Insert 4 apricot halves and ¼ cup (50 mL) of onions into each pocket.

METHOD

1. Soak apricots in warm water for 10 minutes.
2. Cut each lamb chop horizontally through to center bone to form a pocket.
3. Insert 4 apricot halves and ¼ cup (50 mL) of onions into each pocket.
4. Press pockets firmly to close.
5. In a food processor, combine remaining ingredients to form a paste.
6. Rub paste over lamb chops and place on a plate.
7. Cover with plastic wrap and refrigerate for 3 hours.
8. Heat broiler.
9. Place lamb chops on a baking sheet.
10. Broil for 5-6 minutes per side, until browned.
11. Serve hot with rice pilaf.

4 servings

Variation:

- *Soak apricots in brandy for 1 hour before using.*

Approximate nutritional analysis per serving
Calories 574, Protein 69 g, Carbohydrates 13 g, Fat 26 g, Cholesterol 215 mg, Sodium 297 mg

Apricot-Stuffed Lamb Chops

Rack of Lamb with Mustard Crust

An exquisite recipe sure to become a favorite.

INGREDIENTS

2	**racks of lamb, 8 ribs each**
2 tbsp	**(30 mL) honey**
4 tbsp	**(60 mL) country-style Dijon mustard**
2 cups	**(500 mL) fine white bread crumbs**
½ tsp	**(2 mL) salt**
½ tsp	**(2 mL) pepper**

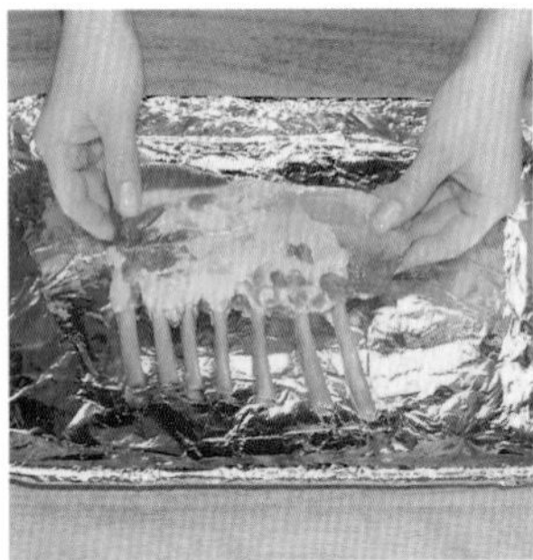

Step 3. Place lamb racks in roasting pan, fat side up.

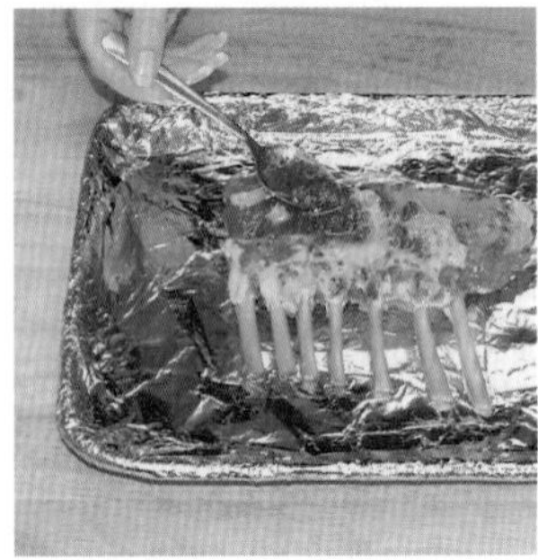

Step 5. Spread mustard mixture evenly onto lamb racks.

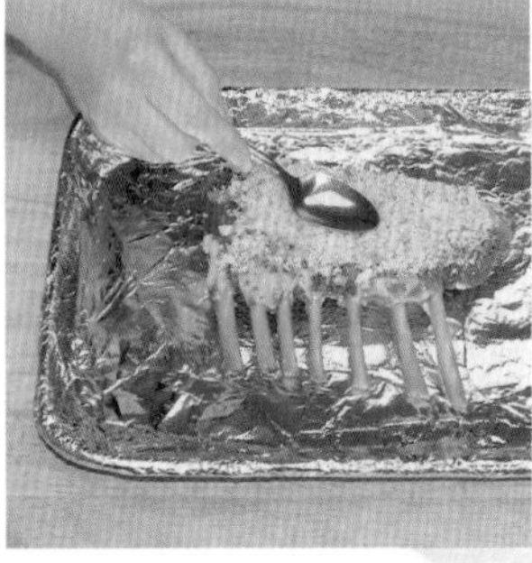

Step 7. Sprinkle lamb racks with bread crumbs, pressing down on crumbs to form a light crust.

METHOD

1. Preheat oven to 450°F (230°C).
2. Line a roasting pan with aluminum foil.
3. Place lamb racks in roasting pan, fat side up.
4. In a small bowl, combine honey and mustard.
5. Spread mustard mixture evenly onto lamb racks.
6. In a medium bowl, combine bread crumbs, salt and pepper.
7. Sprinkle lamb racks with bread crumbs, pressing down on crumbs to form a light crust.
8. Bake until desired degree of doneness is reached. Do not bake for longer than 30 minutes.
9. Allow lamb racks to stand in a warm place for 10 minutes.
10. Slice racks between the ribs into chops.
11. Serve with potatoes, vegetables and mint jelly.

4 servings

Approximate nutritional analysis per serving
Calories 637, Protein 62 g, Carbohydrates 22 g, Fat 32 g, Cholesterol 200 mg, Sodium 943 mg

Rack of Lamb with Mustard Crust

Lamb Kebabs with Zesty Marinade

A unique marinade lends the taste of lemon and fresh herbs to this colorful recipe.

INGREDIENTS

1 cup	**(250 mL) olive oil**
⅓ cup	**(75 mL) lemon juice**
6	**fresh chives, chopped**
1 tbsp	**(15 mL) Dijon mustard**
2 tbsp	**(30 mL) fresh tarragon, chopped or 2 tsp (10 mL) dried tarragon**
1 tsp	**(5 mL) salt**
1½ lbs	**(675 g) boneless lamb shoulder, cut into 1-inch (2.5 cm) cubes**
2	**small zucchini, cut into 1-inch (2.5 cm) cubes**
2	**small banana squash, cut into rounds**

METHOD

1. In a medium glass bowl, combine oil, lemon juice, chives, mustard, tarragon and salt until well blended.
2. Place lamb, zucchini and squash in bowl, tossing to coat pieces with marinade.
3. Cover with plastic wrap and refrigerate overnight.
4. Drain off marinade and reserve.
5. Heat grill.
6. Thread marinated pieces on skewers, alternating lamb, zucchini and squash.
7. Grill kebabs for 8-10 minutes, turning occasionally and brushing with marinade. Kebabs are done when lamb is medium-rare.
8. Serve hot with rice pilaf.

6 servings

Approximate nutritional analysis per serving
Calories 654, Protein 27 g, Carbohydrates 5 g, Fat 59 g, Cholesterol 104 mg, Sodium 205 mg

Lamb Kebabs with Zesty Marinade

Madras Lamb Curry

Make this recipe as mild or spicy as you like by varying the amount of curry.

INGREDIENTS

8	**small red potatoes, halved**
2	**medium carrots, peeled and diced**
1	**small cauliflower head, cut into flowerets**
1½ lbs	**(675 g) boneless leg of lamb, cut into 1-inch (2.5 cm) cubes**
3 tbsp	**(45 mL) Madras curry powder or curry paste to taste**
½ tsp	**(2 mL) black pepper**
2 tbsp	**(30 mL) butter**
2 tbsp	**(30 mL) vegetable oil**
1	**large onion, sliced**
4	**garlic cloves, minced**
1 tbsp	**(15 mL) paprika**
1 tsp	**(5 mL) dry mustard**
¾ cup	**(175 mL) tomato sauce**
1¼ cups	**(300 mL) chicken broth**
3 tbsp	**(45 mL) raisins**
½	**fresh lemon, cut into thin slices**
2 tsp	**(10 mL) salt**
1 tbsp	**(15 mL) fresh coriander or parsley, chopped**

METHOD

1. Preheat oven to 350°F (175°C).
2. Bring a large pot of salted water to a boil.
3. Blanch potatoes and carrots for 3 minutes.
4. Add cauliflower and cook for 2 minutes.
5. Drain cooking liquid from vegetables. Set vegetables aside.
6. In a medium bowl, toss lamb with curry powder and pepper.
7. In a medium skillet, heat butter and oil over medium-high heat.
8. Add lamb and sauté for 3-4 minutes, until browned.
9. Add onions and garlic. Cook for 2 minutes.
10. Stir in paprika, mustard, tomato sauce, chicken broth and raisins.
11. Bring mixture to a boil. Remove from heat.
12. Place lamb mixture in an ovenproof casserole dish.
13. Cover and bake for 1 hour.
14. Add lemon and vegetables to casserole dish.
15. Continue baking for 30 minutes, until vegetables are tender.
16. Season to taste with salt.
17. Garnish with coriander and serve.

6 servings

Approximate nutritional analysis per serving
Calories 507, Protein 32 g, Carbohydrates 21 g, Fat 34 g, Cholesterol 115 mg, Sodium 1360 mg

Madras Lamb Curry

Fish & Seafood

Lime Butter Sauce

A delightful sauce for fish.

INGREDIENTS

¼ cup	**(50 mL) champagne**
¼ cup	**(50 mL) fresh lime juice**
3 tbsp	**(45 mL) sugar**
¼ tsp	**(1 mL) lime peel, grated**
¼ cup	**(50 mL) unsalted butter, cold**

METHOD

1. In a small saucepan, combine champagne, lime juice, sugar and lime peel.
2. Bring to a boil. Reduce heat to medium and simmer until reduced by half.
3. Pour sauce into a small bowl.
4. Whisk butter into sauce, until butter is melted and sauce is the consistency of mayonnaise.
5. Serve with fish, seafood, or cooked, fresh vegetables.

1¼ cups (300 mL)

Approximate nutritional analysis
per 1 tbsp (15 mL) serving
Calories 31, Protein 0 g, Carbohydrates 2 g, Fat 2 g, Cholesterol 6 mg, Sodium 1 mg

Blackened Red Snapper

A Cajun specialty sure to please.

INGREDIENTS

4	**8-oz (225 g) red snapper fillets**
1 cup	**(250 mL) butter**
1 tbsp	**(15 mL) lemon juice**
2 tsp	**(10 mL) thyme**
1 tsp	**(5 mL) black pepper**
1 tsp	**(5 mL) paprika**
½	**lemon, cut into wedges**

METHOD

1. Remove any skin and bones from red snapper fillets.
2. In a large, cast iron skillet, melt butter over medium heat.
3. Stir in lemon juice, thyme, pepper and paprika. Cook for 5 minutes, stirring occasionally. Transfer to a shallow dish.
4. Heat the same skillet over high heat until a white haze forms on the bottom of the skillet.
5. Dip each fillet into butter mixture, then place in skillet.
6. Cook fillets for approximately 1 minute per side.
7. Remove fillets from skillet and place in a serving dish. Cover loosely with aluminum foil and keep warm.
8. Reduce heat to medium-high. Pour remaining butter mixture into skillet.
9. Cook, stirring with a wooden spoon, until butter is dark brown in color.
10. Spoon browned butter over fish.
11. Garnish with lemon wedges and serve.

4 servings

Tip:

- *This recipe produces a great deal of smoke in the kitchen. Try preparing this dish outdoors using a skillet placed on your barbecue grill.*

Approximate nutritional analysis per serving
Calories 641, Protein 47 g, Carbohydrates 2 g, Fat 49 g, Cholesterol 208 mg, Sodium 617 mg

Blackened Red Snapper

Red Snapper Casserole

A delicious, layered trio of onions, red snapper and potatoes.

INGREDIENTS

6	**new potatoes**
1 lb	**(450 g) red snapper fillets**
2 tbsp	**(30 mL) lemon juice**
2 cups	**(500 mL) water**
4½ tbsp	**(70 mL) olive oil**
2	**medium red onions, diced**
1	**garlic clove, chopped**
¼ tsp	**(1 mL) rosemary, crushed**
pinch	**thyme**
	black pepper
¼ cup	**(50 mL) fresh parsley, minced**
1 tsp	**(5 mL) fennel seeds, crushed**
¼ cup	**(50 mL) water**
¼ cup	**(50 mL) white bread crumbs**
	paprika

METHOD

1. Preheat oven to 350°F (175°C).
2. Lightly grease a 9-inch (22 cm) casserole dish.
3. Place potatoes in a medium saucepan.
4. Cover with water and bring to a boil over medium-high heat. Reduce heat to medium.
5. Cook potatoes for 12-15 minutes, until tender.
6. Drain potatoes and allow to cool.
7. Remove any skin and bones from red snapper fillets. Place in a medium skillet.
8. Add 1 tbsp (15 mL) of lemon juice and water to skillet.
9. Poach fillets over medium heat for 3-4 minutes, until fish flakes easily.
10. Peel cooled potatoes and slice thinly. Set aside.
11. In a skillet, heat 3 tbsp (45 mL) of oil over medium heat.
12. Add onions and garlic. Sauté for 5 minutes, stirring occasionally, until golden.
13. Stir in rosemary and thyme. Remove skillet from heat.
14. Spread one-third of the onion mixture into prepared casserole dish.
15. Place half of the red snapper on top of onion mixture.
16. Place half of the potatoes on top of fish.
17. Drizzle with ½ tbsp (7 mL) of oil.
18. Season with pepper. Sprinkle with parsley and fennel.
19. Repeat layering steps, ending with a layer of onions.
20. Combine water and remaining lemon juice in a small bowl. Pour over top of onions.
21. Sprinkle bread crumbs on top of casserole and drizzle with remaining oil.
22. Bake for 35 minutes.
23. Serve hot.

4 servings

Approximate nutritional analysis per serving
Calories 470, Protein 20 g, Carbohydrates 16 g, Fat 37 g, Cholesterol 99 mg, Sodium 400 mg

Red Snapper Casserole

Red Snapper Baked in Grape Leaves

These tasty packages contain red snapper, grapes and seasoned bread crumbs.

INGREDIENTS

4	**6-oz (170 g) red snapper fillets**
2	**garlic cloves, halved**
4 tsp	**(20 mL) olive oil**
	salt and white pepper
4 tbsp	**(60 mL) fresh bread crumbs**
4 tbsp	**(60 mL) Parmesan cheese, grated**
2 tsp	**(10 mL) fresh oregano, chopped**
12	**grape leaves, rinsed thoroughly**
4 tbsp	**(60 mL) seedless black grapes, quartered**

METHOD

1. Preheat oven to 375°F (190°C).

Step 7. Lay out another grape leaf next to first leaf, also rib side up, overlapping first leaf by about ½ inch (1.3 cm).

Step 11. Top fish with a grape leaf, rib side down.

Step 12. Fold sides of lower grape leaves up to enclose fish.

2. Remove any skin and bones from red snapper fillets.
3. Rub one side of each fillet with garlic. Brush with oil.
4. Season fillets with salt and pepper.
5. In a small bowl, combine bread crumbs, Parmesan cheese and oregano.
6. Lay out one grape leaf on work surface, rib side up.
7. Lay out another grape leaf next to first leaf, also rib side up, overlapping first leaf by about ½ inch (1.3 cm).
8. Place 1 tbsp (15 mL) of grapes in center of grape leaves.
9. Sprinkle grape leaves with about 2 tbsp (30 mL) of bread crumb mixture.
10. Place fish, seasoned side down, on top of bread crumb mixture.
11. Top fish with a grape leaf, rib side down.
12. Fold sides of lower grape leaves up to enclose fish.
13. Brush grape leaves with oil.
14. Wrap in aluminum foil, shiny side in, and place on a baking sheet.
15. Repeat steps until all of the grape leaves have been folded.
16. Bake for 20 minutes.
17. Serve hot.

4 servings

Approximate nutritional analysis per serving
Calories 296, Protein 41 g, Carbohydrates 11 g, Fat 10 g, Cholesterol 71 mg, Sodium 358 mg

Red Snapper Baked in Grape Leaves

Baked Salmon Printanière

Fresh, garden vegetables and salmon team up in this magnificent creation.

INGREDIENTS

1	**24-oz (675 g) salmon fillet**
8 cups	**(2 L) water**
2 tbsp	**(30 mL) salt**
6 oz	**(170 g) fresh green beans**
3	**medium carrots, peeled and julienned**
2	**medium onions, julienned**
3	**celery stalks, julienned**
1	**medium red pepper, julienned**
3 tbsp	**(45 mL) butter**
	salt and pepper
¼ tsp	**(1 mL) paprika**

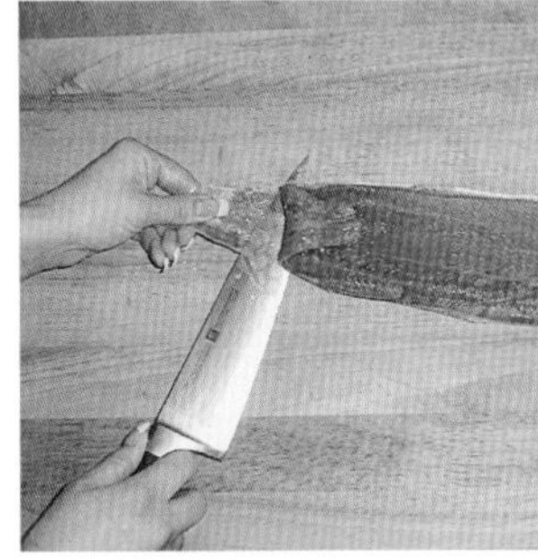

Step 4. Pulling tail end of fillet firmly toward you, use a light sawing motion to remove skin.

Step 6. Cut fillet at a 45° angle into 4 pieces.

METHOD

1. Preheat oven to 400°F (205°C).
2. To remove skin from salmon, position fillet, skin side down, with tail facing toward you. Grasp the fillet by the tail.
3. Using a French knife, position blade at a 10° angle between salmon skin and flesh.
4. Pulling tail end of fillet firmly toward you, use a light sawing motion to remove skin.
5. Run your hand across the fillet, from head to tail, to locate any remaining rib bones. Remove with tweezers or small pliers.
6. Cut fillet at a 45° angle into 4 pieces.
7. Place water and salt in a large saucepan. Bring to a boil over high heat.
8. Remove strings and stem ends from beans. Cut any large beans in half.
9. Add carrots, onions, celery, peppers and beans to saucepan. Blanch for 3 minutes.
10. Drain vegetables and rinse under cold, running water.
11. Transfer vegetables to an ovenproof casserole dish.
12. Pat salmon fillets dry and place on top of vegetables.
13. Dot fillets with butter. Season with salt, pepper and paprika.
14. Cover casserole dish with aluminum foil.
15. Bake on bottom oven rack for 10-12 minutes.
16. Place salmon on a serving platter. Surround with cooked vegetables and serve.

4 servings

Approximate nutritional analysis per serving
Calories 386, Protein 36 g, Carbohydrates 16 g, Fat 20 g, Cholesterol 117 mg, Sodium 309 mg

Baked Salmon Printanière

Poached Salmon En Papillote

Aromas and flavors are sealed in using this French cooking technique.

INGREDIENTS

4	**5-oz (140 g) salmon fillets, bones removed**
1	**onion, thinly sliced**
4	**green onions, thinly sliced**
3 oz	**(85 g) red or green peppers, sliced**
4	**fresh dill weed sprigs**
4	**fresh basil leaves**
4	**lemon slices**
2 tsp	**(10 mL) black pepper**
4 tbsp	**(60 mL) dry white wine**
2 tbsp	**(30 mL) vegetable oil**

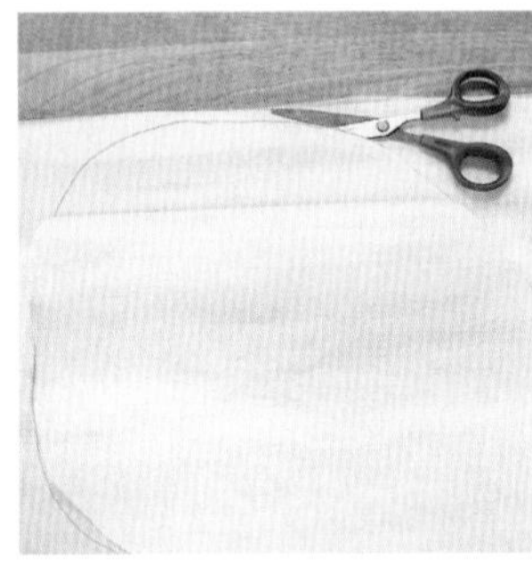

Step 4. Using the cut parchment as a guide, cut the other pieces of folded parchment into equal-sized half heart shapes.

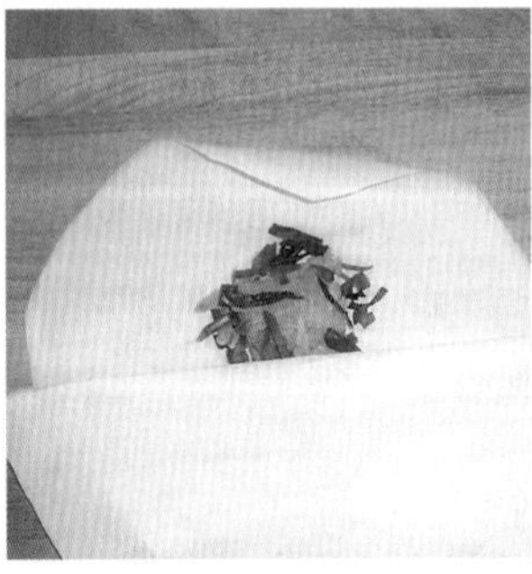

Step 9. Fold one side of paper over salmon and vegetables, forming a half heart shape.

Step 11. Continue folding paper until all edges are sealed and the salmon and vegetables are completely enclosed in the paper.

METHOD

1. Preheat oven to 375°F (190°C).
2. Fold four sheets of parchment paper in half.
3. Cut one sheet of parchment paper into a half heart shape, with one rounded and one pointed end.
4. Using the cut parchment as a guide, cut the other pieces of folded parchment into equal-sized half heart shapes.
5. Unfold all four pieces of parchment paper and lay out on work surface.
6. Place one piece of salmon near the fold of each heart-shaped piece of paper.
7. Divide onions, green onions, peppers, dill, basil and lemon slices evenly onto salmon.
8. Season salmon with pepper and sprinkle with wine.
9. Fold one side of paper over salmon and vegetables, forming a half heart shape.
10. Beginning at the top, round edge of the paper, make one fold along your finger. Place fingertip down to hold the crease, then make another fold alongside your fingertip, slightly overlapping the first fold.
11. Continue folding paper until all edges are sealed and the salmon and vegetables are completely enclosed in the paper.
12. Repeat steps until all parchment papers have been folded into packets.
13. Place packets on a baking sheet, tucking the pointed end underneath each packet.
14. Brush packets with oil.
15. Bake for 20-25 minutes.
16. Carefully cut packets open with scissors or a sharp knife.
17. Serve hot in the parchment packets.

4 servings

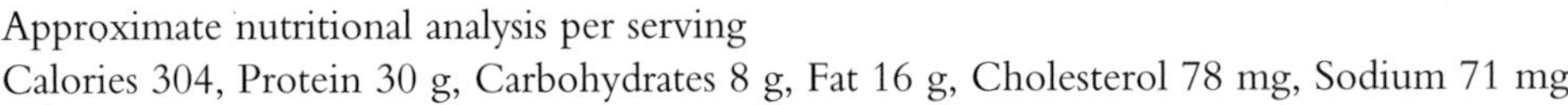

Approximate nutritional analysis per serving
Calories 304, Protein 30 g, Carbohydrates 8 g, Fat 16 g, Cholesterol 78 mg, Sodium 71 mg

Poached Salmon En Papillote

Roasted Salmon with Dill

Dill — a classic companion to salmon.

INGREDIENTS

4	**8-oz (225 g) salmon fillets**
3 tbsp	**(45 mL) fresh lemon juice**
¼ cup	**(50 mL) fresh dill, minced**
1 tsp	**(5 mL) salt**
1 tsp	**(5 mL) freshly ground black pepper**
4 tbsp	**(60 mL) extra virgin olive oil**

METHOD

1. Preheat oven to 400°F (205°C).
2. Brush a roasting pan with oil.
3. Remove any bones from salmon fillets.
4. Place salmon in roasting pan. Sprinkle with lemon juice and dill.
5. Season fillets with salt and pepper.
6. Bake for 10-12 minutes, brushing occasionally with olive oil. Salmon is cooked when fish flakes easily.
7. Serve with lime wedges, salsa or dill butter.

4 servings

Salmon Glazed with Ginger and Lime

Rich, satisfying taste.

INGREDIENTS

4	**6-oz (170 g) salmon steaks, cut 1-inch (2.5 cm) thick**
1 tbsp	**(15 mL) ginger root, peeled and grated**
2 tbsp	**(30 mL) fresh lime juice**
1½ tbsp	**(25 mL) low sodium soy sauce**
2	**garlic cloves, crushed**
1½ tsp	**(7 mL) sesame oil**
1 tsp	**(5 mL) red pepper flakes**
1 tsp	**(5 mL) brown sugar**
1	**lime, cut into wedges**

METHOD

1. Arrange salmon steaks in a shallow baking dish.
2. In a small bowl, whisk together all remaining ingredients except lime.
3. Pour marinade over salmon, turning to coat both sides with liquid.
4. Cover with plastic wrap and refrigerate for 1 hour.
5. Heat broiler.
6. Remove salmon from marinade and place on a wire rack over a roasting pan. Reserve marinade.
7. Broil on middle oven rack for 8-10 minutes, basting frequently with marinade. Salmon is cooked when bone comes out clean.
8. Place salmon on a serving plate and garnish with lime wedges.
9. Serve with lemon butter.

4 servings

Approximate nutritional analysis per serving
Calories 276, Protein 35 g, Carbohydrates 5 g, Fat 13 g, Cholesterol 94 mg, Sodium 265 mg

◀ Approximate nutritional analysis per serving
Calories 446, Protein 45 g, Carbohydrates 1 g, Fat 28 g, Cholesterol 125 mg, Sodium 633 mg

Salmon Glazed with Ginger and Lime

Rolled Sole Fillets with Leeks

A special dish for family and friends.

INGREDIENTS

1 lb	**(450 g) leeks**
4	**6-oz (170 g) sole fillets**
¼ cup	**(50 mL) red peppers, thinly sliced**
3 tbsp	**(45 mL) butter**
2 tbsp	**(30 mL) all-purpose flour**
1 cup	**(250 mL) white wine**
1¼ cups	**(300 mL) whipping cream**
2 tbsp	**(30 mL) lemon juice**
	salt and freshly ground pepper
pinch	**nutmeg, freshly grated**

METHOD

1. Trim leeks and remove any tough, outer leaves.
2. Slice leeks into rounds and wash thoroughly. Drain well and pat dry.
3. Position each sole fillet so tail is facing toward you.
4. Place 1 tbsp (15 mL) of peppers on tail end of each fillet.
5. Roll each fillet around peppers into a tube shape.
6. Pin each roll with a wooden pick.
7. In a heavy skillet, melt 2 tbsp (30 mL) of butter over medium heat.
8. Sauté leeks for 4-5 minutes, until soft.
9. Using a slotted spoon, transfer leeks to a bowl. Set aside.
10. Reduce heat to low and add flour to skillet. Cook for 3 minutes, stirring sauce with a wooden spoon.
11. Whisk in wine until thoroughly combined.
12. Stir in 1 cup (250 mL) of cream and cook gently for 4 minutes.
13. Return leeks to skillet. Simmer gently for 2 minutes, stirring occasionally.
14. Season sauce with 1 tbsp (15 mL) of lemon juice, salt, pepper and nutmeg.
15. Place rolled sole fillets on top of leek mixture.
16. Pour 1 tbsp (15 mL) of cream over each fillet.
17. Sprinkle fillets with remaining lemon juice, salt and pepper.
18. Dot remaining butter on top of sole fillets. Bring to a simmer.
19. Butter a sheet of wax paper large enough to cover skillet.
20. Lay wax paper, buttered side down, on top of skillet.
21. Simmer for 6 minutes, until fish is opaque.
22. Serve garnished with lemon or lime wedges.

4 servings

Approximate nutritional analysis per serving
Calories 784, Protein 22 g, Carbohydrates 50 g, Fat 54 g, Cholesterol 179 mg, Sodium 924 mg

Step 4. Place 1 tbsp (15 mL) of peppers on tail end of each fillet.

Step 5. Roll each fillet around peppers into a tube shape.

Rolled Sole Fillets with Leeks

Grilled Halibut with Nasturtium Butter

Nasturtium butter lends a wonderful, peppery flavor to this dish.

INGREDIENTS

4	**8-oz (225 g) halibut steaks**
1 tbsp	**(15 mL) paprika**
1 tsp	**(5 mL) dry mustard**
	black pepper
2 tbsp	**(30 mL) olive oil**
2	**garlic cloves, minced**
1 tbsp	**(15 mL) vegetable oil**
5 tbsp	**(75 mL) butter, softened**
1	**shallot, minced**
1 tsp	**(5 mL) hot pepper sauce**
	salt and pepper
½ cup	**(125 mL) nasturtium leaves and blossoms, washed well and drained**

METHOD

1. Place halibut steaks in a glass dish.
2. In a small bowl, combine paprika, mustard and pepper. Sprinkle over halibut steaks.
3. In another small bowl, combine olive oil and garlic. Brush on halibut.
4. Cover halibut with plastic wrap and refrigerate for 1 hour.
5. Cream butter in a small bowl until light.
6. Stir in shallots, hot pepper sauce, salt and pepper.
7. Shred nasturtium leaves and blossoms into small pieces.
8. Add nasturtiums to butter, stirring to combine thoroughly.
9. Place nasturtium butter in a piping bag with a star-shaped tip.
10. Pipe butter onto a plate into rosette shapes.
11. Cover butter with plastic wrap and refrigerate.
12. Heat grill and brush with vegetable oil.
13. Grill halibut for 4-5 minutes per side.
14. Test halibut for doneness. Fish is cooked when bone comes out clean.
15. Place halibut steaks on a serving platter.
16. Serve halibut accompanied by nasturtium butter.

4 servings

Step 5. Cream butter in a small bowl until light.

Step 8. Add nasturtiums to butter, stirring to combine thoroughly.

Step 10. Pipe butter onto a plate into rosette shapes.

Tip:

- *Nasturtium butter may be piped into shapes and frozen for later use. Place in a plastic bag and keep in the freezer for up to 3 months.*

Approximate nutritional analysis per serving
Calories 495, Protein 49 g, Carbohydrates 3 g, Fat 31 g, Cholesterol 111 mg, Sodium 319 mg

Grilled Halibut with Nasturtium Butter

Bahamian Fish Pie

Mashed potatoes top a delectable blend of tomatoes, onions and red snapper.

INGREDIENTS

2 tbsp	**(30 mL) vegetable oil**
2	**medium onions, thinly sliced**
8	**mushrooms, sliced**
2 lbs	**(900 g) red snapper fillets**
8 oz	**(250 mL) canned, whole tomatoes, undrained**
1 tbsp	**(15 mL) tomato paste**
1 tsp	**(5 mL) thyme**
½ tsp	**(2 mL) hot pepper sauce**
2½ lbs	**(1.2 kg) potatoes, peeled and diced into 1-inch (2.5 cm) cubes**
⅓ cup	**(75 mL) whipping cream, warm**
2 tbsp	**(30 mL) butter, melted**
	salt and pepper

METHOD

1. Preheat oven to 350°F (175°C).
2. Butter a 13 x 9 x 2-inch (33 x 22 x 5 cm) ovenproof casserole dish.
3. Heat oil in a heavy skillet over medium heat.
4. Sauté onions for 5 minutes, until golden brown.
5. Add mushrooms and cook for 5 more minutes, stirring occasionally.
6. Remove any skin and bones from red snapper fillets. Cut fillets into strips.
7. Add fillets to skillet and cook for 1 minute.
8. Stir in tomatoes with their juice, tomato paste, thyme and hot pepper sauce.
9. Cook for 10 minutes, stirring occasionally, until liquid evaporates and mixture begins to thicken.
10. Place potatoes in a large saucepan.
11. Cover with water and bring to a boil over medium-high heat. Reduce heat to medium.
12. Cook for 12-15 minutes, until potatoes are tender.
13. Drain potatoes and return to saucepan.
14. Add cream and butter to potatoes. Mash well.
15. Season with salt and pepper.
16. Pour fish mixture into prepared casserole dish.
17. Spread mashed potatoes on top of fish.
18. Bake for 30 minutes, until heated through. Switch oven setting to broil.
19. Broil pie until potatoes have browned.
20. Serve hot.

8 servings

Approximate nutritional analysis per serving
Calories 469, Protein 27 g, Carbohydrates 16 g, Fat 35 g, Cholesterol 88 mg, Sodium 239 mg

Bahamian Fish Pie

Crab and Fennel with Dill

The flavors of dill and apple brandy enhance this lovely crab recipe.

INGREDIENTS

2	**fennel bulbs**
¼ cup	**(50 mL) butter**
¼ tsp	**(1 mL) salt**
¼ tsp	**(1 mL) black pepper**
1 lb	**(450 g) cooked crab meat**
1 tbsp	**(15 mL) calvados**
¼ cup	**(50 mL) heavy cream**
1 tbsp	**(15 mL) lemon juice**
3 tbsp	**(45 mL) fresh dill, chopped**

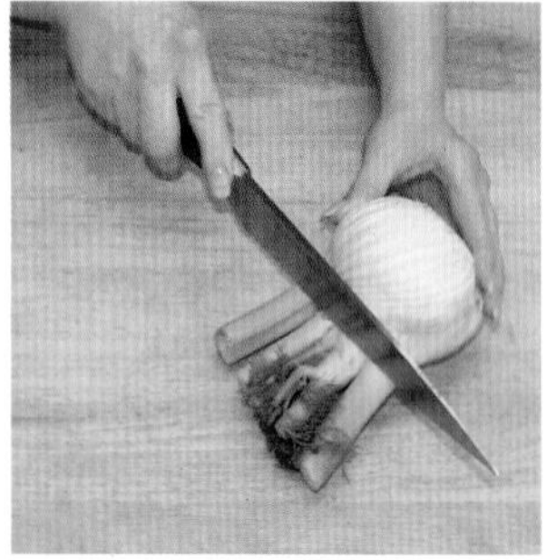

Step 1. Remove leaf end from top of each fennel bulb, leaving ½-inch (1.3 cm) stems.

Step 2. Trim root end of each fennel bulb.

Step 3. Cut fennel into ½-inch (1.3 cm) slices.

METHOD

1. Remove leaf end from top of each fennel bulb, leaving ½-inch (1.3 cm) stems.
2. Trim root end of each fennel bulb.
3. Cut fennel into ½-inch (1.3 cm) slices.
4. Steam fennel for 5 minutes, until lightly cooked but still crisp.
5. Rinse fennel under cold, running water. Drain well.
6. In a skillet, melt 2 tbsp (30 mL) of butter over medium heat.
7. Add fennel to skillet and sauté for 1 minute.
8. Season with salt and pepper.
9. Transfer fennel to a serving dish and keep warm.
10. Using the same skillet, melt remaining butter over medium heat.
11. Stir in crab meat and calvados.
12. Flame calvados and stir in cream. Reduce heat to low.
13. Cook gently for 3 minutes, stirring occasionally, until sauce thickens.
14. Season with salt and pepper to taste.
15. Add lemon juice, stirring to combine. Remove from heat.
16. Spoon crab mixture over fennel.
17. Garnish with dill and serve.

4 servings

Approximate nutritional analysis per serving
Calories 328, Protein 25 g, Carbohydrates 13 g, Fat 19 g, Cholesterol 152 mg, Sodium 697 mg

Crab and Fennel with Dill

Backers (Stuffed Crab)

A crab shell doubles as a unique baking dish in this seafood recipe.

INGREDIENTS

1	**2-lb (900 g) blue crab, cooked**
1 tbsp	**(15 mL) olive oil**
1	**medium onion, diced**
2	**celery stalks, diced**
1	**small red pepper, diced**
3 cups	**(750 mL) fresh white bread crumbs**
2 tbsp	**(30 mL) fresh parsley, chopped**
2 tbsp	**(30 mL) tomato paste**
1	**fresh thyme sprig, chopped**
½ cup	**(125 mL) dry white wine**
1 tsp	**(5 mL) hot pepper sauce**
	salt and pepper

METHOD

1. Preheat oven to 350°F (175°C).
2. Over a bowl, break open crab and remove main body from shell.
3. Set crab shell aside. Reserve liquid from inside shell.
4. Discard spongy gills and stomach sac located just behind the eyes.
5. Pick out meat from crab body and place in a bowl.
6. Crack crab legs and claws. Remove meat and add to crab meat in bowl.
7. Heat oil in a skillet over medium heat.
8. Sauté onions, celery and peppers for 5 minutes, stirring occasionally.
9. Transfer vegetable mixture to a medium bowl. Stir in bread crumbs.
10. Add parsley, tomato paste and just enough reserved crab liquid to moisten. Combine well.
11. Stir in crab meat, thyme, wine, hot pepper sauce, salt and pepper. If crab mixture is too moist, add some bread crumbs.
12. Rinse out reserved crab shell and dry.
13. Spoon crab mixture into crab shell.
14. Place stuffed crab shell on a baking sheet.
15. Bake for 35-40 minutes, until filling is heated through.
16. Spoon filling onto individual plates or serve directly from the shell.
17. Garnish with lemon or lime wedges and serve.

2 servings

Variation:

- *To save time, purchase an empty crab shell from a fish market. Substitute 8 oz (225 g) of canned, undrained crab for crab meat and crab liquid in above recipe.*

Approximate nutritional analysis per serving
Calories 561, Protein 54 g, Carbohydrates 46 g, Fat 13 g, Cholesterol 229 mg, Sodium 1338 mg

Backers (Stuffed Crab)

Broiled Lobster Tails

A classic recipe worthy of this prestigious shellfish.

INGREDIENTS

4	**raw, whole lobster tails**
3 tbsp	**(45 mL) butter, melted**
2 tbsp	**(30 mL) lemon juice**
	salt and pepper
1	**lemon, cut into wedges**

Step 3. Using a sharp pair of scissors, cut each shell down the center leaving meat intact.

Step 4. Pull lobster meat through cut in each shell, leaving meat still attached at tip of tail.

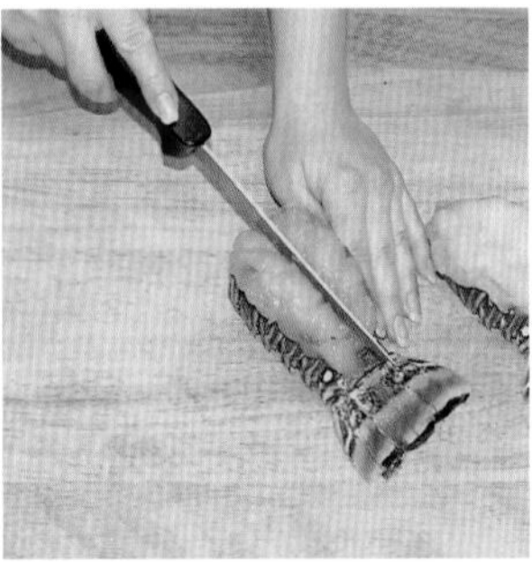

Step 5. Partially slice lobster meat down the center. Do not cut all the way through the meat.

METHOD

1. Preheat broiler.
2. Place lobster tails on work surface, rounded sides up.
3. Using a sharp pair of scissors, cut each shell down the center leaving meat intact.
4. Pull lobster meat through cut in each shell, leaving meat still attached at tip of tail.
5. Partially slice lobster meat down the center. Do not cut all the way through the meat.
6. Fan out meat evenly onto top of each shell.
7. Place lobster tails on a baking sheet and brush with butter.
8. Sprinkle with lemon juice and season with salt and pepper.
9. Broil 6 inches (15 cm) from heat for 6-8 minutes. If lobster tails begin to brown before they are fully cooked, switch oven setting to 375°F (190°C) and bake until cooked.
10. Place lobster tails on a serving platter. Garnish with lemon wedges.
11. Serve accompanied by melted butter.

4 servings

Approximate nutritional analysis per serving
Calories 345, Protein 45 g, Carbohydrates 5 g, Fat 16 g, Cholesterol 195 mg, Sodium 1548 mg

Broiled Lobster Tails

Coquilles St. Jacques St. Albert

An old favorite. Scallops and mushrooms in a rich, white wine sauce.

INGREDIENTS

3 tbsp	**(45 mL) butter**
2	**celery stalks, finely diced**
6	**shallots, finely diced**
2 tbsp	**(30 mL) fresh chives, chopped**
16	**small mushrooms, sliced**
½ cup	**(125 mL) dry white wine**
24	**scallops**
	salt and pepper
pinch	**nutmeg**
1½ cups	**(375 mL) whipping cream**
2 tbsp	**(30 mL) fresh parsley or chives, chopped**

METHOD

1. In a skillet, melt 2 tbsp (30 mL) of butter over medium heat.
2. Add celery and shallots. Cook for 5 minutes, stirring occasionally, until soft.
3. Stir in chives and mushrooms. Cook for an additional 3 minutes.
4. Remove vegetables from skillet with a slotted spoon. Keep warm.
5. In the same skillet, cook wine over medium heat until reduced by half.
6. Stir in scallops and remaining butter. Reduce heat to low.
7. Cook gently for 1 minute. Do not overcook.
8. Return cooked vegetables to skillet. Season with salt, pepper and nutmeg.
9. Stir in cream and cook for 1 minute. Do not boil.
10. Transfer to a serving dish. Sprinkle with parsley and serve.

4 servings

Tip:

- *If a thicker sauce is desired, remove vegetables and scallops from skillet with a slotted spoon after cream is added. Over low heat, cook sauce until it is reduced to desired consistency. Return vegetables and scallops to skillet to reheat before serving.*

Approximate nutritional analysis per serving
Calories 469, Protein 10 g, Carbohydrates 11 g, Fat 42 g, Cholesterol 157 mg, Sodium 737 mg

Coquilles St. Jacques St. Albert

Tea-Smoked Shrimp

The marinade and smoking technique give these shrimp their exotic flavor.

INGREDIENTS

¼ cup	**(50 mL) light soy sauce**
¼ cup	**(50 mL) dry sherry**
6	**ginger root slices, peeled**
4	**garlic cloves, crushed**
1	**lemon grass stem, chopped**
1½ lbs	**(675 g) large, raw shrimp, unpeeled**
¼ cup	**(50 mL) black tea leaves**
2 tbsp	**(30 mL) dark brown sugar**

Step 4. Line a wok and its lid with aluminum foil.

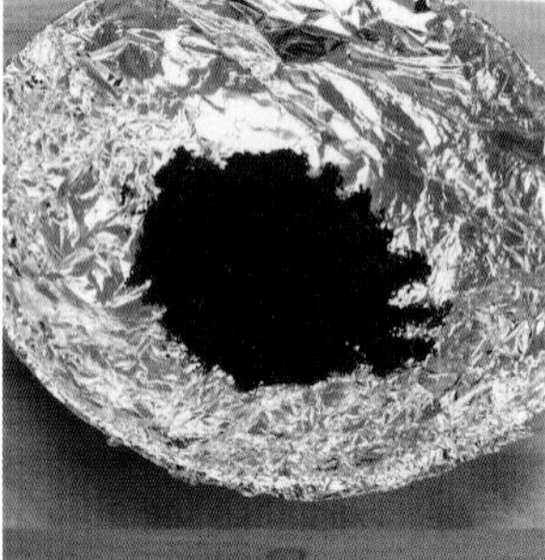

Step 6. Place tea leaf mixture in wok.

Step 7. Position a rack at least 1 inch (2.5 cm) above tea leaf mixture.

METHOD

1. In a glass bowl, combine soy sauce, sherry, ginger, garlic and lemon grass.
2. Add unpeeled shrimp, tossing to coat with marinade.
3. Cover with plastic wrap and refrigerate overnight.
4. Line a wok and its lid with aluminum foil.
5. In a small bowl, combine tea leaves and brown sugar.
6. Place tea leaf mixture in wok.
7. Position a rack at least 1 inch (2.5 cm) above tea leaf mixture.
8. Place half of the shrimp on the rack. Cover wok with lid.
9. Smoke shrimp over medium heat for 5 minutes. Remove from rack and keep warm.
10. Repeat steps with remaining shrimp.
11. Serve with hoisin, plum, teriyaki or soy sauce for dipping.

4 servings

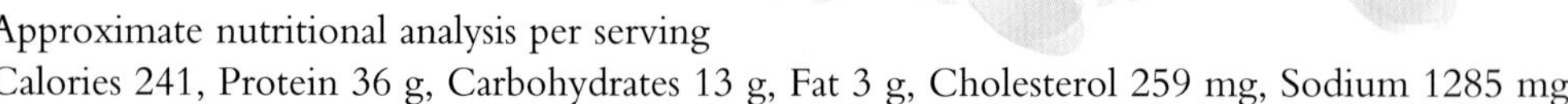

Approximate nutritional analysis per serving
Calories 241, Protein 36 g, Carbohydrates 13 g, Fat 3 g, Cholesterol 259 mg, Sodium 1285 mg

Tea-Smoked Shrimp

Grilled Shrimp Kebabs

Tender shrimp and tangy lemon team up in these magnificent kebabs.

INGREDIENTS

¼ cup	**(50 mL) butter, melted**
2 tbsp	**(30 mL) olive oil**
2 tbsp	**(30 mL) fresh parsley, minced**
1 tbsp	**(15 mL) fresh thyme, minced**
1 tbsp	**(15 mL) fresh cilantro, minced**
1 tbsp	**(15 mL) shallots, minced**
	salt and black pepper
24	**large, raw shrimp, unpeeled**
2	**Swiss chard bunches**
2	**lemons**

METHOD

1. In a large bowl, toss together butter, oil, parsley, thyme, cilantro, shallots, salt, pepper and shrimp.
2. Cover with plastic wrap and refrigerate overnight.
3. Soak 4 wooden skewers in water overnight.
4. Remove shrimp from marinade. Reserve marinade.
5. Heat grill.
6. Separate chard leaves. Wash thoroughly and drain.
7. Steam chard for 7-8 minutes.
8. Cut 1 lemon into slices. Cut each slice into quarters.
9. Alternately thread 6 shrimp and 2 pieces of lemon onto each skewer.
10. Grill kebabs for 2 minutes per side, brushing frequently with reserved marinade.
11. Cut remaining lemon into slices.
12. Place chard on a serving platter and arrange kebabs on top of chard.
13. Garnish with lemon slices and serve.

4 servings

Variation:

- *Red or green peppers are a great addition to this recipe for color and flavor. Cut 1 pepper into strips and thread onto skewers between lemon pieces and shrimp.*

Approximate nutritional analysis per serving
Calories 245, Protein 11 g, Carbohydrates 7 g, Fat 21 g, Cholesterol 97 mg, Sodium 311 mg

Grilled Shrimp Kebabs

Hot Coconut Shrimp

A superb combination of flavors and textures make this recipe a sure hit.

INGREDIENTS

1 cup	**(250 mL) all-purpose flour**
½ tsp	**(2 mL) cayenne pepper**
1 tsp	**(5 mL) red pepper flakes**
3	**medium eggs, beaten**
½ tsp	**(2 mL) hot pepper sauce**
1 cup	**(250 mL) fresh bread crumbs**
1 cup	**(250 mL) sweetened, shredded coconut**
24	**large, raw shrimp, peeled and deveined, with tails attached**
	vegetable oil for deep frying

Step 4. Lightly coat shrimp in seasoned flour.

Step 5. Holding each shrimp by the tail, dip into egg mixture.

Step 6. Roll shrimp in bread crumb mixture.

METHOD

1. In a shallow pan, mix together flour, cayenne pepper and pepper flakes.
2. In a small bowl, combine eggs and hot pepper sauce.
3. In another shallow pan, combine bread crumbs and coconut.
4. Lightly coat shrimp in seasoned flour.
5. Holding each shrimp by the tail, dip into egg mixture.
6. Roll shrimp in bread crumb mixture.
7. For an extra coating of bread crumbs, dip shrimp into egg mixture again and then into bread crumbs.
8. Heat oil to 300°F (150°C).
9. Deep fry shrimp for 1 minute, until golden brown. Drain on paper towels.
10. Serve with chutney or salsa.

4 servings

Approximate nutritional analysis per serving
Calories 453, Protein 21 g, Carbohydrates 49 g, Fat 19 g, Cholesterol 224 mg, Sodium 333 mg

Hot Coconut Shrimp

Garlic Shrimp in Croutons

Toasted bread filled with a luscious mixture of shrimp, garlic and tomatoes.

INGREDIENTS

⅓ cup	**(75 mL) olive oil**
1 lb	**(450 g) large, raw shrimp, peeled and deveined**
2	**garlic cloves, minced**
⅓ cup	**(75 mL) tomatoes, blanched, peeled, seeded and chopped**
⅓ cup	**(75 mL) sun-dried tomatoes, chopped**
2 tbsp	**(30 mL) lemon juice**
1 tbsp	**(15 mL) fresh basil, chopped**
1	**white bread loaf, unsliced**
½ cup	**(125 mL) butter, melted**

Step 6. Cut bread into six 2-inch (5 cm) slices.

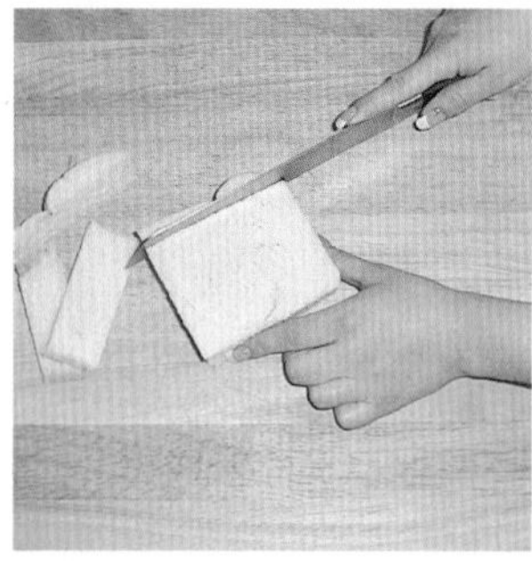

Step 7. Remove crusts from bread slices.

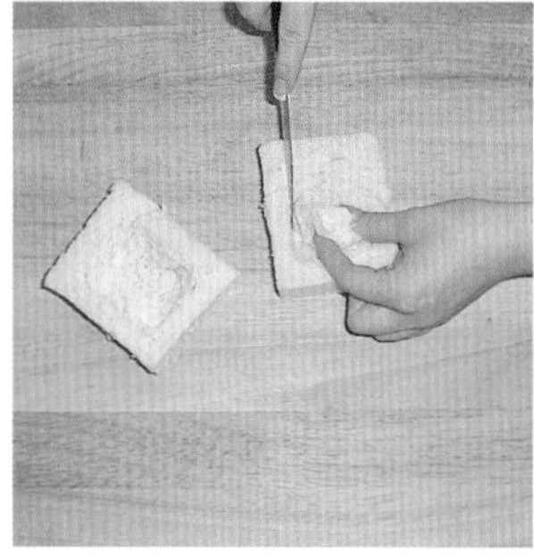

Step 8. Partially hollow out center of each bread slice leaving ¼-inch (0.6 cm) base at the bottom.

METHOD

1. Preheat broiler.
2. In a skillet, heat oil over medium heat.
3. Sauté shrimp for 30 seconds or until they begin to turn pink.
4. Add garlic. Sauté for 30 seconds.
5. Stir in fresh and sun-dried tomatoes, lemon juice and basil. Remove from heat.
6. Cut bread into six 2-inch (5 cm) slices.
7. Remove crusts from bread slices.
8. Partially hollow out center of each bread slice leaving ¼-inch (0.6 cm) base at the bottom.
9. Place bread on a baking sheet and brush top and insides with butter.
10. Broil bread slices on middle rack for 2-3 minutes.
11. Turn and brush bases of bread with remaining butter. Toast for 2 more minutes, until golden brown. Remove from oven.
12. Fill toasted bread with shrimp filling.
13. Serve with fresh basil and lime wedges.

6 servings

Approximate nutritional analysis per serving
Calories 551, Protein 23 g, Carbohydrates 42 g, Fat 33 g, Cholesterol 161 mg, Sodium 557 mg

Garlic Shrimp in Croutons

Chutney Shrimp in Phyllo Shells

Spicy-sweet shrimp nestled in perfect phyllo baskets.

INGREDIENTS

3	**phyllo dough sheets**
4 tbsp	**(60 mL) butter**
1 tsp	**(5 mL) vegetable oil**
1	**medium onion, chopped**
1½ tsp	**(7 mL) curry paste**
½ cup	**(125 mL) mango chutney, chopped**
12	**large, raw shrimp, peeled and deveined**
1	**small apple, peeled, cored and finely diced**
1 tbsp	**(15 mL) fresh parsley, finely chopped**

METHOD

1. Preheat oven to 375°F (190°C).
2. Grease a muffin pan.
3. Melt 3 tbsp (45 mL) of butter.
4. Brush one sheet of phyllo dough with melted butter.
5. Place second sheet of phyllo dough on top of first layer. Brush with butter. Repeat with last sheet of phyllo dough.
6. Cut layered phyllo dough into 4-inch (10 cm) squares.
7. Place phyllo squares into prepared muffin pan.
8. Push each square lightly into muffin pan, leaving a well in the center.
9. Bake for 8-10 minutes, until golden brown.
10. Cool shells for 5 minutes and place on a serving plate.
11. In a skillet, heat oil and remaining butter over medium heat.
12. Sauté onions for 5 minutes, until golden brown.
13. Stir in curry paste and chutney.
14. Add shrimp to skillet, tossing to coat with sauce. Cook for 2 minutes. Do not boil.
15. Spoon shrimp mixture evenly into phyllo shells.
16. Sprinkle with apples and parsley. Serve.

4 servings

Approximate nutritional analysis per serving
Calories 232, Protein 5 g, Carbohydrates 23 g, Fat 14 g, Cholesterol 65 mg, Sodium 239 mg

Chutney Shrimp in Phyllo Shells

Favorite Steamed Clams

A timeless and delicious clam recipe your guests will love.

INGREDIENTS

2 tbsp	**(30 mL) olive oil**
2 tsp	**(10 mL) garlic, minced**
5 cups	**(1.3 L) clam juice**
6	**tomatoes, blanched, peeled, seeded and chopped**
1 cup	**(250 mL) water**
2 cups	**(500 mL) dry white wine**
2 tsp	**(10 mL) red pepper flakes**
2 tsp	**(10 mL) dried oregano**
1 tbsp	**(15 mL) fresh oregano, chopped**
1 tbsp	**(15 mL) fresh parsley, chopped**
72	**littleneck clams**
	salt and black pepper

METHOD

1. In a large stockpot, heat oil over medium heat.
2. Sauté garlic for 2 minutes, taking care that the garlic does not burn. Remove stockpot from heat.
3. Add all remaining ingredients except salt and pepper.
4. Cover and bring to a boil over medium-high heat, stirring occasionally.
5. Cook for 5-6 minutes, until clams are open. Remove from heat.
6. Season with salt and pepper.
7. Let stand, covered, for 5 minutes.
8. Serve hot.

6 servings

Approximate nutritional analysis per serving
Calories 188, Protein 15 g, Carbohydrates 6 g, Fat 6 g, Cholesterol 42 mg, Sodium 606 mg

Favorite Steamed Clams

Moules Marinière

Serve this classic recipe with fresh bread for dunking.

INGREDIENTS

7 lbs	**(3.2 kg) mussels, scrubbed and bearded**
8 oz	**(225 g) shallots, finely chopped**
10	**parsley stems**
1 tsp	**(5 mL) freshly ground black pepper**
2 cups	**(500 mL) dry white wine**
¼ cup	**(50 mL) fresh parsley, chopped**
½ cup	**(125 mL) butter**
	salt
1 tsp	**(5 mL) lemon juice**

METHOD

1. Sort through mussels and discard any with open shells.
2. Place mussels in a large stockpot.
3. Add shallots, parsley, pepper and wine. Cover.
4. Bring to a boil over medium-high heat. Steam mussels for 4 minutes, until shells are barely open.
5. Using a slotted spoon, remove mussels from pot and set aside.
6. Strain cooking liquid through several layers of cheesecloth into a clean saucepan.
7. Add parsley and butter to cooking liquid. Cook over medium heat until butter is melted.
8. Season to taste with salt and lemon juice.
9. Divide mussels evenly into 8 broad soup plates.
10. Pour sauce over mussels and serve.

8 servings

Tips:

- *How To Remove Sand From Mussels: Soak mussels overnight in the refrigerator in a mixture of 4 cups (1 L) of water and 2 tbsp (30 mL) of corn meal. If there is not enough liquid to cover the mussels, double the quantities of water and corn meal. Drain liquid from mussels before using.*
- *How To Select Mussels: When buying mussels, it is best to hand pick them by weight and appearance. Mussels that feel too light or too heavy should be avoided. The light ones may be hollow, and the heavy ones are probably full of sand. Select only mussels with closed shells, or shells that close when tapped.*

Approximate nutritional analysis per serving
Calories 505, Protein 48 g, Carbohydrates 20 g, Fat 21 g, Cholesterol 142 mg, Sodium 1284 mg

Moules Marinière

Pasta, Bread & Rice

Bow Ties with Herb Sauce and Olives

A quick and tasty meal suitable for any occasion.

INGREDIENTS

2 cups	**(500 mL) fresh basil, firmly packed**
2 cups	**(500 mL) fresh parsley, firmly packed**
4	**garlic cloves**
1 cup	**(250 mL) Parmesan cheese, freshly grated**
1 cup	**(250 mL) olive oil**
1 cup	**(250 mL) pitted black olives, coarsely chopped**
4 oz	**(115 g) smoked salmon, diced**
1 tbsp	**(15 mL) lemon juice**
	salt and pepper
pinch	**nutmeg**
1 lb	**(450 g) bow tie pasta, cooked and drained**

METHOD

1. In a food processor, combine basil, parsley, garlic and Parmesan cheese.
2. In a steady stream, add oil to food processor, blending until mixture thickens. Transfer to a large saucepan.
3. Stir in olives, smoked salmon and lemon juice.
4. Season to taste with salt, pepper and nutmeg.
5. Heat mixture gently over low heat for 4-5 minutes to blend flavors.
6. Add pasta to saucepan, tossing to coat with sauce.
7. Serve with toasted bread rounds or bread sticks.

6 servings

Approximate nutritional analysis per serving
Calories 680, Protein 19 g, Carbohydrates 48 g, Fat 48 g, Cholesterol 18 mg, Sodium 968 mg

Bow Ties with Herb Sauce and Olives

Stuffed Cannelloni

Prepare this recipe ahead of time for a hearty pasta dinner sure to please.

INGREDIENTS

16	**cannelloni tubes, uncooked**
2 cups	**(500 mL) cooked ground pork**
3 tbsp	**(45 mL) heavy cream**
1 tbsp	**(15 mL) fresh parsley, minced**
4 cups	**(1 L) tomato sauce**
	salt and black pepper
¼ tsp	**(1 mL) nutmeg, grated**
1 cup	**(250 mL) Parmesan cheese, grated**

METHOD

1. Preheat oven to 400°F (205°C).
2. Cook cannelloni according to package directions. Drain.
3. In a medium bowl, combine ground pork, cream, parsley, 2 tbsp (30 mL) tomato sauce, salt, pepper and nutmeg.
4. Place meat mixture in a piping bag.
5. Pipe meat mixture evenly into each cannelloni tube.
6. Spread half the remaining tomato sauce in the bottom of a baking dish.
7. Place cannelloni in baking dish and cover with remaining tomato sauce.
8. Sprinkle Parmesan cheese evenly over cannelloni.
9. Bake for 6-7 minutes, until cheese is melted and cannelloni is heated through.
10. Serve hot.

8 servings

Variation:

- *Alfredo sauce is a nice addition to this cannelloni for flavor and color contrast.*

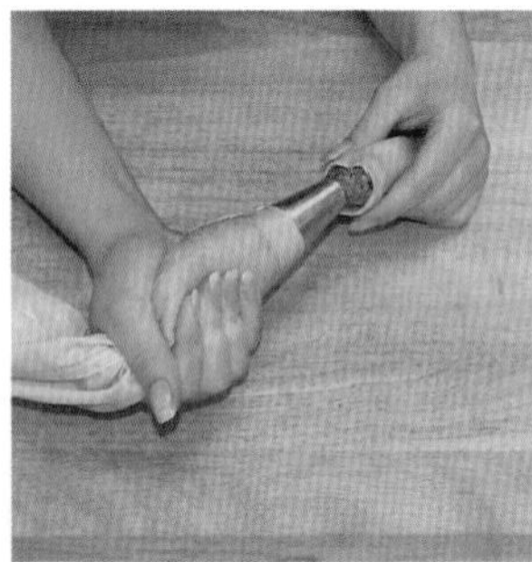

Step 5. Pipe meat mixture evenly into each cannelloni tube.

Step 6. Spread half the remaining tomato sauce in the bottom of a baking dish.

Step 7. Place cannelloni in baking dish and cover with remaining tomato sauce.

Approximate nutritional analysis per serving
Calories 341, Protein 24 g, Carbohydrates 24 g, Fat 17 g, Cholesterol 76 mg, Sodium 1275 mg

Stuffed Cannelloni

Penne with Asparagus

Light-tasting and simple to prepare.

INGREDIENTS

1 lb	**(450 g) asparagus, cut into 1-inch (2.5 cm) pieces**
½ cup	**(125 mL) butter**
2 tbsp	**(30 mL) shallots, chopped**
1	**medium red pepper, thinly sliced**
1 lb	**(450 g) penne pasta, uncooked**
1 tsp	**(5 mL) black pepper**
¾ cup	**(175 mL) Parmesan cheese, grated**

METHOD

1. Cook asparagus in a pot of boiling water for 4 minutes.
2. Rinse asparagus under cold water. Drain well.
3. In a large skillet, melt 6 tbsp (90 mL) butter over medium heat.
4. Add shallots and peppers to skillet. Cook for 4-5 minutes, stirring occasionally.
5. Cook pasta according to package directions. Drain well.
6. Add asparagus to skillet, stirring to combine.
7. Stir penne and remaining butter into skillet.
8. Season with pepper and sprinkle with Parmesan cheese, tossing to combine.
9. Serve hot.

6 servings

Fettucine with Broccoli and Summer Squash

Pasta with crisp, vibrant vegetables.

INGREDIENTS

1	**large broccoli head**
3 tbsp	**(45 mL) olive oil**
2	**medium butternut squash or zucchini, sliced**
3	**garlic cloves, chopped**
2 tbsp	**(30 mL) butter**
½ cup	**(125 mL) chicken broth**
	salt and black pepper
½ lb	**(225 g) fettucine, cooked and drained**

METHOD

1. Cut broccoli into bite-sized flowerets.
2. Cook broccoli in boiling, salted water for 4-5 minutes, until just tender.
3. Drain broccoli. Rinse under cold, running water and set aside.
4. In a large skillet, heat olive oil over medium heat.
5. Sauté zucchini for 4 minutes.
6. Add garlic and butter. Cook for 2 more minutes.
7. Stir broccoli and chicken broth into skillet.
8. Season with salt and pepper to taste.
9. Simmer vegetable mixture for an additional 3 minutes.
10. Serve over warm fettucine.

4 servings

Approximate nutritional analysis per serving
Calories 285, Protein 9 g, Carbohydrates 28 g, Fat 18 g, Cholesterol 16 mg, Sodium 281 mg

◀ Approximate nutritional analysis per serving
Calories 320, Protein 12 g, Carbohydrates 24 g, Fat 21 g, Cholesterol 81 mg, Sodium 419 mg

Fettucine with Broccoli and Summer Squash

Triple Cheese and Macaroni

An old favorite. Rich and full of cheesey goodness.

INGREDIENTS

3 tbsp	**(45 ml) butter**
2 tbsp	**(30 ml) vegetable oil**
4	**green onions, sliced**
1	**medium green pepper, chopped**
1	**medium red pepper, chopped**
1	**garlic clove, minced**
6 tbsp	**(90 mL) all-purpose flour**
1 cup	**(250 mL) milk**
6 oz	**(170 g) medium Cheddar cheese, grated**
4 oz	**(115 g) brick cheese, grated**
3 oz	**(85 g) Parmesan cheese, grated**
1 tbsp	**(15 mL) Worcestershire sauce**
	salt and pepper
pinch	**nutmeg**
1½ lbs	**(675 g) macaroni, cooked and drained**
3 oz	**(85 g) bread crumbs**

METHOD

1. Preheat oven to 400°F (205°C).
2. Grease an ovenproof casserole dish.
3. In a large skillet, heat butter and oil over medium heat.
4. Sauté onions, green peppers, red peppers and garlic for 3-5 minutes, until soft.
5. Stir in flour. Sauté for 2-3 minutes, until lightly browned.
6. Add milk. Cook mixture, stirring occasionally, until thickened. Remove from heat.
7. Slowly stir in Cheddar and brick cheeses, and half the Parmesan cheese.
8. Stir in Worcestershire sauce, salt, pepper and nutmeg.
9. Add macaroni to skillet, stirring to combine.
10. Pour into prepared casserole dish.
11. Sprinkle with bread crumbs and remaining Parmesan cheese.
12. Bake for 30 minutes or until top is brown.
13. Serve hot.

6 servings

Approximate nutritional analysis per serving
Calories 591, Protein 26 g, Carbohydrates 51 g, Fat 32 g, Cholesterol 81 mg, Sodium 769 mg

Triple Cheese and Macaroni

Vegetarian Lasagna

A meatless recipe with flavor to spare.

INGREDIENTS

12 oz	**(340 g) lasagna noodles, uncooked**
4	**medium zucchini, thinly sliced**
4	**medium carrots, thinly sliced**
¼ cup	**(50 mL) butter**
2 tbsp	**(30 mL) all-purpose flour**
½ cup	**(125 mL) milk**
	salt and white pepper
2 cups	**(500 mL) chunky-style tomato sauce**
¼ cup	**(50 mL) fresh basil, chopped**
	freshly ground pepper
2 tbsp	**(30 mL) butter, melted**
½ cup	**(125 mL) mozzarella cheese, shredded**

METHOD

1. Preheat oven to 350°F (175°C).
2. Cook lasagna noodles according to package directions until just tender.
3. Drain noodles and rinse under cold water.
4. Steam or boil zucchini and carrots for 5 minutes, until tender. Cool.
5. In a small saucepan, melt butter over medium heat.
6. Whisk flour into butter. Cook for 2 minutes, stirring constantly.
7. Whisk milk into sauce. Simmer until thickened, stirring constantly. Season with salt and pepper to taste. Remove from heat.
8. Lightly butter a 6 x 10 x 12-inch (15 x 25 x 30 cm) casserole or baking dish.
9. Spread ⅓ cup (75 mL) tomato sauce on bottom of baking dish.
10. Sprinkle one-third of the basil and some pepper on top of sauce.
11. Place one-third of vegetable mixture on top of basil.
12. Place a layer of noodles on top of vegetable mixture.
13. Repeat layers of tomato sauce, basil, vegetables and noodles twice more.
14. Brush top layer of noodles with melted butter.
15. Top with white sauce, then mozzarella cheese.
16. Bake until cheese is bubbling, about 35 minutes.
17. Serve remaining tomato sauce as an accompaniment to lasagna.

4 servings

Approximate nutritional analysis per serving
Calories 368, Protein 12 g, Carbohydrates 47 g, Fat 16 g, Cholesterol 44 mg, Sodium 1476 mg

Vegetarian Lasagna

Ricciolini with Onions, Bacon and Olives

A perfect balance of ingredients gives this recipe all the flavors of Italy.

INGREDIENTS

8	**side bacon slices, diced into ½-inch (1.3 cm) pieces**
4 tbsp	**(60 mL) olive oil**
2	**medium onions, diced**
3	**garlic cloves, minced**
1 cup	**(250 mL) chicken broth**
⅓ cup	**(75 mL) white wine**
4 cups	**(1 L) ricciolini pasta, uncooked**
	salt and black pepper
¼ cup	**(50 mL) fresh parsley, chopped**
1 cup	**(250 mL) Parmesan cheese, freshly grated**
½ cup	**(125 mL) pitted green olives**
½ cup	**(125 mL) pitted black olives, sliced**

METHOD

1. In a large skillet, cook bacon over medium heat until browned.
2. Remove bacon from skillet with a slotted spoon. Drain on paper towels and set aside.
3. Pour most of the bacon fat from the skillet, leaving about 2 tbsp (30 mL) of fat in skillet.
4. Add oil to skillet and heat over medium heat.
5. Cook onions and garlic in skillet for 5 minutes, until onions are soft. Reduce heat to low.
6. Cover and cook for 4-5 minutes.
7. Stir in chicken broth and wine. Bring to a boil.
8. Cook, uncovered, over medium heat for 3-4 minutes, stirring occasionally.
9. Cook pasta according to package directions. Drain.
10. Add pasta to sauce in skillet.
11. Stir in salt, pepper, parsley and ½ cup (125 mL) Parmesan cheese.
12. Add bacon, green olives and black olives, tossing to combine.
13. Sprinkle with remaining Parmesan cheese and serve.

6 servings

Approximate nutritional analysis per serving
Calories 422, Protein 17 g, Carbohydrates 32 g, Fat 25 g, Cholesterol 28 mg, Sodium 1585 mg

Ricciolini with Onions, Bacon and Olives

Cheese Biscuits

These light, soft biscuits are the ideal accompaniment to soup or pasta.

INGREDIENTS

2 cups	**(500 mL) all-purpose flour, sifted**	**½ cup**	**(125 mL) Cheddar cheese, grated**
1 tbsp	**(15 mL) baking powder**	**¾ cup**	**(175 mL) milk**
½ tsp	**(2 mL) salt**	**1**	**large egg**
¼ cup	**(50 mL) margarine or butter**	**2 tbsp**	**(30 mL) water**

Step 10. Using a rolling pin, roll out dough into a ½-inch (1.3 cm) thick circle.

Step 11. Dip the edges of a 4-inch (10 cm) round biscuit cutter in flour.

Step 12. Cut dough into circles, taking care not to twist cutter.

METHOD

1. Preheat oven to 400°F (205°C).
2. In a large bowl, combine flour, baking powder and salt.
3. Cut margarine into flour mixture until it resembles corn meal.
4. Stir in cheese.
5. Make a well in the middle of the mixture.
6. Pour all of the milk into center of mixture.
7. Mix dough quickly with a fork until it forms a ball. Dough should be soft.
8. Turn dough onto a floured surface.
9. Knead dough gently for about 30 seconds.
10. Using a rolling pin, roll out dough into a ½-inch (1.3 cm) thick circle.
11. Dip the edges of a 4-inch (10 cm) round biscuit cutter in flour.
12. Cut dough into circles, taking care not to twist cutter.
13. Place dough circles on an ungreased baking sheet.
14. In a small bowl, beat together egg and water.
15. Brush dough circles with egg mixture.
16. Bake for 10-12 minutes, until golden brown.
17. Serve biscuits hot or cold.

1 dozen biscuits

Variation:

- *Herb Biscuits: Substitute 1 tsp (5 mL) mixed, dried herbs for the Cheddar cheese.*

Approximate nutritional analysis per biscuit
Calories 148, Protein 4 g, Carbohydrates 17 g, Fat 7 g, Cholesterol 23 mg, Sodium 253 mg

Cheese Biscuits

Oatmeal Raisin Bread

Healthy goodness in every bite.

INGREDIENTS

2 cups	**(500 mL) whole wheat flour**
2 cups	**(500 mL) rolled oats**
1½ cups	**(375 mL) raisins**
1 cup	**(250 mL) brown sugar, firmly packed**
2 tbsp	**(30 mL) baking soda**
2 tbsp	**(30 mL) baking powder**
¼ tsp	**(1 mL) cinnamon**
3	**medium eggs**
2 cups	**(500 mL) buttermilk**

METHOD

1. Preheat oven to 350°F (175°C).
2. Grease a 9 x 5 x 3-inch (22 x 12 x 7 cm) loaf pan.
3. In a large bowl, combine flour, rolled oats, raisins, brown sugar, baking soda, baking powder and cinnamon.
4. In a medium bowl, whisk together eggs and buttermilk.
5. Add buttermilk mixture to dry ingredients. Combine thoroughly.
6. Fill prepared loaf pan three-quarters full of batter.
7. Bake for 1 hour, until a wooden pick inserted into center of bread comes out clean.
8. Invert bread onto a wire rack. Remove pan and cool bread right side up.

10 servings

◀ Approximate nutritional analysis per serving
Calories 313, Protein 10 g, Carbohydrates 65 g, Fat 3 g, Cholesterol 58 mg, Sodium 1126 mg

Cheese Straws

Serve with soup or as a tasty snack.

INGREDIENTS

½ lb	**(225 g) Puff Pastry Dough (see page 314)**
4 tbsp	**(60 mL) butter, melted**
½ cup	**(125 mL) Parmesan or Cheddar cheese, finely grated**

METHOD

1. Preheat oven to 400°F (205°C).
2. Lightly grease a baking sheet.
3. Using a rolling pin, flatten dough into a 7 x 9-inch (18 x 22 cm) rectangle, ¼-inch (0.6 cm) thick.
4. Brush dough with butter.
5. Sprinkle half the cheese onto surface of dough.
6. Cut dough lengthwise into ¼-inch (0.6 cm) strips.
7. Twist dough strips.
8. Coat twisted dough with remaining cheese and place on prepared baking sheet.
9. Bake for 7 minutes, until golden brown.
10. Cool cheese straws.
11. Cut into desired lengths and serve.

28 straws

Variations:

- *Herb Straws: Substitute 2 tbsp (30 mL) of dried, mixed herbs for the grated cheese.*
- *Pepper Straws: Substitute 2 tbsp (30 mL) of dried pepper flakes for the grated cheese.*

Approximate nutritional analysis per straw
Calories 63, Protein 2 g, Carbohydrates 5 g, Fat 4 g, Cholesterol 7 mg, Sodium 80 mg

Cheese Straws

Corn Cakes with Swiss Cheese and Herbs

This recipe is sure to become a family favorite.

INGREDIENTS

½ cup	**(125 mL) yellow corn meal**
2 tbsp	**(30 mL) all-purpose flour**
½ tsp	**(2 mL) baking powder**
pinch	**salt**
½ cup + 2 tbsp	**(155 mL) milk**
4 tbsp	**(60 mL) butter, melted**
1 tbsp	**(15 mL) vegetable oil**
2 oz	**(55 g) Swiss cheese, grated**
1 tbsp	**(15 mL) fresh basil, minced**
1 tbsp	**(15 mL) fresh cilantro, minced**

Step 3. Make a well in the center of the corn meal mixture.

Step 4. Add milk and melted butter to corn meal mixture, stirring to combine.

METHOD

1. Preheat broiler.
2. In a medium bowl, combine corn meal, flour, baking powder and salt. Mix well.
3. Make a well in the center of the corn meal mixture.
4. Add milk and melted butter to corn meal mixture, stirring to combine.
5. In a heavy skillet, heat oil over medium heat.
6. Spoon batter into skillet to make 4 to 5 equal-sized pancakes.
7. Fry on first side for 4 minutes, until edges turn brown. Turn and fry for 4 more minutes, until golden brown.
8. Drain cakes on paper towels.
9. Repeat process with remaining batter.
10. Place pancakes on a baking sheet and top with Swiss cheese.
11. Broil until cheese melts, about 2 minutes.
12. Sprinkle with basil and cilantro. Serve.

4 servings

Approximate nutritional analysis per serving
Calories 331, Protein 8 g, Carbohydrates 29 g, Fat 21 g, Cholesterol 48 mg, Sodium 241 mg

Corn Cakes with Swiss Cheese and Herbs

Polenta

Tomato sauce is a natural accompaniment to this versatile Italian classic.

INGREDIENTS

8 cups	**(2 L) water**
2 tsp	**(10 mL) salt**
1 lb	**(450 g) corn meal**
3 tbsp	**(45 mL) olive oil**

Step 4. Spread corn meal mixture into damp tray to a depth of ¾ inch (1.9 cm).

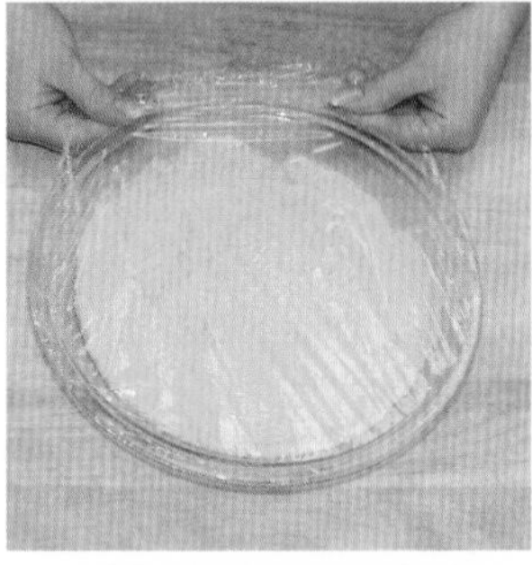

Step 5. Cover tray with plastic wrap and refrigerate overnight.

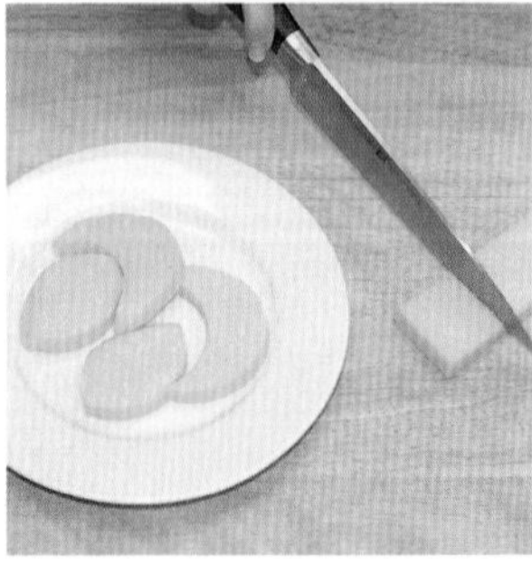

Step 6. Cut polenta into desired shapes with a cookie cutter or knife.

METHOD

1. In a heavy saucepan, combine water, salt and corn meal.
2. Cook corn meal mixture over medium heat for about 5 minutes, stirring occasionally. Mixture is cooked when it leaves the sides of the saucepan.
3. Rinse a shallow tray with water.
4. Spread corn meal mixture into damp tray to a depth of ¾ inch (1.9 cm).
5. Cover tray with plastic wrap and refrigerate overnight.
6. Cut polenta into desired shapes with a cookie cutter or knife.
7. Brush polenta pieces with 2 tbsp (30 mL) olive oil.
8. Heat remaining oil in a large skillet over low heat.
9. Sauté polenta for 5-6 minutes, until heated through.
10. Serve hot.

8 servings

Variations:

- *Cheese Polenta: After brushing polenta pieces with olive oil, top with 4 oz (115 g) grated Parmesan or mozzarella cheese. Place on a baking sheet and broil on middle oven rack until cheese is melted.*
- *Sun-Dried Tomato Polenta: Chop 6 sun-dried tomato halves. Stir into corn meal mixture just before spreading mixture in tray.*

Approximate nutritional analysis per serving
Calories 250, Protein 5 g, Carbohydrates 44 g, Fat 7 g, Cholesterol 0 mg, Sodium 553 mg

Polenta

Cranberry Tea Bread

Serve with your favorite cup of coffee or tea for a perfect afternoon.

INGREDIENTS

2 cups	**(500 mL) all-purpose flour**
2 tsp	**(10 mL) baking powder**
¼ tsp	**(1 mL) salt**
4 tbsp	**(60 mL) butter**
¾ cup + 1 tbsp	**(190 mL) sugar**
¾ cup	**(175 mL) walnuts, chopped**
1 tbsp	**(15 mL) lemon peel, grated**
1	**medium egg**
⅔ cup	**(150 mL) orange juice**
2 cups	**(500 mL) fresh cranberries**
1 tbsp	**(15 mL) milk**

METHOD

1. Preheat oven to 350°F (175°C).
2. Lightly grease a 9 x 5 x 3-inch (22 x 12 x 7 cm) loaf pan.
3. Cut a piece of wax paper to fit bottom of pan. Grease and place in pan.
4. In a large bowl, combine flour, baking powder and salt.
5. Cut butter into flour mixture until it resembles coarse sand.
6. Add ¾ cup (175 mL) sugar, walnuts and lemon peel. Mix lightly.
7. In a small bowl, whisk egg until light and frothy.
8. Whisk orange juice into egg.
9. Pour egg mixture over dry ingredients. Stir just until batter starts to form.
10. Before batter is thoroughly mixed, stir in cranberries.
11. Scrape batter into prepared loaf pan.
12. Using a spatula, spread batter evenly in pan.
13. Brush top of batter with milk.
14. Sprinkle with remaining sugar.
15. Bake for 75 minutes, until a wooden pick inserted into center of bread comes out clean. Loaf should be crusty and golden brown.
16. Transfer bread to a cooling rack.
17. Run a thin-bladed knife around edge of pan to loosen bread.
18. Invert onto cooling rack and remove pan.
19. Peel off wax paper and turn bread right side up.
20. Allow bread to cool.
21. Serve, or place in an airtight container.

10 servings

Approximate nutritional analysis per serving
Calories 287, Protein 5 g, Carbohydrates 41 g, Fat 12 g, Cholesterol 31 mg, Sodium 206 mg

Cranberry Tea Bread

Apricot and Pear Bran Muffins

These moist, nutritious muffins are the perfect snack for any time of the day.

INGREDIENTS

3 cups	**(750 mL) all-bran cereal**
1 cup	**(250 mL) boiling water**
½ cup	**(125 mL) vegetable oil**
½ cup	**(125 mL) molasses**
2	**medium eggs**
2 cups	**(500 mL) buttermilk**
½ cup	**(125 mL) dried apricots, chopped**
½ cup	**(125 mL) dried pears, chopped**
2½ cups	**(625 mL) all-purpose flour**
1 tbsp	**(15 mL) baking soda**
½ tsp	**(2 mL) cinnamon**
½ tsp	**(2 mL) salt**

METHOD

1. In a large bowl, combine bran and water.
2. Allow bran mixture to cool for 15 minutes.
3. In a medium bowl, combine oil, molasses and eggs.
4. Stir molasses mixture into bran mixture.
5. Add buttermilk, apricots and pears.
6. Sift in flour, baking soda, cinnamon and salt.
7. Stir with a wooden spoon or spatula until just blended. Do not over mix.
8. Cover batter and refrigerate overnight.
9. Heat oven to 425°F (220°C).
10. Line muffin pans with paper muffin cups.
11. Remove batter from refrigerator. Do not stir.
12. Spoon batter into muffin cups until three-quarters full.
13. Bake for 15 minutes, until a wooden pick inserted into center comes out clean.

2 dozen muffins

Approximate nutritional analysis per muffin
Calories 158, Protein 4 g, Carbohydrates 27 g, Fat 5 g, Cholesterol 16 mg, Sodium 354 mg

Apricot and Pear Bran Muffins

Scrumptious Blueberry Muffins

These fresh-baked treats won't last long. Melt-in-your mouth goodness.

INGREDIENTS

2	**large eggs**
1 cup	**(250 mL) milk**
¼ cup	**(50 mL) butter, melted**
1¾ cups	**(425 mL) all-purpose flour**
1 tbsp	**(15 mL) baking powder**
½ tsp	**(2 mL) salt**
½ cup + 2 tbsp	**(155 mL) sugar**
pinch	**nutmeg**
1 cup	**(250 mL) blueberries**

METHOD

1. Preheat oven to 400°F (205°C).
2. Line muffin pan with paper muffin cups.
3. In a small bowl, whisk together eggs, milk and butter.
4. In a large bowl, combine 1½ cups (375 mL) flour, baking powder, salt, 2 tbsp (30 mL) sugar and nutmeg.
5. Add egg mixture to dry ingredients, stirring until batter is well combined.
6. In a medium bowl, gently stir together remaining flour, blueberries and remaining sugar.
7. Carefully fold blueberry mixture into batter.
8. Spoon batter into muffin cups until three-quarters full.
9. Bake for 20 minutes, until a wooden pick inserted into center comes out clean.

1 dozen large muffins

Tip:

- *Fresh or frozen blueberries may be used for this recipe. If using fresh blueberries, wash well and pat dry. If using frozen blueberries, add to batter while still frozen.*

Approximate nutritional analysis per muffin
Calories 176, Protein 4 g, Carbohydrates 27 g, Fat 6 g, Cholesterol 49 mg, Sodium 233 mg

Scrumptious Blueberry Muffins

Raisin Baking Powder Biscuits

Try these biscuits toasted for breakfast. A fabulous way to start your day.

INGREDIENTS

2 cups	**(500 mL) all-purpose flour, sifted**	**¼ cup**	**(50 mL) margarine or butter**
1 tbsp	**(15 mL) baking powder**	**½ cup**	**(125 mL) raisins**
½ tsp	**(2 mL) salt**	**¾ cup**	**(175 mL) milk**

METHOD

1. Preheat oven to 400°F (205°C).
2. In a large bowl, combine flour, baking powder and salt.
3. Cut margarine into flour mixture until it resembles corn meal.
4. Stir in raisins.
5. Make a well in the middle of the mixture.
6. Pour all of the milk into center of mixture.
7. Mix dough quickly with a fork until it forms a ball. Dough should be soft.
8. Turn dough onto a floured surface.
9. Knead dough gently for about 30 seconds.
10. Using a rolling pin, roll out dough into a ½-inch (1.3 cm) thick circle.
11. Dip the edges of a 4-inch (10 cm) round biscuit cutter in flour.
12. Cut dough into circles, taking care not to twist cutter.
13. Place dough circles on an ungreased baking sheet.
14. Bake for 10-12 minutes, until golden brown.
15. Serve biscuits hot or cold.

1 dozen biscuits

Tip:

- *How To Glaze Biscuits: Brush with a mixture of 1 beaten egg and 2 tbsp (30 mL) of milk just before baking.*

Variation:

- *Drop Biscuits: Increase milk to 1 cup (250 mL) and omit raisins. Instead of rolling, kneading and cutting dough into circles, drop from a tablespoon onto a greased baking sheet.*

Approximate nutritional analysis per biscuit
Calories 144, Protein 3 g, Carbohydrates 22 g, Fat 5 g, Cholesterol 2 mg, Sodium 220 mg

Raisin Baking Powder Biscuits

Brown Rice Pilaf with Dates and Carrots

This recipe is a delicate blend of textures and sweet flavors.

INGREDIENTS

1	**small onion, thinly sliced**
1	**carrot, peeled and thinly sliced**
1 cup	**(250 mL) long grain brown rice, uncooked**
1 tsp	**(5 mL) olive oil**
¼ cup	**(50 mL) pitted dates, coarsely chopped**
1 tsp	**(5 mL) lemon peel, grated**
1½ cups	**(375 mL) chicken broth**
½ cup	**(125 mL) water**
	black pepper
1 tsp	**(5 mL) lemon juice**
2 tbsp	**(30 mL) green onions, chopped**

METHOD

1. Place onions, carrots, rice and oil in a heavy saucepan.
2. Cook over medium heat for 1 minute, stirring occasionally.
3. Stir in dates, lemon peel, chicken broth and water.
4. Season with pepper.
5. Bring rice mixture to a boil. Reduce heat to low.
6. Cover and simmer for 45 minutes, until all the liquid is absorbed.
7. Fluff pilaf with a fork.
8. Stir in lemon juice.
9. Sprinkle with green onions and serve.

4 servings

Approximate nutritional analysis per serving
Calories 256, Protein 8 g, Carbohydrates 49 g, Fat 4 g, Cholesterol 1 mg, Sodium 543 mg

Brown Rice Pilaf with Dates and Carrots

Smoked Salmon and Artichoke Pilaf

A delightful pilaf brimming with subtle, smoky flavors.

INGREDIENTS

3 tbsp	**(45 mL) vegetable oil**
¼ cup	**(50 mL) onions, small diced**
1	**garlic clove, minced**
1 cup	**(250 mL) long grain rice, uncooked**
2½ cups	**(625 mL) chicken broth**
1	**bay leaf**
3 tbsp	**(45 mL) butter**
2 tbsp	**(30 mL) Parmesan cheese, freshly grated**
	black pepper
3 oz	**(85 g) smoked salmon, diced**
10 oz	**(284 mL) canned artichoke hearts, drained and quartered**
2 tbsp	**(30 mL) fresh parsley, chopped**

METHOD

1. In a saucepan, heat oil over medium heat.
2. Cook onions for 5 minutes, until translucent.
3. Add garlic and cook for 1 minute, stirring occasionally.
4. Add rice to saucepan, stirring until all the rice is coated with oil.
5. Stir in chicken broth. Bring to a boil.
6. Add bay leaf to saucepan. Reduce heat to low.
7. Cover and cook for 20-25 minutes, until all the liquid is absorbed and rice is cooked but not too soft.
8. Remove from heat. Discard bay leaf.
9. Stir in butter and Parmesan cheese.
10. Season with pepper to taste.
11. Stir in smoked salmon, artichokes and parsley. Serve.

4 servings

Tip:

- *This dish makes a lovely appetizer. Serve on warm plates with pita bread or small whole wheat buns.*

Approximate nutritional analysis per serving
Calories 456, Protein 17 g, Carbohydrates 47 g, Fat 23 g, Cholesterol 33 mg, Sodium 1256 mg

Smoked Salmon and Artichoke Pilaf

Vegetables

Stuffed Zucchini Slices

Crisp zucchini rounds filled with mouth-watering, savory bread stuffing.

INGREDIENTS

2	**large zucchini**
2 tbsp	**(30 mL) vegetable oil**
1	**medium onion, finely diced**
2	**celery stalks, small diced**
3 tbsp	**(45 mL) fresh parsley, chopped**
1 tsp	**(5 mL) thyme**
2 tbsp	**(30 mL) tomato paste**
½ cup	**(125 mL) bread crumbs**
1	**large egg, lightly beaten**
½ cup	**(125 mL) chicken broth**
	salt and pepper

METHOD

1. Preheat oven to 375°F (190°C).
2. Cut each zucchini into 2 equal pieces.
3. Using an apple corer or melon baller, hollow out center of each zucchini half. Discard pulp.
4. Blanch zucchini halves in boiling, salted water for 2 minutes.
5. Rinse zucchini under cold, running water. Drain well.
6. In a skillet, heat oil over medium heat.
7. Sauté onions, celery and parsley for 5 minutes. Remove skillet from heat.
8. Stir in thyme and tomato paste.
9. Add bread crumbs and mix well.
10. Stir in egg and ¼ cup (50 mL) of chicken broth.
11. Season with salt and pepper.
12. Place vegetable mixture in a piping bag.
13. Pipe vegetable mixture evenly into each zucchini half.
14. Place zucchini in an ovenproof casserole dish.
15. Add remaining chicken broth to casserole dish. Cover with aluminum foil.
16. Bake for 10-12 minutes, until zucchini is cooked but still crisp.
17. Cool slightly. Slice and serve.

4 servings

Step 2. Cut each zucchini into 2 equal pieces.

Step 3. Using an apple corer or melon baller, hollow out center of each zucchini half. Discard pulp.

Step 13. Pipe vegetable mixture evenly into each zucchini half.

Approximate nutritional analysis per serving
Calories 156, Protein 5 g, Carbohydrates 15 g, Fat 9 g, Cholesterol 47 mg, Sodium 917 mg

Stuffed Zucchini Slices

Spaghetti Squash Napolitain

A unique and nutritious vegetable dish.

INGREDIENTS

2 lbs	**(900 g) spaghetti squash**
¼ cup	**(50 mL) water**
1 tbsp	**(15 mL) butter, melted**
1 tsp	**(5 mL) salt**
1 tsp	**(5 mL) black pepper**
2 cups	**(500 mL) spaghetti sauce**
4 tbsp	**(60 mL) Parmesan cheese, grated**

METHOD

1. Preheat oven to 350°F (175°C).
2. Split squash in half lengthwise.
3. Using a spoon, remove seeds from squash and discard.
4. Place squash halves, cut sides down, in an ovenproof casserole dish.
5. Add water to casserole dish.
6. Bake for 45 minutes.
7. Turn squash halves and bake for 10 minutes, until squash skin is tender.
8. Using a fork, remove pulp from squash and place in a serving dish. Discard outer shell of squash.
9. Serve topped with butter, salt, pepper, spaghetti sauce and Parmesan cheese.

6 servings

Savoy Cabbage Alberta

Caraway seeds add spunk to this recipe.

INGREDIENTS

2 tbsp	**(30 mL) vegetable oil**
½ lb	**(225 g) Canadian back bacon, cut into ¼-inch (0.6 cm) pieces**
2	**garlic cloves, minced**
1	**zucchini, julienned**
2	**carrots, peeled and julienned**
1	**medium onion, sliced**
2 lbs	**(900 g) Savoy cabbage, finely shredded**
1 tsp	**(5 mL) caraway seeds**
	salt and pepper

METHOD

1. In a large skillet, heat oil over medium heat.
2. Cook bacon for 1 minute, stirring occasionally.
3. Add garlic to skillet. Cook for 30 seconds, stirring frequently.
4. Stir in zucchini, carrots, onions, cabbage and caraway seeds.
5. Season vegetable mixture with salt and pepper.
6. Cook for 8-10 minutes, stirring occasionally, until vegetables are cooked but still crisp. Do not overcook.
7. Transfer to a serving dish.
8. Serve hot.

6 servings

Approximate nutritional analysis per serving
Calories 183, Protein 13 g, Carbohydrates 17 g, Fat 8 g, Cholesterol 22 mg, Sodium 998 mg

◀ Approximate nutritional analysis per serving
Calories 106, Protein 4 g, Carbohydrates 16 g, Fat 4 g, Cholesterol 10 mg, Sodium 981 mg

Savoy Cabbage Alberta

Stuffed Green Cabbage

These colorful and delicious cabbage balls complement any dinner.

INGREDIENTS

16 cups	**(4 L) water**
2 lbs	**(900 g) green cabbage**
1	**medium onion, sliced**
1	**medium red pepper, sliced**
1	**medium green pepper, sliced**
1	**large carrot, peeled and grated**
2 tbsp	**(30 mL) fresh parsley, chopped**
1 tsp	**(5 mL) caraway seeds**
	salt and pepper

Step 10. Cut a v-shape at the bottom of each cabbage leaf to remove center core.

Step 14. Twist ends of towel tightly until cabbage is molded into a tight ball.

Step 15. Remove towel from cabbage. The cabbage will remain in a ball shape.

METHOD

1. Place water in a large stockpot. Bring to a boil over medium-high heat.
2. Using a sharp knife, remove core from cabbage by cutting out a cone shape.
3. Add cabbage to stockpot. Reduce heat to low.
4. As the cabbage cooks, the outer leaves will loosen. Using a slotted spoon, remove loose leaves and place in a bowl of cold water.
5. When all of the loose leaves have been removed from the stockpot, remove remaining cabbage. Drain, chop and set aside.
6. Place blanched cabbage leaves on a towel to drain.
7. Using the same stockpot and cooking liquid, blanch onions, red peppers, green peppers and carrots for 4 minutes.
8. Drain vegetable mixture and transfer to a medium bowl. Discard cooking liquid.
9. Add parsley, caraway seeds, salt, pepper and reserved cabbage to vegetable mixture, stirring to combine.
10. Cut a v-shape at the bottom of each cabbage leaf to remove center core.
11. Lay out cabbage leaves on a dry towel.
12. Place 2 tbsp (30 mL) of vegetable mixture in center of each cabbage leaf.
13. Fold edges of cabbage leaf into the center around vegetable mixture. Gather towel around cabbage to form a round ball.
14. Twist ends of towel tightly until cabbage is molded into a tight ball.
15. Remove towel from cabbage. The cabbage will remain in a ball shape.
16. Repeat steps until all cabbage leaves and filling are used up.
17. Place cabbage balls in a steamer basket and steam for 10-12 minutes, until cabbage is cooked.
18. Serve hot or cold.

6 servings

Approximate nutritional analysis per serving
Calories 63, Protein 3 g, Carbohydrates 14 g, Fat 1 g, Cholesterol 0 mg, Sodium 390 mg

Stuffed Green Cabbage

Glazed Carrots with Cloves and Honey

Wonderful, sweet flavor.

INGREDIENTS

1 lb	**(450 g) carrots, peeled**
1 tbsp	**(15 mL) butter**
pinch	**cloves**
2 tbsp	**(30 mL) honey**

METHOD

1. Slice carrots or cut into baton shapes.
2. Blanch carrots in boiling water for 5 minutes. Do not overcook.
3. Rinse carrots under cold, running water. Drain well.
4. In a skillet, melt butter over medium heat.
5. Stir in cloves and honey.
6. Add carrots to skillet, tossing to coat with glaze.
7. Serve hot.

4 servings

◀ Approximate nutritional analysis per serving
Calories 107, Protein 1 g, Carbohydrates 20 g, Fat 3 g, Cholesterol 8 mg, Sodium 70 mg

Cauliflower Polonaise

A classic topping for cauliflower.

INGREDIENTS

1	**medium cauliflower head**
1 tbsp	**(15 mL) lemon juice**
1 cup	**(250 mL) fresh, white bread crumbs**
2 tbsp	**(30 mL) fresh parsley, chopped**
2	**hard-boiled eggs, chopped**
2 tbsp	**(30 mL) butter, melted**
	salt and pepper

METHOD

1. Chop cauliflower into bite-sized pieces. Place in a medium saucepan.
2. Cover cauliflower with water and add lemon juice.
3. Bring to a boil over medium-high heat. Reduce heat to medium.
4. Cook cauliflower for 5 minutes. Do not overcook.
5. Drain cauliflower and place in a serving dish.
6. In a medium bowl, combine bread crumbs, parsley, eggs, butter, salt and pepper to taste.
7. Sprinkle bread crumb mixture over cauliflower and serve.

6 servings

Approximate nutritional analysis per serving
Calories 94, Protein 4 g, Carbohydrates 7 g, Fat 6 g, Cholesterol 81 mg, Sodium 202 mg

Cauliflower Polonaise

Green Beans with Cashews

Rich, buttery flavor.

INGREDIENTS

2 lbs	**(900 g) fresh green beans**
2 tbsp	**(30 mL) butter**
1 cup	**(250 mL) roasted cashew nuts**
	salt and pepper

METHOD

1. Remove strings and stem ends from beans. Cut any large beans in half.
2. Blanch beans in boiling, lightly salted water for 5 minutes.
3. Rinse beans under cold, running water. Drain well and dry with paper towels.
4. In a skillet, melt butter over medium heat.
5. Stir in cashews and cook for 4 minutes, until cashews are lightly browned.
6. Add beans, tossing to coat with butter.
7. Season with salt and pepper to taste.
8. Serve hot.

6 servings

◀Approximate nutritional analysis per serving
Calories 213, Protein 6 g, Carbohydrates 19 g, Fat 15 g, Cholesterol 10 mg, Sodium 407 mg

Mediterranean Poached Fennel

A very special side dish.

INGREDIENTS

¾ cup	**(175 mL) olive oil**
½ cup	**(125 mL) dry white wine**
⅓ cup	**(75 mL) tarragon vinegar**
1 tsp	**(5 mL) thyme**
1 tsp	**(5 mL) tarragon**
2 tbsp	**(30 mL) lemon juice**
1 tsp	**(5 mL) salt**
1 tsp	**(5 mL) black pepper**
2	**large garlic cloves, halved**
1	**bay leaf**
4	**fennel bulbs, trimmed and quartered**

METHOD

1. In a large skillet, combine all ingredients except fennel.
2. Add fennel and slowly bring to a boil over medium heat. Reduce heat to low.
3. Poach for 15-20 minutes, turning occasionally, until fennel is tender. Test root end of fennel with a small, sharp knife for doneness.
4. Season broth, if necessary, with salt and pepper to taste.
5. Remove skillet from heat. Allow fennel to cool in poaching liquid.
6. Place fennel on a serving plate.
7. Ladle some of the poaching liquid over fennel and serve.

6 servings

Approximate nutritional analysis per serving
Calories 308, Protein 2 g, Carbohydrates 13 g, Fat 27 g, Cholesterol 0 mg, Sodium 439 mg

Mediterranean Poached Fennel

Sautéed Cucumbers and Dill

This recipe is light and tasty.

INGREDIENTS

2	**medium English cucumbers**
2 tbsp	**(30 mL) butter**
3 tbsp	**(45 mL) fresh dill, chopped**
	salt and white pepper

METHOD

1. Peel cucumbers and cut into quarters.
2. Remove seeds from cucumbers and cut into slices.
3. Blanch cucumbers in boiling, lightly salted water for 5 minutes, until tender. Do not overcook.
4. Rinse cucumbers under cold, running water. Drain well.
5. In a skillet, melt butter over medium heat.
6. Place cucumbers in skillet and sauté to reheat.
7. Add dill to cucumbers. Season to taste with salt and pepper.
8. Serve hot.

6 servings

Dal (Curried Lentils)

An East Indian specialty.

INGREDIENTS

4 cups	**(1 L) water**
2 cups	**(500 mL) dried lentils**
1 tsp	**(5 mL) curry paste**
⅔ cup	**(150 mL) butter**
1	**large onion, chopped**
1 tsp	**(5 mL) cumin seed**
½ cup	**(125 mL) tomatoes, chopped**
¼ cup	**(50 mL) light cream**
1 tbsp	**(15 mL) fresh cilantro, chopped**
1 tsp	**(5 mL) paprika**
2 tbsp	**(30 mL) fresh parsley, chopped**

METHOD

1. In a large saucepan, combine water and lentils. Bring to a boil over medium-high heat. Reduce heat to medium.
2. Add curry paste to lentils.
3. Cook for 8-10 minutes, until lentils are soft and most of the water has been absorbed.
4. While lentils are cooking, melt butter in a skillet over medium heat.
5. Add onions to skillet and sauté for 5 minutes, until golden.
6. Stir in cumin. Reduce heat to low.
7. Add tomatoes and cream, stirring to combine. Remove from heat.
8. Remove lentils from saucepan with a slotted spoon and place in a serving bowl.
9. Pour onion mixture over lentils.
10. Garnish with cilantro, paprika and parsley. Serve.

6 servings

Approximate nutritional analysis per serving
Calories 426, Protein 19 g, Carbohydrates 41 g, Fat 22 g, Cholesterol 58 mg, Sodium 221 mg

◀ Approximate nutritional analysis per serving
Calories 47, Protein 1 g, Carbohydrates 3 g, Fat 4 g, Cholesterol 10 mg, Sodium 130 mg

Dal (Curried Lentils)

Minted Tomatoes

This recipe is very easy to prepare.

INGREDIENTS

2 tbsp	**(30 ml) cider vinegar**
1 tbsp	**(15 ml) sugar**
	salt and pepper
2 tsp	**(10 ml) fresh mint leaves, minced**
2 lbs	**(900 g) Roma tomatoes**

METHOD

1. In a small saucepan, combine vinegar, sugar, salt and pepper.
2. Bring mixture to a boil over medium-high heat.
3. Stir in mint. Remove from heat and allow to cool.
4. Slice tomatoes and place in a medium bowl.
5. Pour vinegar mixture over tomatoes.
6. Cover with plastic wrap and refrigerate for 1 hour before serving.

6 servings

Brussels Sprouts with Grapes

Grapes add sweet flavor to this recipe.

INGREDIENTS

1 lb	**(450 g) Brussels sprouts, cleaned and trimmed**
4 cups	**(1 L) water**
2 tbsp	**(30 mL) butter**
1 cup	**(250 mL) seedless black grapes**
1 cup	**(250 mL) seedless green grapes**
	salt and black pepper
1 tbsp	**(15 mL) lime juice**

METHOD

1. Using a paring knife, cut a cross in the bottom of each Brussels sprout.
2. Place Brussels sprouts and water in a medium saucepan.
3. Bring to a boil over medium-high heat. Reduce heat to medium.
4. Cook for 7-10 minutes, until Brussels sprouts are tender.
5. Drain Brussels sprouts and keep warm.
6. In a saucepan, melt butter over medium heat.
7. Add black and green grapes to saucepan. Reduce heat to low.
8. Cover and cook for 1 minute. Remove from heat.
9. Place Brussels sprouts and grapes in a serving dish.
10. Season to taste with salt and pepper. Toss together.
11. Drizzle with lime juice and serve.

4 servings

Approximate nutritional analysis per serving
Calories 144, Protein 4 g, Carbohydrates 22 g, Fat 6 g, Cholesterol 16 mg, Sodium 355 mg

◀ Approximate nutritional analysis per serving
Calories 43, Protein 1 g, Carbohydrates 10 g, Fat 1 g, Cholesterol 0 mg, Sodium 104 mg

Brussels Sprouts with Grapes

Poached Leeks Black Forest

Succulent Black Forest ham is hidden within each tender leek bundle.

INGREDIENTS

6	**leeks**
6	**Black Forest ham slices**
3 cups	**(750 mL) canned chicken broth**
1 tbsp	**(15 mL) lemon juice**

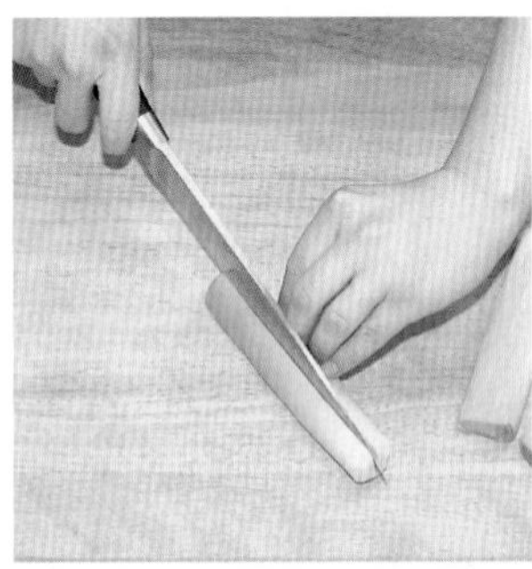

Step 7. Carefully cut leeks in half lengthwise, leaving insides of leeks intact.

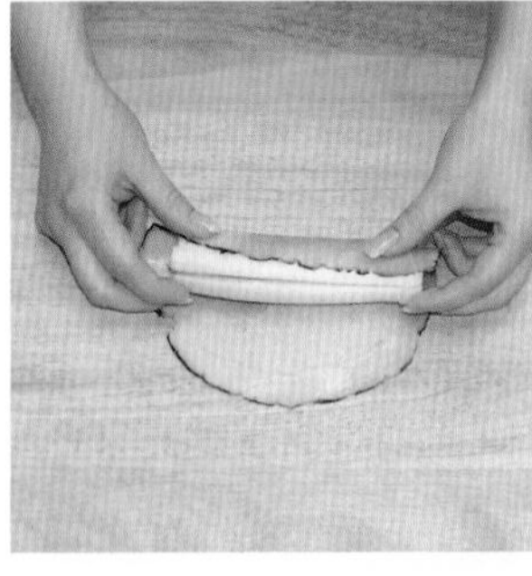

Step 9. Place leek halves back together. Wrap each leek with a slice of ham.

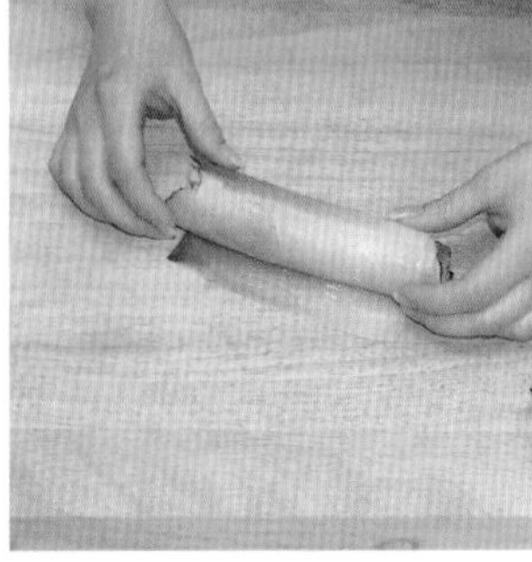

Step 10. Wrap outer leek leaves around ham and tie with string.

METHOD

1. Preheat oven to 375°F (190°C).
2. Remove tough, outer leaves from leeks.
3. Wash leeks and separated outer leaves carefully.
4. Blanch leeks and outer leaves in boiling, salted water for 5 minutes.
5. Rinse under cold, running water. Drain well.
6. Trim ends of leeks, leaving 2-3 inches (5-7 cm) of green.
7. Carefully cut leeks in half lengthwise, leaving insides of leeks intact.
8. Wash leek halves thoroughly to remove any additional grit. Dry well.
9. Place leek halves back together. Wrap each leek with a slice of ham.
10. Wrap outer leek leaves around ham and tie with string.
11. Arrange leeks in a single layer in a shallow casserole dish.
12. Place chicken broth in a saucepan. Bring to a boil over medium-high heat.
13. Remove chicken broth from heat and pour over leeks.
14. Add lemon juice and cover casserole dish.
15. Place in the oven and poach for 45 minutes, until leeks are tender.
16. Remove leeks from poaching liquid. Remove string carefully from each leek.
17. Serve hot.

6 servings

Approximate nutritional analysis per serving
Calories 168, Protein 13 g, Carbohydrates 20 g, Fat 5 g, Cholesterol 22 mg, Sodium 1222 mg

Poached Leeks Black Forest

Vegetable Noodles with Salsa

A fun recipe with flavor to spare.

INGREDIENTS

1 lb	**(450 g) English cucumbers**
1 lb	**(450 g) zucchini**
1 tbsp	**(15 mL) salt**
1½ cups	**(375 mL) chunky-style salsa**

METHOD

1. Using a sharp knife, slice cucumbers and zucchini lengthwise into flat noodle shapes. Place in a medium bowl.
2. Add salt and toss together. Let stand for 10 minutes.
3. Drain vegetables and rinse under cold, running water.
4. Pat vegetables dry with paper towels.
5. Top with salsa and serve.

6 servings

Approximate nutritional analysis per serving
Calories 39, Protein 1 g, Carbohydrates 8 g, Fat 0 g, Cholesterol 0 mg, Sodium 1315 mg

Fabulous Stuffed Peppers

Little treasure chests of taste.

INGREDIENTS

1	**red bell pepper**
1	**green bell pepper**
1	**yellow bell pepper**
1	**large carrot, peeled and grated**
10 oz	**(284 mL) canned kernel corn, drained**
¼ cup	**(50 mL) walnuts, chopped**
¼ cup	**(50 mL) raisins**
4 tbsp	**(60 mL) butter**
3 tbsp	**(45 mL) bread crumbs**
2 tbsp	**(30 mL) sunflower seeds**
2 tbsp	**(30 mL) onions, grated**
	salt and pepper
½ cup	**(125 mL) Cheddar cheese, grated**

METHOD

1. Preheat oven to 350°F (175°C).
2. Blanch red, green and yellow peppers in boiling, salted water for 5 minutes.
3. Rinse peppers under cold, running water. Drain well.
4. Cut peppers in half lengthwise and remove seeds.
5. Butter an ovenproof, glass baking dish.
6. In a large bowl, combine carrots, corn, walnuts, raisins, 2 tbsp (30 mL) butter, 1 tbsp (15 mL) bread crumbs, sunflower seeds, onions, salt and pepper. Mix well.
7. Divide filling mixture evenly into peppers.
8. Top peppers with remaining bread crumbs. Dot with remaining butter.
9. Sprinkle peppers with cheese and place in prepared baking dish.
10. Bake for 30 minutes, until peppers are heated through.
12. Serve immediately.

6 servings

Approximate nutritional analysis per serving
Calories 243, Protein 6 g, Carbohydrates 22 g, Fat 16 g, Cholesterol 31 mg, Sodium 678 mg

Fabulous Stuffed Peppers

Pea Pancakes

Easy and so delicious.

INGREDIENTS

2 cups	**(500 mL) frozen peas, thawed and drained**
2	**large eggs**
¼ cup	**(50 mL) all-purpose flour**
1 tsp	**(5 mL) sugar**
½ tsp	**(2 mL) baking powder**
	salt
⅓ cup	**(75 mL) milk, scalded and cooled**
2 tbsp	**(30 mL) vegetable oil**

METHOD

1. Preheat griddle.
2. In a food processor, purée peas. Add eggs, flour, sugar, baking powder and salt.
3. On medium speed, add milk and blend well.
4. Brush heated griddle with oil as needed.
5. Spoon 2 tbsp (30 mL) of batter onto griddle for each pancake.
6. Cook pancakes for 4 minutes, until bubbles form on top.
7. Turn pancakes and cook for 30 seconds, until golden brown. Serve hot.

6 servings

Approximate nutritional analysis per serving
Calories 132, Protein 6 g, Carbohydrates 12 g, Fat 7 g, Cholesterol 73 mg, Sodium 477 mg

Apple Yams

An exquisite combination of flavors.

INGREDIENTS

6	**medium yams or sweet potatoes or 2½ lbs (1.2 kg) canned yams, drained**
1 tsp	**(5 mL) cinnamon**
¾ cup	**(175 mL) brown sugar, firmly packed**
¼ cup	**(50 mL) butter**
4	**apples, peeled, cored and sliced**
4 tbsp	**(60 mL) butter, melted**

METHOD

1. Preheat oven to 400°F (205°C).
2. Place yams on a baking sheet and bake for 45-60 minutes, until tender when pressed. Do not overcook.
3. Cool yams slightly and remove skins. Cut into slices or dice.
4. Reduce oven temperature to 350°F (175°C).
5. Grease a 9 x 9 x 2-inch (22 x 22 x 5 cm) baking dish.
6. In a small bowl, combine cinnamon and brown sugar.
7. Place a layer of yams in prepared baking dish.
8. Sprinkle yams with some of the brown sugar mixture and dot with a small amount of butter.
9. Place a layer of apples on top of yams. Sprinkle with brown sugar mixture and dot with butter.
10. Continue alternating layers of yams and apples, sprinkling each layer with brown sugar, cinnamon and butter. Finish with a layer of apples.
11. Pour melted butter over top.
12. Cover and bake for 20 minutes.
13. Remove cover and bake for an additional 15 minutes.
14. Serve hot.

8 servings

Approximate nutritional analysis per serving
Calories 350, Protein 3 g, Carbohydrates 59 g, Fat 13 g, Cholesterol 32 mg, Sodium 170 mg

Apple Yams

Braised Celery with Bacon

A wonderful accompaniment to any meal.

INGREDIENTS

4	**bacon strips, diced**
1	**medium red onion, diced**
8	**celery stalks, cut into 3-inch (7 cm) pieces**
14 oz	**(398 mL) canned chicken broth**
¼ tsp	**(1 mL) celery seeds**
2 tbsp	**(30 mL) butter, room temperature**
2 tbsp	**(30 mL) all-purpose flour**
	salt and pepper
1 tbsp	**(15 mL) fresh parsley, chopped**

METHOD

1. Preheat oven to 350°F (175°C).
2. In an ovenproof skillet, sauté bacon over medium heat for 6-8 minutes, until lightly browned.
3. Remove bacon from skillet with a slotted spoon and reserve.
4. Place onions in skillet. Sauté over medium heat for 5 minutes, until soft.
5. Add celery and cook for 3 more minutes.
6. Stir in chicken broth and celery seeds. Bring to a boil. Reduce heat to low.
7. Cook vegetable mixture for an additional 3 minutes. Remove from heat and cover.
8. Transfer skillet to oven and bake for 30 minutes, until celery is tender.
9. In a small bowl, combine butter and flour to form a smooth paste. Keep at room temperature.
10. Remove skillet from oven. Using a slotted spoon, transfer vegetable mixture to a serving dish. Keep warm.
11. Place skillet and cooking liquid on the stove. Bring to a gentle boil over medium heat.
12. Stirring constantly, add pieces of flour/butter mixture until sauce begins to thicken.
13. Season sauce with salt and pepper to taste. Pour sauce over vegetables.
14. Garnish with reserved bacon.
15. Sprinkle with parsley and serve.

4 servings

Approximate nutritional analysis per serving
Calories 157, Protein 8 g, Carbohydrates 9 g, Fat 10 g, Cholesterol 22 mg, Sodium 985 mg

Braised Celery with Bacon

Sweet Potato Turnip Gratin

Rich, satisfying flavor.

INGREDIENTS

1½ lbs	**(675 g) sweet potatoes, peeled and diced**
1½ lbs	**(675 g) turnips, peeled and diced**
1 tbsp	**(15 mL) cornstarch**
1 cup	**(250 mL) milk**
1 cup	**(250 mL) heavy cream**
½ tsp	**(2 mL) salt**
½ tsp	**(2 mL) nutmeg**
1 tsp	**(5 mL) white pepper**

METHOD

1. Preheat oven to 350°F (175°C).
2. Steam potatoes and turnips for 12-15 minutes, until barely tender.
3. Drain vegetables and place in a large, ovenproof casserole dish.
4. In a medium bowl, combine cornstarch and ¼ cup (50 mL) milk.
5. Stir in remaining milk, cream, salt, nutmeg and pepper.
6. Pour milk mixture over vegetables.
7. Bake on top oven rack for 25-30 minutes, until golden brown.
8. Serve hot.

8 servings

Tip:

- *This dish may be prepared the night before and refrigerated before baking.*

Approximate nutritional analysis per serving
Calories 232, Protein 4 g, Carbohydrates 28 g, Fat 12 g, Cholesterol 45 mg, Sodium 213 mg

Chick Peas with Pumpkin Seeds

Nutritious and tasty.

INGREDIENTS

1	**jalapeño pepper**
1 cup	**(250 mL) frozen lima beans, thawed and drained**
1 cup	**(250 mL) roasted pumpkin seeds**
14 oz	**(398 mL) canned chick peas, drained**
4	**green onions, minced**
	salt and black pepper

METHOD

1. Preheat broiler.
2. Place jalapeño pepper on a baking sheet.
3. Broil on top oven rack for 8-10 minutes, turning frequently, until pepper skin is blackened.
4. Remove skin and seeds from pepper.
5. Chop pepper and set aside.
6. Dry lima beans well.
7. In an ungreased skillet, toast pumpkin seeds over medium heat for 4-5 minutes, stirring constantly.
8. Stir in reserved peppers, lima beans, chick peas and green onions.
9. Season to taste with salt and pepper. Reduce heat to low.
10. Cook, stirring gently, until mixture is dry. Do not break the beans.
11. Transfer mixture to a serving dish.
12. Serve hot.

6 servings

Approximate nutritional analysis per serving
Calories 135, Protein 7 g, Carbohydrates 21 g, Fat 3 g, Cholesterol 0 mg, Sodium 356 mg

Chick Peas with Pumpkin Seeds

Potato Cheese Pie

A layered masterpiece of cheese and seasoned mashed potatoes.

INGREDIENTS

3 lbs	**(1.4 kg) potatoes, peeled and diced**
2	**garlic cloves, minced**
6 tbsp	**(90 mL) butter**
¾ cup	**(175 mL) Parmesan cheese, grated**
½ cup	**(125 mL) green onions, minced**
⅓ cup	**(75 mL) light cream**
2	**eggs, beaten**
	salt and white pepper
½ tsp	**(2 mL) cayenne pepper**
1¼ cups	**(300 mL) aged Cheddar cheese, grated**
2 tbsp	**(30 mL) dry bread crumbs**
2 tbsp	**(30 mL) butter, cut into pieces**

METHOD

1. Preheat oven to 350°F (175°C).
2. Butter a 10-inch (25 cm) glass pie plate.
3. Place potatoes and garlic in a large saucepan.
4. Cover potatoes with cold water and bring to a boil over medium-high heat. Reduce heat to medium.
5. Cook potatoes for 12-15 minutes, until tender.
6. Drain potatoes and return to saucepan.
7. Over medium heat, cook potatoes, shaking frequently, until potatoes are dry. Remove from heat.
8. Add butter to saucepan and mash potatoes.
9. Stir in ½ cup (125 mL) Parmesan cheese, green onions, cream and eggs. Mash until fluffy.
10. Season with salt, pepper, and cayenne pepper.
11. Spoon half the potato mixture into prepared pie plate.
12. Top with 1 cup (250 mL) Cheddar cheese and press down lightly with the back of a spoon.
13. Place remaining potato mixture on top of cheese.
14. Sprinkle remaining Parmesan cheese and bread crumbs on top of potato mixture.
15. Top with remaining Cheddar cheese.
16. Dot with butter and bake for 10 minutes, until golden brown.
17. Cut into wedges and serve.

6 servings

Approximate nutritional analysis per serving
Calories 477, Protein 18 g, Carbohydrates 34 g, Fat 31 g, Cholesterol 157 mg, Sodium 1535 mg

Potato Cheese Pie

Potatoes with Tri-Colored Peppers

A delightful and colorful recipe.

INGREDIENTS

4	**medium potatoes, peeled and sliced**
2	**medium onions, sliced**
2	**small yellow peppers, sliced**
2	**small green peppers, sliced**
2	**small red peppers, sliced**
3 oz	**(85 g) Italian sausage, cooked and julienned**
1 tbsp	**(15 mL) fresh parsley, chopped**
1 tbsp	**(15 mL) fresh chives, chopped**
	salt and pepper
¼ cup	**(50 mL) olive oil**

METHOD

1. Preheat oven to 400°F (205°C).
2. In a casserole dish, combine potatoes, onions, yellow peppers, green peppers, red peppers and sausage.
3. Stir in parsley, chives, salt and pepper.
4. Add oil to casserole dish and toss with vegetables.
5. Bake for 35-40 minutes, stirring occasionally, until potatoes are tender.
6. Serve hot.

4 servings

Canadian Bacon Cheddar Potatoes

Delicious, twice-baked potatoes.

INGREDIENTS

4	**large baking potatoes**
2 tbsp	**(30 mL) vegetable oil**
	salt and pepper
1 cup	**(250 mL) sour cream**
3	**green onions, chopped**
4 tbsp	**(60 mL) butter, melted**
1 cup	**(250 mL) Canadian Cheddar cheese, grated**
1	**medium tomato, seeded and diced**
6	**bacon slices, cooked until crisp and crumbled**

METHOD

1. Preheat oven to 375°F (190°C).
2. Brush potatoes with oil.
3. Puncture potato skins once or twice with the point of a sharp knife.
4. Place potatoes on a baking sheet. Bake for 1 hour, until tender. Remove from oven.
5. Carefully holding in a dry towel, lay each potato sideways on a cutting board.
6. Cut a slice off the flat side of each potato.
7. Using a spoon, scoop potato pulp into a mixing bowl, taking care not to break potato skins.
8. Add salt, pepper and sour cream to potato pulp.
9. Mix in green onions and butter, stirring to combine.
10. Spoon mixture into empty potato shells.
11. Sprinkle cheese, tomatoes and bacon on top of potatoes.
12. Return potatoes to baking sheet.
13. Bake until cheese begins to melt. Serve hot.

4 servings

Approximate nutritional analysis per serving
Calories 625, Protein 16 g, Carbohydrates 31 g, Fat 50 g, Cholesterol 97 mg, Sodium 1722 mg

◀ Approximate nutritional analysis per serving
Calories 360, Protein 7 g, Carbohydrates 39 g, Fat 21 g, Cholesterol 16 mg, Sodium 172 mg

Canadian Bacon Cheddar Potatoes

Almond Potato Croquettes

Tasty potato morsels coated with almonds and fried until golden brown.

INGREDIENTS

1¼ lbs	**(565 g) potatoes, peeled**
2 tbsp	**(30 mL) butter**
pinch	**nutmeg**
	salt and white pepper
3	**egg yolks, beaten**
3 tbsp	**(45 mL) all-purpose flour**
	vegetable oil for deep frying
3	**large eggs, beaten**
1 cup	**(250 mL) almonds, slivered**

METHOD

1. Preheat oven to 350°F (175°C).
2. Cut potatoes into small, even-sized pieces and place in a medium saucepan.
3. Cover potatoes with water. Bring to a boil over medium-high heat. Reduce heat to medium.
4. Cook for 12-15 minutes, until potatoes are tender.
5. Drain potatoes and place on a baking sheet.
6. Bake potatoes for 5 minutes, until they are dry.
7. Transfer potatoes to a medium bowl and mash well.
8. Add butter to potatoes and mix to form a smooth paste. Season with nutmeg, salt and pepper.
9. Place potato mixture in a heavy saucepan.
10. Cook over medium heat, stirring frequently, until mixture dries. Remove from heat.
11. Add egg yolks and combine well. Allow mixture to cool.
12. Form potato mixture into cylinder, ball or pear shapes.
13. Heat oil to 350°F (175°C).
14. Place flour in a shallow pan.
15. Place eggs in a medium bowl.
16. Place almonds in another shallow pan.
17. Dip potato shapes first in flour, then eggs and roll in almonds.
18. Deep fry for 2-3 minutes, until golden brown.
19. Remove croquettes from oil and drain on paper towels.
20. Serve hot.

4 servings

Approximate nutritional analysis per serving
Calories 439, Protein 15 g, Carbohydrates 37 g, Fat 28 g, Cholesterol 178 mg, Sodium 1071 mg

Almond Potato Croquettes

Garlic Herb Potatoes

A simple potato dish rich in taste.

INGREDIENTS

4 tbsp	**(60 mL) butter**
4 tbsp	**(60 mL) olive oil**
2	**garlic cloves, chopped**
4	**large potatoes, peeled and sliced**
1 tsp	**(5 mL) salt**
1 tsp	**(5 mL) black pepper**
1 tsp	**(5 mL) paprika**
2 tbsp	**(30 mL) fresh parsley, chopped**
1 tbsp	**(15 mL) fresh mint leaves, chopped**

METHOD

1. In a heavy skillet, heat butter and oil over medium heat.
2. Add garlic to skillet. Sauté for 2 minutes, until golden. Remove garlic from skillet and discard.
3. Place potatoes in skillet. Cook, stirring occasionally, for 8-10 minutes, until potatoes are tender and golden brown.
4. Season with salt and pepper.
5. Remove potatoes from skillet and place in a serving dish.
6. Sprinkle potatoes with paprika, parsley and mint.
7. Serve hot.

4 servings

Approximate nutritional analysis per serving
Calories 250, Protein 1 g, Carbohydrates 6 g, Fat 25 g, Cholesterol 31 mg, Sodium 745 mg

Garlic Herb Potatoes

Desserts

Puff Pastry Dough

A time-tested recipe for rich and flaky puff pastry.

INGREDIENTS

3 cups	**(750 mL) bread flour**
pinch	**salt**
1 cup	**(250 mL) butter**
1 cup	**(250 mL) margarine**
1 cup	**(250 mL) ice water**
dash	**lemon juice**

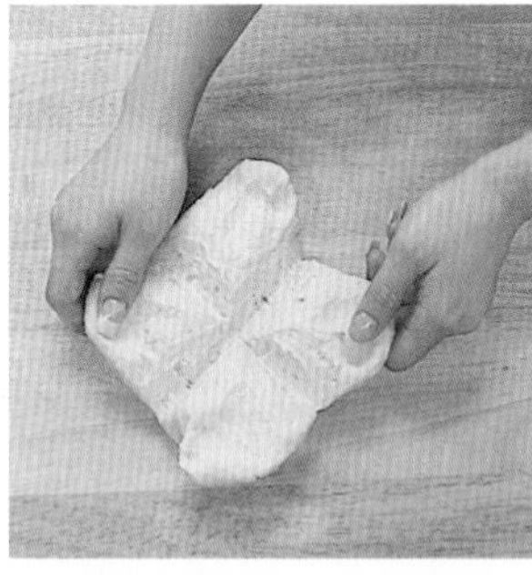

Step 10. Pull out corners of dough to form a star shape.

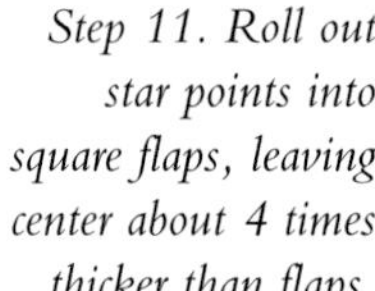

Step 11. Roll out star points into square flaps, leaving center about 4 times thicker than flaps.

Step 13. Place butter mixture in center of dough.

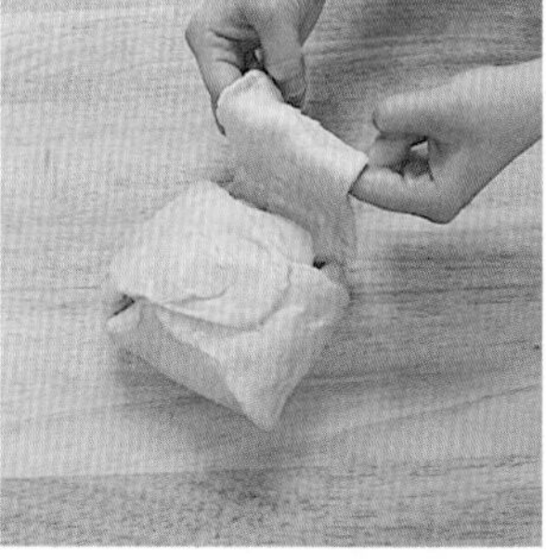

Step 14. Fold dough flaps over butter mixture.

METHOD

1. In a large bowl, sift together flour and salt.
2. In a medium bowl, combine butter and margarine until well blended.
3. Rub 4 tbsp (60 mL) butter mixture into flour mixture.
4. Make a well in the middle of the mixture.
5. Add water and lemon juice to flour mixture.
6. Knead mixture to make a smooth dough.
7. Form dough into a ball.
8. Refrigerate for 30 minutes.
9. Cut a cross halfway through the dough.
10. Pull out corners of dough to form a star shape.
11. Roll out star points into square flaps, leaving center about 4 times thicker than flaps.
12. Soften remaining butter mixture until it is the same texture as dough.
13. Place butter mixture in center of dough.
14. Fold dough flaps over butter mixture.
15. Roll dough into a 24 x 12-inch (60 x 30 cm) rectangle.
16. Cover dough with a cloth. Allow dough to rest for 15 minutes.
17. Roll dough into a 30 x 18-inch (75 x 45 cm) rectangle.
18. Fold the two long ends of the dough so that they meet in the center of the rectangle.
19. Fold in half again to form a square.
20. Allow dough to rest in a cool place for 20 minutes.
21. Half turn the dough to the right or left.
22. Roll dough into a 24 x 12-inch (60 x 30 cm) rectangle. Allow dough to rest again for 20 minutes.

Puff Pastry Dough (continued)

23. Repeat rolling procedure, making sure that sides of dough are always kept as square as possible.
24. Allow dough to rest again before using.
25. Dough may be wrapped in plastic wrap, sealed in a plastic bag and frozen for up to 3 months.

Makes 2 lbs (900 g) dough

Pâte Brisée

A classic sweet pastry dough.

INGREDIENTS

1¼ cups	**(300 mL) all-purpose flour**
6 tbsp	**(90 mL) cold, unsalted butter, cut into small pieces**
2 tbsp	**(30 mL) cold vegetable shortening**
¼ tsp	**(1 mL) salt**
3 tbsp	**(45 mL) ice water**

METHOD

1. In a medium bowl, combine flour, butter, shortening and salt until mixture resembles corn meal.
2. Add ice water. Lightly toss mixture to form a dough.
3. Turn dough out onto a smooth surface.
4. Lightly knead dough for a few seconds to distribute the fat.
5. Shape dough into a ball and wrap in wax paper.
6. Chill for 1 hour before using.
7. Dough may be wrapped in plastic wrap, sealed in a plastic bag and frozen for up to 3 months.

Makes 10 oz (285 g) dough

Flaky Pie Pastry

For light and delicious pie crusts.

INGREDIENTS

pinch	**salt**
½ cup	**(125 mL) cold water**
2 cups	**(500 mL) all-purpose flour**
¾ cup	**(175 mL) shortening**

METHOD

1. In a small bowl, dissolve salt in water.
2. Place flour and shortening in a medium bowl.
3. Work shortening into flour until shortening is broken into pea-size pieces.
4. Add water to mixture.
5. Mix together until dough forms a ball.
6. Dough may be wrapped in plastic wrap, sealed in a plastic bag and frozen for up to 3 months.

Makes 18 oz (510 g) dough

Classic Apple Pie

Serve this extra-special treat with a slice of aged Cheddar cheese.

INGREDIENTS

18 oz	**(510 g) Flaky Pie Pastry (see page 315)**
7	**tart apples**
2 tbsp	**(30 mL) all-purpose flour**
1 cup	**(250 mL) brown sugar, lightly packed**
1 tsp	**(5 mL) cinnamon**
pinch	**cloves**
pinch	**salt**
2 tbsp	**(30 mL) butter**
1	**egg, beaten**

METHOD

1. Preheat oven to 375°F (190°C).
2. Divide dough into two portions, one slightly larger than the other.
3. Form each portion of dough into a ball.
4. Wrap smaller ball of dough in plastic wrap and refrigerate.
5. On a lightly floured surface, roll out larger ball of dough into an 11-inch (28 cm) circle, ⅛-inch (0.3 cm) thick.
6. Line a 9-inch (22 cm) pie plate with dough.
7. Trim away excess dough from edges.
8. Peel and core apples. Slice thinly.
9. In a large bowl, combine flour, brown sugar, cinnamon, cloves and salt.
10. Add apples to flour mixture. Toss lightly to coat.
11. Fill pie shell with apple mixture.
12. Dot apple filling with butter.
13. Brush edge of crust with egg.
14. Roll remaining dough into an 11-inch (28 cm) circle, ⅛-inch (0.3 cm) thick.
15. Cut slits in dough, and place on top of pie.
16. Crimp edges of pie.
17. Brush top of pie with egg.
18. Bake for 45-50 minutes, until crust is golden brown.

8 servings

Tip:

- *Do not allow apple mixture to sit too long as mixture will become syrupy.*

Approximate nutritional analysis per serving
Calories 456, Protein 3 g, Carbohydrates 65 g, Fat 21 g, Cholesterol 48 mg, Sodium 377 mg

Classic Apple Pie

Strawberry Kiwi Flan

The perfect dessert for a summer afternoon.

INGREDIENTS

½ cup	**(125 mL) sugar**
4	**medium eggs, room temperature**
¾ cup	**(175 mL) all-purpose flour, sifted**
¼ cup	**(50 mL) butter, melted**
2 cups	**(500 mL) lemon custard**
2 cups	**(500 mL) fresh strawberries, sliced**
2	**kiwi fruit, thinly sliced**
3 oz	**(85 g) strawberry glaze**

Step 11. Fill center of cooled flan with lemon custard.

Step 12. Decorate top of flan with strawberries and kiwi.

Step 13. Brush flan with strawberry glaze.

METHOD

1. Preheat oven to 150°F (65°C).
2. Grease and flour a 10-inch (25 cm) flan ring.
3. Spread sugar on a baking sheet. Place in oven and warm for 3 minutes.
4. Remove sugar from oven. Increase oven temperature to 375°F (190°C).
5. In a double boiler, combine eggs and warm sugar. Beat with an electric mixer at medium speed until doubled in bulk. Remove from heat.
6. Gently fold flour into sugar mixture.
7. Fold in butter.
8. Pour mixture into prepared flan ring.
9. Bake for 30-35 minutes.
10. Invert pan on wire rack. When cool, remove flan ring.
11. Fill center of cooled flan with lemon custard.
12. Decorate top of flan with strawberries and kiwi.
13. Brush flan with strawberry glaze.
14. Serve with ice cream or custard.

10 servings

Variations:

- *Vary above recipe by substituting 2 cups (500 mL) vanilla custard or 2 cups (500 mL) applesauce for lemon custard.*

Approximate nutritional analysis per serving
Calories 378, Protein 6 g, Carbohydrates 65 g, Fat 11 g, Cholesterol 159 mg, Sodium 75 mg

Strawberry Kiwi Flan

Fresh Strawberry Tarts

Irresistible chocolate and strawberries.

INGREDIENTS

10 oz	**(285 g) Pâte Brisée (see page 315)**
3 oz	**(85 g) semisweet chocolate**
2 cups	**(500 mL) fresh strawberries, sliced**
2 oz	**(55 g) strawberry glaze**

METHOD

1. Preheat oven to 375°F (190°C).
2. On a lightly floured surface, roll dough into a circle, ⅛-inch (0.3 cm) thick.
3. Using a 3-inch (7 cm) round cookie cutter, cut 12 dough circles.
4. Line 3-inch (7 cm) aluminum foil tart containers with dough.
5. Place paper muffin cups into tart containers.
6. Fill muffin cups with uncooked rice.
7. Place tart containers on a baking sheet.
8. Bake for 5 minutes. Remove baking sheet from oven.
9. Carefully remove muffin cups and rice.
10. Return tart shells to oven. Bake for 3 minutes, until golden brown.
11. Allow tart shells to cool.
12. In a double boiler, melt chocolate.
13. Brush insides of tart shells with chocolate.
14. Fill tart shells with strawberries.
15. Brush with strawberry glaze and serve.

1 dozen tarts

Coconut Walnut Pie

A delectable crustless pie.

INGREDIENTS

1½ cups	**(375 mL) milk**
1 cup	**(250 mL) sugar**
1 cup	**(250 mL) unsweetened, shredded coconut**
½ cup	**(125 mL) all-purpose flour**
½ cup	**(125 mL) walnuts, chopped**
¼ cup	**(50 mL) butter**
4	**medium eggs**
1½ tsp	**(7 mL) almond extract**
¾ tsp	**(4 mL) baking powder**
¼ tsp	**(1 mL) salt**
½ cup	**(125 mL) toasted, shredded coconut**

METHOD

1. Preheat oven to 325°F (160°C).
2. Grease and flour a 9-inch (22 cm) pie plate.
3. In a food processor, blend all ingredients, except toasted coconut, until well combined.
4. Pour mixture into prepared pie plate.
5. Bake for 30 minutes, until golden brown.
6. Cool pie for 15 minutes.
7. Sprinkle with toasted coconut.
8. Serve warm or cold with ice cream or fresh whipped cream.

8 servings

Variation:

- *To make individual pies, pour mixture into 6 small, ovenproof casserole dishes.*

Approximate nutritional analysis per serving
Calories 366, Protein 7 g, Carbohydrates 42 g, Fat 20 g, Cholesterol 115 mg, Sodium 254 mg

◀ Approximate nutritional analysis per tart
Calories 187, Protein 2 g, Carbohydrates 25 g, Fat 9 g, Cholesterol 0 mg, Sodium 86 mg

Coconut Walnut Pie

Marvellous Cherry Pie

Serve with ice cream for a dessert as rich and fragrant as a spring breeze.

INGREDIENTS

18 oz	**(510 g) Flaky Pie Pastry (see page 315)**
20 oz	**(568 mL) canned cherry pie filling**

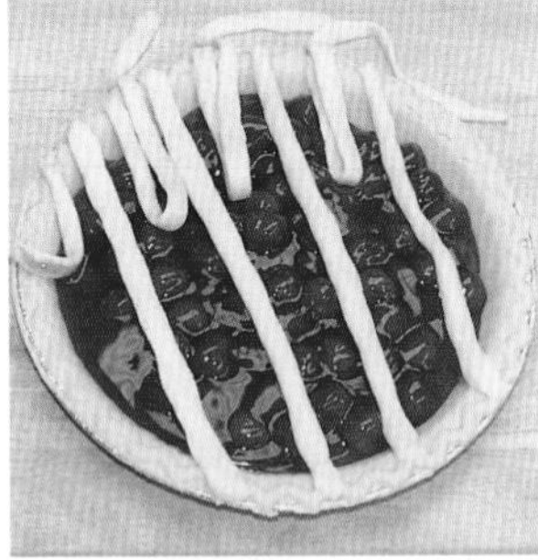

Step 12. Fold back every second strip of dough.

Step 14. Unfold folded strips to weave dough strips into a lattice.

Step 15. Fold back alternate dough strips and repeat weaving process until lattice top has been constructed.

METHOD

1. Preheat oven to 375°F (190°C).
2. Divide pie pastry dough into two portions, one slightly larger than the other.
3. Form each portion of dough into a ball.
4. Wrap smaller ball of dough in plastic wrap and refrigerate.
5. On a lightly floured surface, roll out larger ball of dough into an 11-inch (28 cm) circle, ⅛-inch (0.3 cm) thick.
6. Line a 9-inch (22 cm) pie plate with dough.
7. Trim pie crust ½-inch (1.3 cm) past edge of pie plate.
8. Place cherry pie filling in pie shell.
9. Roll remaining dough into a 12-inch (30 cm) circle, ⅛-inch (0.3 cm) thick.
10. Cut dough into 14 strips, each strip ½-inch (1.3 cm) wide.
11. Place half the dough strips on top of pie at 1-inch (2.5 cm) intervals.
12. Fold back every second strip of dough.
13. Place one strip of dough at right angles to dough strips.
14. Unfold folded strips to weave dough strips into a lattice.
15. Fold back alternate dough strips and repeat weaving process until lattice top has been constructed.
16. Trim dough strips even with edge of pie plate.
17. Seal edge and crimp to finish.
18. Bake for 35-40 minutes, until crust is golden brown.

8 servings

Approximate nutritional analysis per serving
Calories 365, Protein 4 g, Carbohydrates 45 g, Fat 20 g, Cholesterol 0 mg, Sodium 9 mg

Marvellous Cherry Pie

Apple Orange Tart

All the fresh goodness of summer fruits.

INGREDIENTS

10 oz	**(285 g) Pâte Brisée (see page 315)**
1 cup	**(250 mL) graham cracker crumbs**
pinch	**cinnamon**
pinch	**cloves**
⅓ cup	**(75 mL) butter, melted**
1¼ cups	**(300 mL) canned applesauce**
2	**Granny Smith apples**
4	**large navel oranges, peeled, segmented, seeds removed**
½ cup	**(125 mL) orange marmalade**

METHOD

1. Preheat oven to 400°F (205°C).
2. On a lightly floured surface, roll dough into an 11-inch (28 cm) circle, ⅛-inch (0.3 cm) thick.
3. Line a 9-inch (22 cm) removable rim tart pan with dough.
4. Trim away excess dough from edges.
5. Prick pie shell with a fork.
6. Line pie shell with wax paper and fill with uncooked rice.
7. Bake for 12 minutes. Remove pie shell from oven.
8. Carefully remove wax paper and rice.
9. Return pie shell to oven. Bake for 5 minutes, until golden brown.
10. Allow pie shell to cool.
11. Reduce oven temperature to 375°F (190°C).
12. In a medium bowl, combine graham cracker crumbs, cinnamon, cloves and butter.
13. Spread crumb mixture onto base of pie shell.
14. Spread applesauce on top of crumb mixture.
15. Peel and core apples. Slice thinly.
16. Layer sliced apples on top of applesauce.
17. Arrange orange segments on top of apple slices.
18. Spread marmalade over oranges.
19. Bake for 35 minutes.
20. Cool tart on a rack.
21. Transfer tart to a cake stand or serving plate.
22. Serve with fresh cream.

8 servings

Approximate nutritional analysis per serving
Calories 371, Protein 4 g, Carbohydrates 53 g, Fat 18 g, Cholesterol 27 mg, Sodium 373 mg

Apple Orange Tart

Best Ever Butter Tarts

Brings home the golden memories of Grandma's kitchen.

INGREDIENTS

10 oz	**(285 g) Pâte Brisée (see page 315)**
½ cup	**(125 mL) raisins**
¼ cup	**(50 mL) butter, softened**
¼ cup	**(50 mL) sugar**
⅓ cup	**(75 mL) white corn syrup**
2 tbsp	**(30 mL) maple syrup**
2	**medium eggs, lightly beaten**
½ tsp	**(2 mL) vanilla extract**
pinch	**salt**

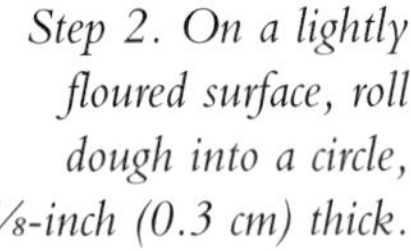

Step 2. On a lightly floured surface, roll dough into a circle, ⅛-inch (0.3 cm) thick.

Step 3. Using a 3-inch (7 cm) round cookie cutter, cut 12 dough circles.

Step 9. Spoon filling into tart shells until three-quarters full. Do not overfill.

METHOD

1. Preheat oven to 325°F (160°C).
2. On a lightly floured surface, roll dough into a circle, ⅛-inch (0.3 cm) thick.
3. Using a 3-inch (7 cm) round cookie cutter, cut 12 dough circles.
4. Line 3-inch (7 cm) aluminum foil tart containers with dough.
5. Soak raisins in warm water for 10 minutes.
6. In a medium bowl, cream butter and sugar with an electric mixer until light and creamy.
7. Slowly stir in corn syrup and maple syrup.
8. Add eggs, vanilla and salt. Stir to blend.
9. Spoon filling into tart shells until three-quarters full. Do not overfill.
10. Drain water from raisins. Pat dry with paper towels.
11. Place a few raisins into filling of each tart. Using a small spoon, push raisins into filling until they are covered with filling mixture.
12. Place tart shells on a baking sheet.
13. Bake for 40-45 minutes, until tart shells are golden brown.
14. Allow tarts to cool.
15. Remove tarts, right side up, from their aluminum foil containers.

1 dozen tarts

Approximate nutritional analysis per tart
Calories 375, Protein 5 g, Carbohydrates 40 g, Fat 23 g, Cholesterol 42 mg, Sodium 179 mg

Best Ever Butter Tarts

Zesty Lemon Tarts

These tangy tarts are little pieces of heaven.

INGREDIENTS

10 oz	**(285 g) Pâte Brisée (see page 315)**
5 tbsp	**(75 mL) cornstarch**
1½ cups	**(375 mL) sugar**
¼ tsp	**(1 mL) salt**
1 cup	**(250 mL) orange juice**
6 tbsp	**(90 mL) lemon juice**
1 tsp	**(5 mL) lemon peel, grated**
1 tbsp	**(15 mL) butter**
3	**egg yolks, lightly beaten**
1 cup	**(250 mL) whipping cream**

METHOD

1. Preheat oven to 375°F (190°C).
2. On a lightly floured surface, roll dough into a circle, ⅛-inch (0.3 cm) thick.
3. Using a 2-inch (5 cm) round cookie cutter, cut 24 dough circles.
4. Line 2-inch (5 cm) aluminum foil tart containers with dough.
5. Place paper muffin cups into tart containers.
6. Fill muffin cups with uncooked rice. The rice prevents the tart shells from rising when baked.
7. Place tart containers on a baking sheet.
8. Bake for 5 minutes. Remove baking sheet from oven.
9. Carefully remove muffin cups and rice.
10. Return tart shells to oven. Bake for 3 minutes, until golden brown.
11. Allow tart shells to cool.
12. In a double boiler, combine cornstarch, sugar and salt.
13. Stir in orange juice, lemon juice, lemon peel and butter.
14. Cook for about 5 minutes, stirring constantly.
15. Cover and cook for 8-10 minutes over gently simmering water. Do not stir.
16. Remove from heat.
17. Gently stir in egg yolks.
18. Return double boiler to heat and cook for 2 minutes longer.
19. Spoon filling into tart shells until three-quarters full.
20. Allow filled tarts to cool.
21. In a medium bowl, beat whipping cream until it holds soft peaks.
22. Top tarts with whipped cream and serve.

2 dozen tarts

Approximate nutritional analysis per tart
Calories 365, Protein 4 g, Carbohydrates 37 g, Fat 23 g, Cholesterol 42 mg, Sodium 150 mg

Zesty Lemon Tarts

Apple Fritters

Soft and crisp, these fritters will quickly disappear.

INGREDIENTS

1¼ cups	**(300 mL) all-purpose flour**
1 cup	**(250 mL) dry white wine**
2 tbsp	**(30 mL) sugar**
½ tsp	**(2 mL) lemon peel, grated**
pinch	**cinnamon**
1	**large egg white**
3	**large apples**
3 tbsp	**(45 mL) all-purpose flour**
	vegetable oil for deep frying

METHOD

1. In a medium bowl, mix first five ingredients until well blended.
2. Cover batter with plastic wrap and refrigerate overnight.
3. Just before using batter, beat egg white until stiff.
4. Gently fold beaten egg white into batter.
5. Peel and core apples. Cut into rings.
6. Dust apple rings with flour.
7. Heat oil to 325°F (160°C).
8. Dip apple rings in batter.
9. Using a wooden skewer, hold rings in deep fryer until they float. This will prevent fritters from sinking to the bottom of the deep fryer.
10. Deep fry for 2 minutes until golden brown, turning with a slotted spoon to fry evenly.
11. Remove fritters from oil and drain on paper towels.
12. While still hot, roll in cinnamon sugar, or serve hot with fruit sauce or custard sauce.

1 dozen fritters

Variations:

- *Pear Fritters: Replace apples with 3 peeled, cored and sliced pears.*
- *Banana Fritters: Replace apples with 2 quartered bananas.*
- *Pineapple Fritters: Replace apples with 8 oz (250 mL) canned, drained pineapple rings.*

Approximate nutritional analysis per fritter
Calories 99, Protein 2 g, Carbohydrates 19 g, Fat 0 g, Cholesterol 0 mg, Sodium 6 mg

Apple Fritters

Apple Strudel

Light, flaky pastry filled with apples, raisins and almonds.

INGREDIENTS

1 lb	**(450 g) Puff Pastry Dough (see page 314)**
1 cup	**(250 mL) graham cracker crumbs**
1 tbsp	**(15 mL) cinnamon**
3 tbsp	**(45 mL) sugar**
1 tbsp	**(15 mL) lemon peel, grated**
¾ cup	**(175 mL) raisins**
½ cup	**(125 mL) ground almonds**
4	**large apples, sliced**
1	**medium egg, beaten**
2 tbsp	**(30 mL) icing sugar**

METHOD

1. Preheat oven to 350°F (190°C).

Step 7. Place apples on top of raisin mixture.

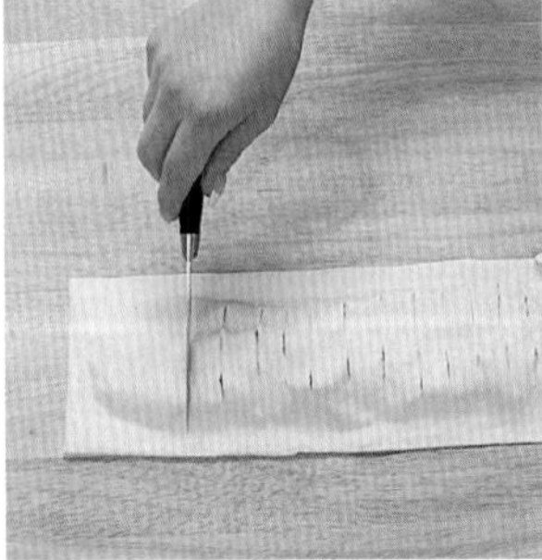

Step 11. Make a series of sideways cuts ½-inch (1.3 cm) apart on top layer of dough. Do not cut closer than 1 inch (2.5 cm) from edges.

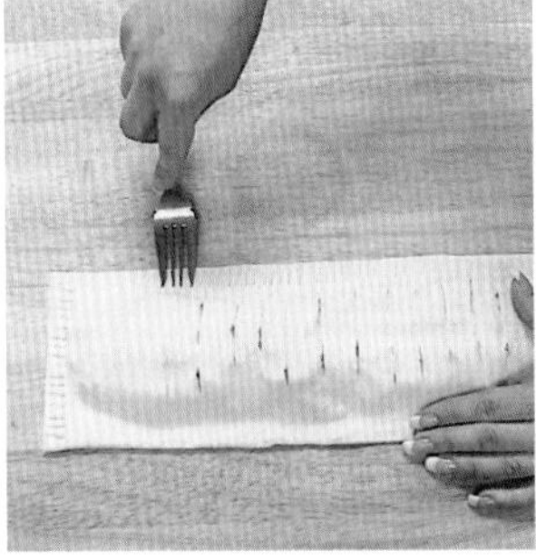

Step 12. Crimp edges of strudel with a fork to seal.

2. Lightly grease a baking sheet.
3. Using a rolling pin, roll half of puff pastry dough into a 12 x 6-inch (30 x 15 cm) rectangle. Place on prepared baking sheet.
4. Sprinkle graham cracker crumbs, cinnamon and sugar on dough up to ½ inch (1.3 cm) from edges.
5. In a small bowl, mix lemon peel, raisins and almonds.
6. Spread raisin mixture evenly over graham cracker crumbs.
7. Place apples on top of raisin mixture.
8. Roll out remaining half of pastry dough into a 13 x 7-inch (33 x 18 cm) rectangle.
9. Brush edges of bottom pastry dough with egg.
10. Gently place top layer of dough on top of bottom layer.
11. Make a series of sideways cuts ½-inch (1.3 cm) apart on top layer of dough. Do not cut closer than 1 inch (2.5 cm) from edges.
12. Crimp edges of strudel with a fork to seal.
13. Brush strudel with egg.
14. Bake for 45 minutes, until golden brown.
15. Cool. Dust with icing sugar.
16. Slice strudel into 6 pieces.
17. Serve with custard or ice cream.

6 servings

Approximate nutritional analysis per serving
Calories 818, Protein 15 g, Carbohydrates 90 g, Fat 46 g, Cholesterol 31 mg, Sodium 324 mg

Apple Strudel

Puff Pastry Treasures

Delightful puff pastry boxes brimming with fresh fruit.

INGREDIENTS

1 lb	**(450 g) Puff Pastry Dough (see page 314)**
1	**large egg, beaten**
2 cups	**(500 mL) applesauce**
2	**kiwi fruits, diced**
1 cup	**(250 mL) fresh blueberries**
1 cup	**(250 mL) fresh raspberries**
1 cup	**(250 ml) fresh strawberries, sliced**

Step 5. Using a knife, score a square shape in the center of one dough square, leaving a ½-inch (1.3 cm) border around the outside.

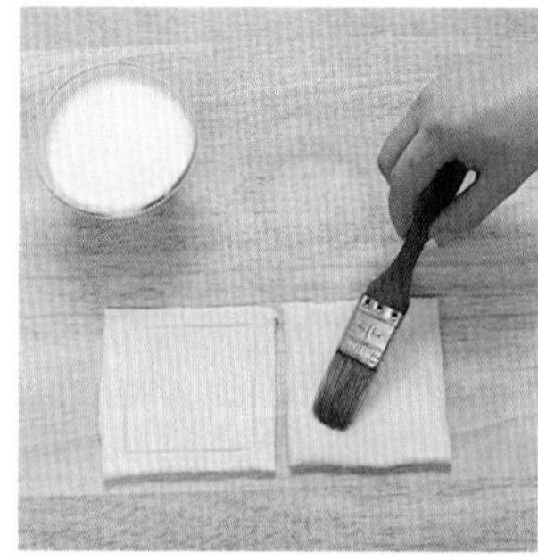

Step 6. Brush another dough square evenly with egg.

Step 7. Place scored dough square on top of second square and brush with egg.

METHOD

1. Preheat oven to 375°F (190°C).
2. Lightly grease a baking sheet.
3. Using a rolling pin, roll puff pastry dough into a 12 x 9-inch (30 x 22 cm) rectangle.
4. Cut dough into twelve 3 x 3-inch (7 x 7 cm) squares.
5. Using a knife, score a square shape in the center of one dough square, leaving a ½-inch (1.3 cm) border around the outside.
6. Brush another dough square evenly with egg.
7. Place scored dough square on top of second square and brush with egg.
8. Place on prepared baking sheet.
9. Repeat steps until 6 double layer squares have been made.
10. Bake 8-10 minutes, until golden brown.
11. Allow squares to cool.
12. Remove scored square "lid" from top of each stack.
13. Place ⅓ cup (75 mL) applesauce in center cavity of each square.
14. Fill squares with kiwi, blueberries, raspberries and strawberries.
15. Replace lids of squares and serve.

6 servings

Approximate nutritional analysis per serving
Calories 520, Protein 7.5 g, Carbohydrates 56 g, Fat 30 g, Cholesterol 36 mg, Sodium 203 mg

Puff Pastry Treasures

Phyllo Shells

A tasty dessert heaping with luscious berries.

INGREDIENTS

3	**phyllo dough sheets**
3 tbsp	**(45 mL) butter, melted**
2 tbsp	**(30 mL) icing sugar**
1 cup	**(250 mL) vanilla custard**
½ cup	**(125 mL) fresh berries**

METHOD

1. Preheat oven to 375°F (190°C).
2. Grease a muffin pan.
3. Brush one sheet of phyllo dough with butter.
4. Place second sheet of phyllo dough on top of first layer. Brush with butter.
5. Place last sheet of phyllo dough on top of first two layers. Brush with butter.
6. Cut layered phyllo dough into 4-inch (10 cm) squares.
7. Place phyllo squares into prepared muffin pan.
8. Push each phyllo square lightly into muffin pan, leaving a well in the center.
9. Bake for 8-10 minutes, until golden brown.
10. Cool shells for 5 minutes.
11. Place phyllo shells on a plate.
12. Dust edges of shells with icing sugar.
13. Place 2 tbsp (30 mL) custard and 1 tbsp (15 mL) berries in each shell.
14. Serve.

8 servings

Variations:

- *Ice cream may be substituted for vanilla custard.*
- *Substitute other types of chopped fruit, such as kiwi or peaches, for berries.*

Step 6. Cut layered phyllo dough into 4-inch (10 cm) squares.

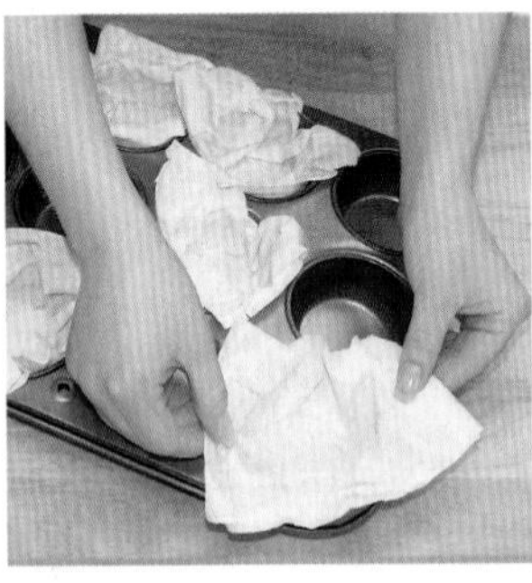

Step 7. Place phyllo squares into prepared muffin pan.

Step 8. Push each phyllo square lightly into muffin pan, leaving a well in the center.

Approximate nutritional analysis per serving
Calories 109, Protein 1 g, Carbohydrates 13 g, Fat 6 g, Cholesterol 12 mg, Sodium 59 mg

Phyllo Shells

Blueberry Lemon Pound Cake

Old-fashioned goodness in every bite.

INGREDIENTS

1 cup	**(250 mL) butter, softened**
2 cups	**(500 mL) sugar**
6	**large egg yolks**
4 tsp	**(20 mL) lemon peel, grated**
2 tbsp	**(30 mL) lemon juice**
3 cups	**(750 mL) cake flour, sifted**
1 tsp	**(5 mL) baking soda**
1 cup	**(250 mL) lemon yogurt**
6	**large egg whites**
pinch	**cream of tartar**
1½ cups	**(375 mL) fresh blueberries**

METHOD

1. Preheat oven to 375°F (190°C).
2. Grease and flour an 8 x 4 x 3-inch (20 x 10 x 7 cm) loaf pan.
3. In a large bowl, cream butter with an electric mixer.
4. Slowly add sugar, beating until mixture is light and fluffy.
5. Beat in egg yolks, one at a time.
6. Add lemon peel and lemon juice.
7. In a medium bowl, combine flour and baking soda.
8. Add to creamed butter mixture alternately with yogurt.
9. In a clean, medium bowl, combine egg whites with cream of tartar. Beat until mixture holds soft peaks.
10. Stir one-quarter of beaten egg whites into batter.
11. Fold remaining egg whites into mixture.
12. Fold in blueberries.
13. Spoon mixture into prepared loaf pan.
14. Bake for 1 hour, until a wooden pick inserted into center of cake comes out clean.
15. Cool cake for 5 minutes in pan.
16. Invert onto a wire rack and cool.

10 servings

Tips:

- *Frozen blueberries may be used in place of fresh. If using frozen, choose small berries. Dust with flour and add to batter while still frozen.*
- *This pound cake may be toasted under the broiler.*

Approximate nutritional analysis per serving
Calories 548, Protein 9 g, Carbohydrates 80 g, Fat 22 g, Cholesterol 178 mg, Sodium 375 mg

Blueberry Lemon Pound Cake

Decadent Chocolate Sponge Cake

A chocolate lover's delight, this cake will be gone before you know it!

INGREDIENTS

Chocolate Sponge Cake

4 oz	**(115 g) semisweet chocolate**
1 cup	**(250 mL) milk**
1¼ cups	**(300 mL) cake flour**
½ tsp	**(2 mL) salt**
2½ tsp	**(12 mL) double-acting baking powder**
½ tsp	**(2 mL) baking soda**
4	**large egg yolks, beaten**
2 cups	**(500 mL) icing sugar, sifted**
1½ tsp	**(7 mL) vanilla extract**
4	**large egg whites**

Chocolate Frosting

8 oz	**(225 g) semisweet chocolate**
6 tbsp	**(90 mL) butter**
5½ cups	**(1.4 L) icing sugar, sifted**
2 tsp	**(10 mL) vanilla extract**
¾ cup	**(175 mL) light cream**

METHOD

Chocolate Sponge Cake

1. Preheat oven to 350°F (175°C).
2. Grease and flour two 9-inch (22 cm) round baking pans.
3. In a small saucepan, heat chocolate and milk over low heat until chocolate melts. Remove from heat.
4. In a medium bowl, sift together flour, salt, baking powder and baking soda.
5. In a large bowl, beat egg yolks, icing sugar and vanilla with an electric mixer until light and fluffy.
6. Add chocolate to icing sugar mixture.
7. Stir in flour mixture.
8. In a clean, medium bowl, beat egg whites until stiff.
9. Gently fold beaten egg whites into chocolate mixture in thirds.
10. Spoon batter into prepared baking pans.
11. Bake for 45-50 minutes, until a wooden pick inserted into center of cake comes out clean.
12. Cool cake for 5 minutes in pans.
13. Invert onto a wire rack and cool.

Chocolate Frosting

14. In a double boiler, melt chocolate and butter.
15. In a medium bowl, mix icing sugar, vanilla and cream with an electric mixer until combined.
16. Add to chocolate in double boiler. Cook for 5 minutes. If mixture becomes too stiff, add a little more cream.
17. Remove from heat.
18. Use to frost cooled Chocolate Sponge Cake.

12 servings

Approximate nutritional analysis per serving
Calories 610, Protein 6 g, Carbohydrates 93 g, Fat 26 g, Cholesterol 119 mg, Sodium 421 mg

Decadent Chocolate Sponge Cake

Home-Style Gingerbread Cake

For an amazing taste sensation, serve this cake warm with cold whipped cream.

INGREDIENTS

1½ tsp	**(7 mL) ginger**
1½ tsp	**(7 mL) cinnamon**
¼ tsp	**(1 mL) nutmeg**
¼ tsp	**(1 mL) cloves**
¼ tsp	**(1 mL) allspice**
1 tsp	**(5 mL) baking soda**
½ cup	**(125 mL) molasses**
⅓ cup	**(75 mL) butter**
½ cup	**(125 mL) dark brown sugar, firmly packed**
¼ cup	**(50 mL) water**
3	**medium eggs**
2 cups	**(500 mL) all-purpose flour**

METHOD

1. Preheat oven to 350°F (175°C).
2. Grease an 8-inch (20 cm) round baking pan.
3. In a medium bowl, combine ginger, cinnamon, nutmeg, cloves, allspice and baking soda.
4. In a small saucepan, heat molasses over medium-low heat until it begins to bubble.
5. Remove saucepan from heat. Stir in butter.
6. Scrape molasses into a large bowl.
7. Using an electric mixer, add spice mixture, brown sugar and water to molasses.
8. Add eggs, one at a time, beating on medium-high speed until well blended.
9. Sift flour into mixture. Blend on low speed for 1 minute.
10. Increase speed to medium and mix for 1 minute.
11. Pour batter into prepared baking pan.
12. Bake for 45-50 minutes, until a wooden pick inserted into center comes out clean.
13. Cool cake for 5 minutes in pan.
14. Invert onto a wire rack and cool.

8 servings

Approximate nutritional analysis per serving
Calories 325, Protein 5 g, Carbohydrates 46 g, Fat 14 g, Cholesterol 101 mg, Sodium 311 mg

Home-Style Gingerbread Cake

Speechless Lemon Sponge Cake

A delicate, airy creation as light as a cloud.

INGREDIENTS

Lemon Sponge Cake

1 cup	**(250 mL) shortening**
2¼ cups	**(550 mL) sugar**
2 tsp	**(10 mL) vanilla extract**
1 tbsp	**(15 mL) lemon juice**
1 tsp	**(5 mL) lemon peel, grated**
6	**large eggs, separated**
3 cups	**(750 mL) all-purpose flour, sifted**
1 tsp	**(5 mL) baking powder**
1 tsp	**(5 mL) baking soda**
pinch	**salt**
¾ cup	**(175 mL) buttermilk**

Butter Frosting

⅓ cup	**(75 mL) butter, softened**
4 cups	**(1 L) icing sugar**
1	**large egg yolk**
1 tsp	**(5 mL) vanilla extract**
2 tbsp	**(30 mL) light cream**

METHOD

Lemon Sponge Cake

1. Preheat oven to 350°F (175°C).
2. Grease and flour two 9-inch (22 cm) round baking pans.
3. In a large bowl, beat shortening and 1½ cups (375 mL) sugar with an electric mixer.
4. Stir in vanilla, lemon juice and lemon peel.
5. Add egg yolks, one at a time, beating after each addition.
6. In a medium bowl, sift together flour, baking powder, baking soda and salt.
7. Add flour mixture and buttermilk alternately to batter, blending until smooth.
8. In a clean, medium bowl, beat egg whites until frothy.
9. Gradually add remaining sugar, beating until stiff peaks form.
10. Gently fold beaten egg whites into batter.
11. Spoon batter into prepared baking pans.
12. Bake for 1 hour, until a wooden pick inserted into center of cake comes out clean.
13. Cool cake for 5 minutes in pans.
14. Invert onto a wire rack and cool.

Butter Frosting

15. In a large bowl, cream butter with an electric mixer.
16. Gradually blend in half the icing sugar.
17. Beat in egg yolk and vanilla.
18. Gradually blend in remaining icing sugar until thoroughly combined.
19. Add enough cream to make mixture spreadable.
20. Use to frost cooled Lemon Sponge Cake.

12 servings

Approximate nutritional analysis per serving
Calories 640, Protein 7 g, Carbohydrates 96 g, Fat 26 g, Cholesterol 140 mg, Sodium 248 mg

Speechless Lemon Sponge Cake

Raisin-Laced Spice Cake

A rich, moist cake with glorious spice flavors in every bite.

INGREDIENTS

¾ cup	**(175 mL) butter, softened**
1 cup	**(250 mL) sugar**
1	**large egg**
2½ cups	**(625 mL) all-purpose flour**
1 tsp	**(5 mL) baking soda**
1 tbsp	**(15 mL) cinnamon**
1 tbsp	**(15 mL) allspice**
1 cup	**(250 mL) lukewarm milk**
1 tbsp	**(15 mL) white vinegar**
½ cup	**(125 mL) molasses**
1 cup	**(250 mL) raisins**

METHOD

1. Preheat oven to 350°F (175°C).
2. Grease a 9-inch (22 cm) square baking pan.
3. Using an electric mixer, cream together butter and sugar in a large bowl. Beat until light and fluffy.
4. Add egg. Beat until combined.
5. In a medium bowl, sift together flour, baking soda, cinnamon and allspice.
6. In a small bowl, combine milk and vinegar. Let stand for 5 minutes.
7. Stir flour mixture into creamed butter mixture.
8. Stir in molasses and milk in two batches, mixing well after each addition.
9. Add raisins. Stir until combined.
10. Spoon batter into prepared baking pan.
11. Bake for 45-50 minutes, until a wooden pick inserted into center of cake comes out clean.
12. Cool cake in pan for 5 minutes.
13. Invert onto a wire rack and cool.

20 servings

Approximate nutritional analysis per serving
Calories 217, Protein 3 g, Carbohydrates 35 g, Fat 8 g, Cholesterol 34 mg, Sodium 112 mg

Raisin-Laced Spice Cake

Spiced Carrot Cake with Orange Icing

Moist and flavorful, this cake is topped off with a marvellous cream cheese icing.

INGREDIENTS

Cake

2 cups	**(500 mL) all-purpose flour**
2 cups	**(500 mL) sugar**
2 tsp	**(10 mL) baking soda**
1 tsp	**(5 mL) cinnamon**
1 tsp	**(5 mL) cloves**
1 tsp	**(5 mL) nutmeg**
4	**medium eggs, room temperature**
1 cup	**(250 mL) vegetable oil**
1 cup	**(250 mL) raisins**
4 cups	**(1 L) carrots, peeled and finely grated**

Orange Icing

8 oz	**(225 g) cream cheese, softened**
2 tbsp	**(30 mL) whipping cream**
1 cup	**(250 mL) icing sugar, sifted**
2 tbsp	**(30 mL) orange peel, grated**
½ tsp	**(2 mL) cinnamon**
1 oz	**(30 mL) orange liqueur**

METHOD

Cake

1. Preheat oven to 350°F (175°C).
2. Grease and flour a 13 x 9-inch (33 x 22 cm) baking pan.
3. In a medium bowl, combine flour, sugar, baking soda, cinnamon, cloves and nutmeg.
4. In a large bowl, beat eggs with an electric mixer until light and frothy.
5. Slowly beat oil into eggs.
6. Add flour mixture to egg mixture. Beat until smooth.
7. Stir in raisins and carrots. Combine thoroughly.
8. Pour batter into prepared baking pan.
9. Bake for 1 hour, until a wooden pick inserted into center of cake comes out clean.
10. Cool cake in pan.

Orange Icing

11. In a medium bowl, combine cream cheese and whipping cream until soft.
12. Slowly beat in icing sugar.
13. Add orange peel and cinnamon.
14. Add orange liqueur. Mix until well combined.
15. Use to frost cooled Spiced Carrot Cake.

24 servings

Approximate nutritional analysis per serving
Calories 278, Protein 3 g, Carbohydrates 37 g, Fat 14 g, Cholesterol 42 mg, Sodium 154 mg

Spiced Carrot Cake with Orange Icing

Apple Lover's Pizza

A fresh and tasty dessert idea.

INGREDIENTS

2	**9-inch (22 cm) pizza shells, unbaked**
14 oz	**(398 mL) canned applesauce**
4	**small apples, peeled, cored and sliced**
1 tbsp	**(15 mL) cinnamon**
½ cup	**(125 mL) brown sugar**
2 tbsp	**(30 mL) butter, melted**
1¼ cups	**(300 mL) Cheddar or blue cheese, grated**

METHOD

1. Bake pizza shells according to package directions.
2. Switch oven to broil setting.
3. Place pizza shells on a baking sheet.
4. Spread applesauce on pizza shells.
5. Layer apple slices on top of applesauce.
6. Sprinkle pizzas with cinnamon, brown sugar and butter.
7. Top each pizza with cheese.
8. Broil until sugar and cheese are just melted.
9. Serve hot.

12 servings

Approximate nutritional analysis per serving
Calories 203, Protein 6 g, Carbohydrates 30 g, Fat 7 g, Cholesterol 20 mg, Sodium 244 mg

Snappy Ginger Snaps

Timeless and perfect for any occasion.

INGREDIENTS

1 cup	**(250 mL) brown sugar, firmly packed**
1 cup	**(250 mL) butter**
1 cup	**(250 mL) molasses**
4¼ cups	**(1.1 L) all-purpose flour, sifted**
1 tbsp	**(15 mL) ginger**
1 tsp	**(5 mL) salt**
1 tsp	**(5 mL) baking soda**
2 tbsp	**(30 mL) hot water**
1 tbsp	**(15 mL) white vinegar**
1	**medium egg**
1 cup	**(250 mL) sugar**

METHOD

1. Preheat oven to 300°F (150°C).
2. Lightly grease a baking sheet.
3. In a heavy saucepan, combine brown sugar, butter and molasses. Bring to a boil over medium-high heat, stirring constantly.
4. Remove saucepan from heat. Cool for 10 minutes.
5. Add flour, ginger and salt. Mix well.
6. In a small bowl, dissolve baking soda in water. Stir into saucepan.
7. Add vinegar and egg to dough mixture. Mix until well blended.
8. Form mixture into 2-inch (5 cm) balls.
9. Roll balls in sugar.
10. Place cookies 1 inch (2.5 cm) apart on prepared baking sheets.
11. Bake for 15 minutes until edges are lightly browned.

4 dozen cookies

Approximate nutritional analysis per cookie
Calories 120, Protein 1 g, Carbohydrates 20 g, Fat 4 g, Cholesterol 14 mg, Sodium 116 mg

Snappy Ginger Snaps

Irresistible Oatmeal Cookies

A wonderful accompaniment to a good cup of coffee.

INGREDIENTS

½ cup	**(125 mL) brown sugar, firmly packed**
½ cup	**(125 mL) sugar**
½ cup	**(125 mL) butter, softened**
1	**large egg**
1 tsp	**(5 mL) vanilla extract**
1 tbsp	**(15 mL) milk**
1 cup	**(250 mL) all-purpose flour**
½ tsp	**(2 mL) baking soda**
½ tsp	**(2 mL) double-acting baking powder**
½ tsp	**(2 mL) salt**
1 cup	**(250 mL) uncooked quick rolled oats**
½ tsp	**(2 mL) cinnamon**
¾ cup	**(175 mL) raisins**
1 tsp	**(5 mL) lemon peel, grated**

METHOD

1. Preheat oven to 350°F (175°C).
2. Lightly grease a baking sheet.
3. In a large bowl, cream together brown sugar, sugar and butter with an electric mixer.
4. Add egg, vanilla and milk. Beat until smooth.
5. In a medium bowl, sift together flour, baking soda, baking powder and salt.
6. Add to creamed butter mixture. Beat until smooth.
7. Stir in rolled oats, cinnamon, raisins and lemon peel until well combined.
8. Drop cookies from a spoon 3 inches (7 cm) apart onto prepared baking sheet.
9. Bake 8-10 minutes, until light brown.

1½ dozen cookies

Approximate nutritional analysis per cookie
Calories 152, Protein 2 g, Carbohydrates 23 g, Fat 6 g, Cholesterol 31 mg, Sodium 172 mg

Irresistible Oatmeal Cookies

Grandma's Chocolate Chip Cookies

Hide the cookie jar. These won't last long!

INGREDIENTS

1 cup	**(250 mL) shortening**
1 cup	**(250 mL) sugar**
½ cup	**(125 mL) dark brown sugar, lightly packed**
2	**medium eggs**
2 tsp	**(10 mL) vanilla extract**
2 cups	**(500 mL) all-purpose flour, sifted**
1½ tsp	**(7 mL) salt**
1 tsp	**(5 mL) baking soda**
2 cups	**(500 mL) semisweet chocolate chips**
1 cup	**(250 mL) pecans or walnuts, chopped**
4 oz	**(115 g) semisweet chocolate**

METHOD

1. Preheat oven to 375°F (190°C).
2. Lightly grease a baking sheet.
3. In a medium bowl, combine shortening, sugar, brown sugar, eggs and vanilla.
4. Cream mixture with an electric mixer until light and fluffy.
5. In a medium bowl, sift together flour, salt and baking soda
6. Stir dry ingredients into creamed mixture until batter is well blended.
7. Add chocolate chips and pecans to batter. Stir to combine.
8. Using a tablespoon, drop cookies 3 inches (7 cm) apart onto prepared baking sheet.
9. Press cookies lightly with a fork.
10. Bake for 10-12 minutes.
11. Remove cookies from baking sheet while still warm.
12. Cool on a wire rack.
13. In a double boiler, melt chocolate.
14. Place melted chocolate in a small piping bag.
15. Pipe chocolate onto tops of cookies.

1½ dozen cookies

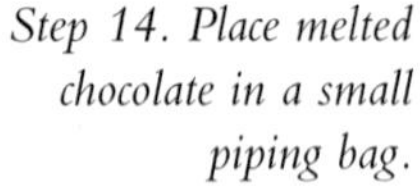

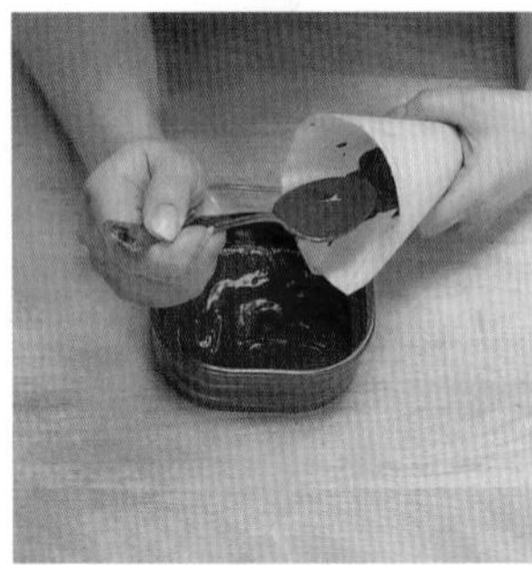

Step 14. Place melted chocolate in a small piping bag.

Step 15. Pipe chocolate onto tops of cookies.

Approximate nutritional analysis per cookie
Calories 382, Protein 4 g, Carbohydrates 43 g, Fat 24 g, Cholesterol 21 mg, Sodium 258 mg

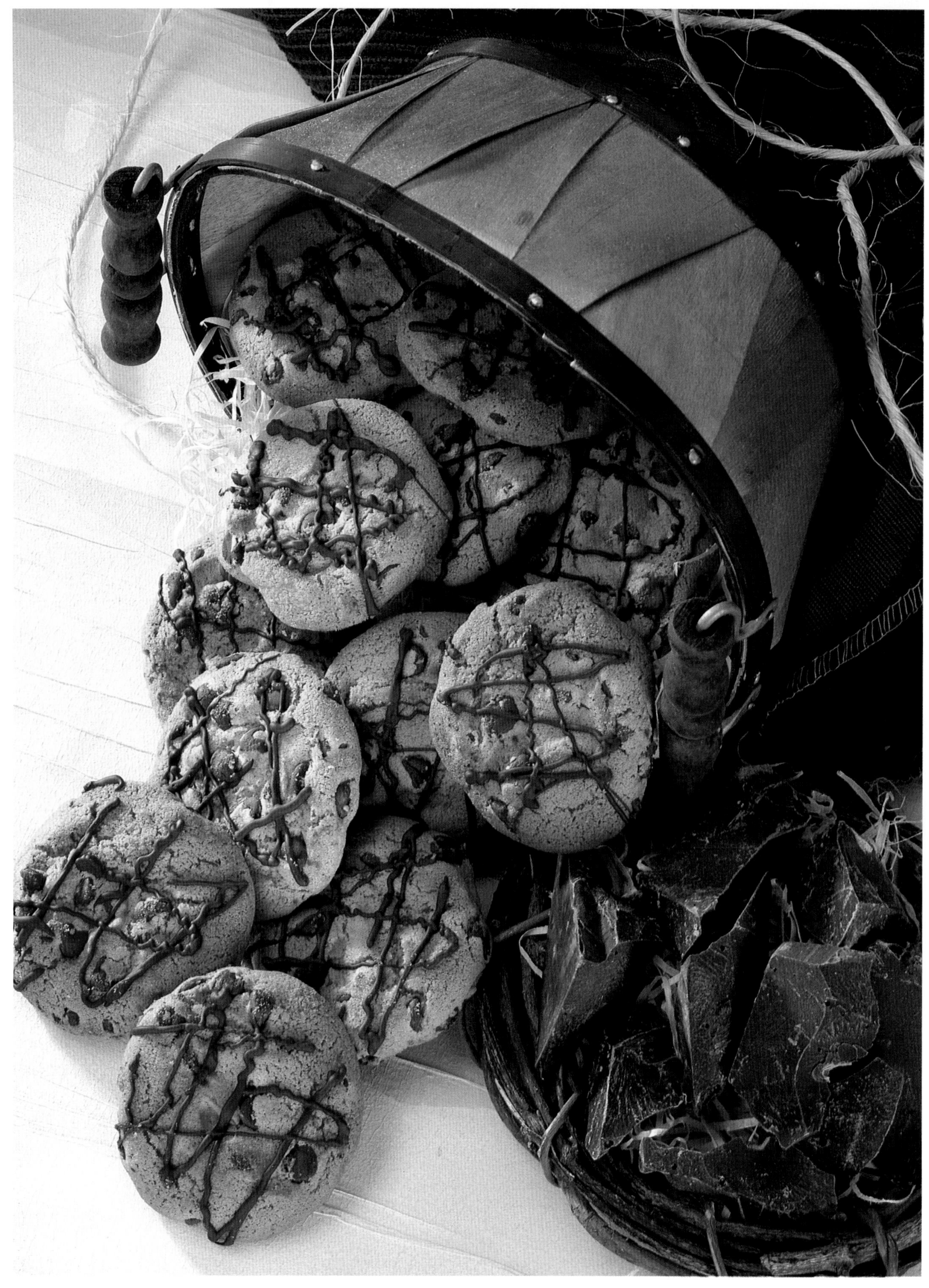

Grandma's Chocolate Chip Cookies

Palmiers

Delicate, caramelized pastry pieces joined together with fresh whipped cream.

INGREDIENTS

1 cup	**(250 mL) sugar**
8 oz	**(225 g) Puff Pastry Dough (see page 314)**
1 cup	**(250 mL) whipping cream**

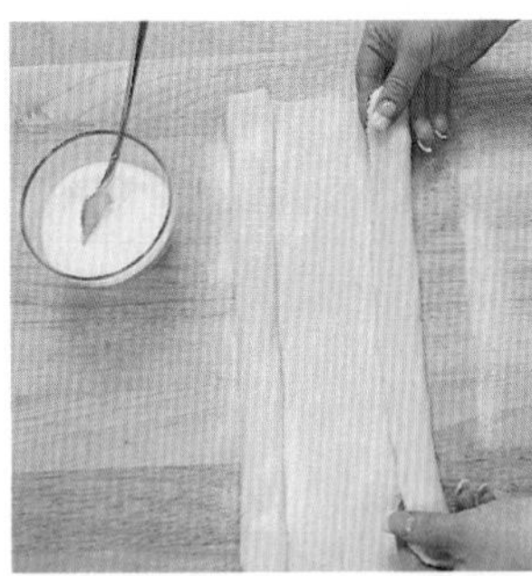

Step 6. Starting at top edge of dough, alternately fold top and bottom edges in 3 equal portions toward the middle.

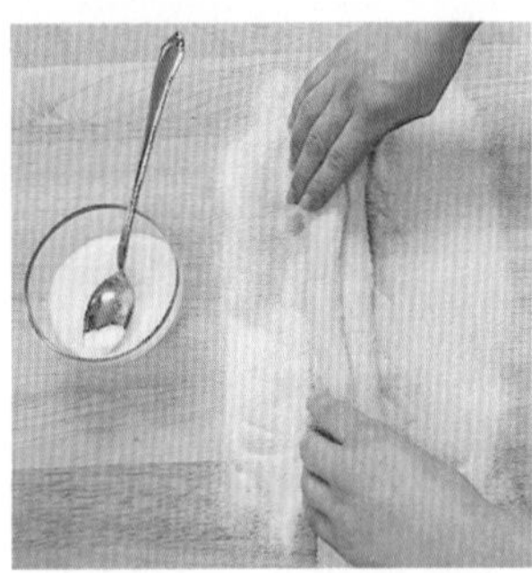

Step 7. Fold top half of folded dough over bottom half.

Step 9. Separate slices and lay out flat. Flatten pieces slightly with a flat-bladed spatula.

METHOD

1. Preheat oven to 450°F (230°C).
2. Lightly grease a baking sheet and sprinkle work surface with sugar.
3. Using a rolling pin, roll puff pastry dough into a 12 x 12-inch (30 x 30 cm) square on sugared surface. Square should be about ⅛-inch (0.3 cm) thick.
4. Sprinkle top of dough liberally with sugar. Roll sugar into dough.
5. Using a dull knife, make a small mark on left and right edges of dough 6 inches (15 cm) from top. Use these marks as guides to mark middle of dough.
6. Starting at top edge of dough, alternately fold top and bottom edges in 3 equal portions toward the middle.
7. Fold top half of folded dough over bottom half.
8. Using a sharp knife, cut folded dough into 1-inch (2.5 cm) slices.
9. Separate slices and lay out flat. Flatten pieces slightly with a flat-bladed spatula.
10. Dust pieces with sugar and place on prepared baking sheet.
11. Bake for 6 minutes.
12. Turn pieces with a spatula. Bake for 6 more minutes, until both sides are golden brown and sugar has caramelized.
13. Allow pieces to cool.
14. In a small bowl, beat whipping cream until stiff peaks form.
15. Join cooled pieces together with whipped cream.

6 servings

Variation:

- *Tips of cooled pastry may be dipped in 4 oz (115 g) melted semisweet chocolate.*

Approximate nutritional analysis per serving
Calories 474, Protein 4 g, Carbohydrates 52 g, Fat 29 g, Cholesterol 54 mg, Sodium 109 mg

Palmiers

Dreamy Éclairs

For a classic dessert, try these rich French pastries.

INGREDIENTS

1 cup	**(250 mL) all-purpose flour**
1 tbsp	**(15 mL) sugar**
pinch	**salt**
1 cup	**(250 mL) water or milk**
⅓ cup	**(75 mL) butter**
5	**medium eggs, room temperature**
2 cups	**(500 mL) whipping cream**
4 oz	**(115 g) semisweet chocolate, melted**

METHOD

1. Preheat oven to 400°F (205°C).
2. Lightly grease a baking sheet.
3. In a small bowl, sift flour.
4. In a heavy saucepan, mix sugar, salt and water or milk. Bring to a boil over high heat.
5. Stir in butter.
6. As liquid boils, add flour, stirring quickly with a wooden spoon.
7. Dough will not mix immediately. Keep stirring. Mixture will suddenly become smooth.
8. Keep stirring mixture until it leaves the spoon and no longer sticks to sides of saucepan. It will form a smooth ball.
9. Remove from heat and allow to cool for 2-3 minutes.
10. Stirring briskly, add eggs, one at a time. Stir mixture back to a smooth paste after each addition. Dough will be quite stiff after eggs have been added.
11. Place dough in a piping bag with a large star tip.
12. Pipe dough in 4-inch (10 cm) strips 4 inches (10 cm) apart onto prepared baking sheet.
13. Bake for 20 minutes. Reduce oven temperature to 325°F (160°C).
14. Bake shells for 15 more minutes, until centers are no longer moist.
15. Allow shells to cool.
16. In a medium bowl, beat whipping cream until stiff peaks form.
17. Split cooled éclair shells in half lengthwise.
18. Fill shells with whipped cream. Replace tops.
19. Drizzle tops of éclairs with chocolate.

10 éclairs

Tips:

- *Milk produces a moister dough than water.*
- *Have baking sheet, piping bag and large star tip in place before making dough.*

Variation:

- *Dreamy Cream Puffs: Pipe dough into round shapes instead of strips.*

Approximate nutritional analysis per éclair

Calories 370, Protein 7 g, Carbohydrates 19 g, Fat 31 g, Cholesterol 178 mg, Sodium 122 mg

Dreamy Éclairs

Frosted Fudge Brownies

Moist brownies smothered in decadent chocolate frosting.

INGREDIENTS

Brownies

2½ cups	**(625 mL) butter**
4 oz	**(115 g) semisweet chocolate**
4	**medium eggs, room temperature**
¼ tsp	**(1 mL) salt**
2 cups	**(500 mL) sugar**
1 tsp	**(5 mL) vanilla extract**
1 cup	**(250 mL) all-purpose flour**
1 cup	**(250 mL) walnuts or pecans, chopped**

Chocolate Frosting

4 oz	**(115 g) semisweet chocolate**
3 tbsp	**(45 mL) butter**
2¾ cups	**(675 mL) icing sugar, sifted**
1 tsp	**(5 mL) vanilla extract**
6 tbsp	**(90 mL) light cream**

METHOD

Brownies

1. Preheat oven to 350°F (175°C).
2. Grease a 13 x 9-inch (33 x 22 cm) baking pan.
3. In a double boiler, melt butter and chocolate. Remove from heat.
4. Cool chocolate for 5 minutes.
5. Using an electric mixer, beat eggs and salt in a large bowl until lemon colored and foamy.
6. Add sugar and continue beating until mixture is well blended.
7. Stir in vanilla.
8. Add cooled chocolate to mixture.
9. Fold in flour. Do not overmix.
10. Gently fold nuts into batter.
11. Pour batter into prepared baking pan.
12. Bake for 20-25 minutes until a wooden pick inserted into center comes out clean.
13. Cool in baking pan.

Chocolate Frosting

14. In a double boiler, melt chocolate and butter.
15. In a medium bowl, mix icing sugar, vanilla and cream with an electric mixer until combined.
16. Add to chocolate in double boiler. Cook for 5 minutes. If mixture becomes too stiff, add a little more cream.
17. Remove from heat.
18. Spread frosting on cooled brownies.

2 dozen brownies

Approximate nutritional analysis per brownie
Calories 405, Protein 3 g, Carbohydrates 39 g, Fat 28 g, Cholesterol 88 mg, Sodium 245 mg

Frosted Fudge Brownies

Delectable Meringues

These incredibly light morsels will melt in your mouth.

INGREDIENTS

4	**large egg whites, room temperature**	**1 cup**	**(250 mL) sugar**
pinch	**cream of tartar**		

METHOD

1. Preheat oven to 250°F (120°C).
2. Cut a piece of parchment paper to fit the bottom of a baking sheet. Place paper on baking sheet.
3. In a medium bowl, beat egg whites and cream of tartar at low speed.
4. When egg whites begin to foam, increase speed to high.
5. Beat until soft peaks begin to form.
6. Still beating at high speed, slowly add half the sugar, 1 tbsp (15 mL) at a time.
7. Turn off mixer. Egg whites should stand in stiff peaks.
8. Sprinkle remaining sugar over egg whites.
9. Using a spatula, fold sugar into egg whites until thoroughly blended.
10. Turn oven off. Turn on oven light.
11. While oven is cooling, place meringue mixture in a piping bag.
12. Pipe meringue mixture into desired shapes onto prepared baking sheet.
13. Place meringues in oven overnight. The heat from the oven light will dry, rather than bake, meringues.
14. Serve meringues filled with whipped cream or fruit.

8 large meringues

Tips:

- *Make sure all utensils are free of oil or grease.*
- *Choose a dry day for making meringues. Excess humidity will cause meringues to be soft.*
- *Experiment piping different meringue shapes using a variety of piping bag tips.*

Variations:

- *Chocolate Meringues: Add 2 tbsp (30 mL) sifted cocoa to remaining half of sugar before folding into beaten egg whites.*
- *Coffee Meringues: Add 1 tbsp (15 mL) dissolved instant coffee to beaten egg whites before folding in remaining sugar.*

Approximate nutritional analysis per meringue
Calories 105, Protein 2 g, Carbohydrates 25 g, Fat 0 g, Cholesterol 0 mg, Sodium 28 mg

Delectable Meringues

Fruit Fool

Cool and simple dessert.

INGREDIENTS

2	**large egg whites, room temperature**
1 tbsp	**(15 mL) lemon juice**
1⅓ cups	**(325 mL) sugar**
2 cups	**(500 mL) whipping cream**
2 cups	**(500 mL) fresh blueberries**

METHOD

1. In a medium bowl, combine egg whites and lemon juice with an electric mixer.
2. Gradually add sugar. Beat until soft peaks form.
3. In a clean, medium bowl, beat whipping cream until soft peaks form.
4. Fold blueberries into whipped cream.
5. Fold beaten egg whites into whipped cream mixture.
6. Pour into 6 glasses. Chill for 1 hour
7. Garnish with fresh fruit and serve with ladyfingers.

6 servings

Variation:

- *Replace blueberries with 2 cups (500 mL) of any combination of small, fresh fruit. Canned fruit should not be used, as it will sink to the bottom of the dessert.*

Approximate nutritional analysis per serving
Calories 478, Protein 3 g, Carbohydrates 54 g, Fat 30 g, Cholesterol 109 mg, Sodium 52 mg

Timeless Nanaimo Bars

Magic for your taste buds.

INGREDIENTS

Base

½ cup	**(125 mL) butter, melted**
¼ cup	**(50 mL) sugar**
⅓ cup	**(75 mL) cocoa**
1	**medium egg**
2 cups	**(500 mL) graham cracker crumbs**
1 cup	**(250 mL) flaked coconut**
½ cup	**(125 mL) walnuts, chopped**

Filling

½ cup	**(125 mL) butter, softened**
4 tbsp	**(60 mL) custard powder**
2 tsp	**(10 mL) vanilla extract**
6 tbsp	**(90 mL) milk**
4 cups	**(1 L) icing sugar, sifted**

Icing

3 oz	**(85 g) semisweet chocolate**
1 tbsp	**(15 mL) butter**

METHOD

1. In a medium bowl, combine first seven ingredients until well blended.
2. Press mixture into a 9-inch (22 cm) square pan.
3. Refrigerate for 1 hour.
4. In a large bowl, cream together butter, custard powder and vanilla.
5. Gradually blend in milk and icing sugar alternately in thirds.
6. When filling is smooth, spread onto chilled base and refrigerate for 1 hour.
7. In a double boiler, melt chocolate and butter.
8. Spread melted chocolate evenly over chilled filling.
9. Refrigerate until chocolate is set.
10. Cut into squares and serve.

20 squares

Approximate nutritional analysis per square
Calories 298, Protein 2 g, Carbohydrates 39 g, Fat 16 g, Cholesterol 36 mg, Sodium 188 mg

Timeless Nanaimo Bars

Lemon Zabaglione

Scrumptious and smooth.

INGREDIENTS

2	**large eggs**
6	**large egg yolks**
1 cup	**(250 mL) sugar**
1 tbsp	**(15 mL) lemon peel, grated**
¼ cup	**(50 mL) lemon juice**
½ cup	**(125 mL) Madeira wine or cream sherry**

METHOD

1. In a double boiler, combine eggs, egg yolks, sugar and lemon peel.
2. Beat with an electric mixer until light and very thick.
3. Stir in lemon juice and Madeira.
4. Beat mixture until doubled in volume. Remove from heat.
5. Divide into 6 stemmed glasses.
6. Serve with ladyfingers.

6 servings

Approximate nutritional analysis per serving
Calories 253, Protein 6 g, Carbohydrates 37 g, Fat 7 g, Cholesterol 305 mg, Sodium 39 mg

Mango Mousse

A tropical masterpiece.

INGREDIENTS

3	**medium mangoes, peeled and sliced**
2 tbsp	**(30 mL) fresh lime juice**
1 tbsp	**(15 mL) orange liqueur**
2	**large egg whites, room temperature**
2 tbsp	**(30 mL) sugar**
1 cup	**(250 mL) whipping cream**

METHOD

1. In a food processor, blend mangoes, lime juice and orange liqueur.
2. In a medium bowl, beat egg whites until soft peaks form.
3. Gradually add sugar to egg whites. Beat until stiff, but not dry.
4. In a large bowl, whip cream until soft peaks form.
5. Gently fold half the beaten egg whites into whipped cream.
6. Fold mango purée into whipped cream mixture.
7. Fold remaining egg whites into mixture.
8. Pour into 6 serving dishes.
9. Chill for 1 hour and serve.

6 servings

Tip:

- *To reduce the amount of time required to whip cream, chill beaters and bowl in the refrigerator for 1 hour.*

Approximate nutritional analysis per serving
Calories 214, Protein 2 g, Carbohydrates 18 g, Fat 15 g, Cholesterol 54 mg, Sodium 35 mg

Mango Mousse

English Trifle

Make this colorful, layered dessert for your next special gathering.

INGREDIENTS

4 tbsp	**(60 mL) custard powder**
2 cups	**(500 mL) milk**
¼ cup	**(50 mL) sugar**
3 cups	**(750 mL) sponge cake or yellow cake, cubed**
2 tbsp	**(30 mL) sherry**
4 tbsp	**(60 mL) raspberry jam or raspberry sauce**
1 cup	**(250 mL) canned fruit cocktail, in heavy syrup, drained**
1 cup	**(250 mL) whipping cream**

Step 10. Pour cooled custard on top of fruit cocktail.

Step 14. Decorate trifle with whipped cream.

Step 15. If desired, garnish trifle with maraschino cherries, almonds or choice of decorating pieces.

METHOD

1. In a medium bowl, mix custard powder with 1 cup (250 mL) milk.
2. Stir in sugar.
3. In a heavy saucepan, heat remaining 1 cup (250 mL) milk over medium heat until hot.
4. Stir heated milk into custard mixture.
5. Place custard mixture in saucepan.
6. Over low heat, slowly bring custard to a boil, stirring constantly. Cook for 1 minute. Remove from heat. Cool.
7. Place cake cubes in a large bowl. Sprinkle with sherry.
8. Dot cake cubes with raspberry jam or pour raspberry sauce over cake.
9. Place fruit cocktail on top of cake cubes.
10. Pour cooled custard on top of fruit cocktail.
11. Cover trifle with plastic wrap. Refrigerate for 1 hour.
12. In a medium bowl, beat whipping cream until stiff peaks form.
13. Place whipped cream into a piping bag with a star-shaped tip.
14. Decorate trifle with whipped cream.
15. If desired, garnish trifle with maraschino cherries, almonds or choice of decorating pieces.

8 servings

Approximate nutritional analysis per serving
Calories 298, Protein 4 g, Carbohydrates 40 g, Fat 14 g, Cholesterol 66 mg, Sodium 88 mg

English Trifle

Bavarian Cream

A fresh fruit sauce is the perfect accompaniment to this luxurious dessert.

INGREDIENTS

4	**medium eggs, separated**
½ cup	**(125 mL) sugar**
2 cups	**(500 mL) milk**
1 oz	**(30 g) gelatin**
¼ cup	**(50 mL) cold water**
1 cup	**(250 mL) whipping cream**

METHOD

1. In a medium bowl, cream egg yolks and sugar with an electric mixer until almost white in color.
2. In a heavy saucepan, heat milk over medium heat. Bring to a boil. Remove from heat.
3. Whisk hot milk into egg yolk mixture.
4. Return custard mixture to saucepan.
5. Stirring continuously, heat mixture over low heat for 8-10 minutes, until it lightly coats the back of a metal spoon. Do not boil the mixture. Remove from heat.
6. In a small bowl, soak gelatin in water for 5 minutes.
7. Stir softened gelatin into warm custard mixture.
8. Transfer custard mixture to a clean bowl. Cool until custard begins to set.
9. In a medium bowl, beat whipping cream until it holds soft peaks.
10. In a clean, medium bowl, beat egg whites until stiff peaks form.
11. Fold whipped cream into partially set custard mixture.
12. Gently fold in egg whites.
13. Pour mixture into a serving bowl or 8 individual molds.
14. Refrigerate for 1 hour. Serve.

8 servings

Variations:

- *Vanilla Bavarian Cream: Add ½ tsp (2 mL) vanilla extract to hot milk.*
- *Coffee Bavarian Cream: Add 1 tsp (5 mL) dissolved instant coffee to hot milk.*
- *Chocolate Bavarian Cream: Melt 2 oz (55 g) semisweet chocolate in hot milk.*
- *Strawberry Bavarian Cream: Add ½ tsp (2 mL) strawberry extract to hot milk.*

Approximate nutritional analysis per serving
Calories 240, Protein 8 g, Carbohydrates 18 g, Fat 15 g, Cholesterol 143 mg, Sodium 76 mg

Bavarian Cream

Poached Pears

Wonderful with vanilla ice cream.

INGREDIENTS

4	**firm pears**
1½ cups	**(375 mL) sugar**
1½ cups	**(375 mL) water**
½	**lemon, sliced**
1	**cinnamon stick**

METHOD

1. Peel pears. Cut in half lengthwise and remove cores.
2. In a large saucepan, bring sugar and water to a boil over high heat.
3. Add pears, flat side down, to saucepan.
4. Add lemon and cinnamon stick. Reduce heat to medium.
5. Simmer for 10 minutes, until pears are tender. Remove from heat.
6. Remove lemon slices and cinnamon stick.
7. Place pears on a serving dish. Top with syrup.
8. Serve hot or cold.

8 servings

Variations:

- *Ginger Pears: Add 4 whole cloves and ⅓ tsp (2 mL) ginger to poaching liquid.*
- *Blush Pears: Brush cooked pears with red food coloring or add ¼ cup (50 mL) sweet red wine to poaching liquid.*

◄ Approximate nutritional analysis per serving
Calories 380, Protein 0 g, Carbohydrates 98 g, Fat 0 g, Cholesterol 0 mg, Sodium 1 mg

Coffee Parfait

Serve with crispy cookies for dipping.

INGREDIENTS

2 tbsp	**(30 mL) cornstarch**
⅔ cup	**(150 mL) sugar**
pinch	**salt**
2 tbsp	**(30 mL) milk**
2	**large egg yolks**
2 tsp	**(10 mL) instant coffee**
1 tbsp	**(15 mL) water**
1½ cups	**(375 mL) whipping cream**

METHOD

1. In a medium bowl, mix together cornstarch, sugar and salt.
2. Stir in milk.
3. In a small bowl, beat egg yolks with an electric mixer. Stir into sugar mixture.
4. In a small bowl, mix instant coffee with water. Add to sugar mixture.
5. Transfer mixture to a double boiler.
6. Over medium heat, cook for 5 minutes, stirring constantly, until thickened. Remove from heat.
7. Cover mixture. Refrigerate for 30 minutes.
8. In a medium bowl, beat whipping cream until thickened but not stiff.
9. Fold whipped cream into cooled custard mixture.
10. Divide custard into 6 tall glasses.
11. Garnish with coffee beans or grated chocolate and whipped cream.

6 servings

Approximate nutritional analysis per serving
Calories 326, Protein 2 g, Carbohydrates 27 g, Fat 24 g, Cholesterol 153 mg, Sodium 31 mg

Coffee Parfait

Cocada

A delightful coconut custard recipe your guests will love.

INGREDIENTS

1 cup	**(250 mL) sugar**
2½ cups	**(625 mL) grated coconut**
3 cups	**(750 mL) milk**
pinch	**salt**
4	**large eggs**
1 tsp	**(5 mL) vanilla extract**
¼ cup	**(50 mL) medium-dry sherry**
1 cup	**(250 mL) whipping cream**
⅔ cup	**(150 mL) sliced, toasted almonds**

METHOD

1. In a large saucepan, combine sugar, coconut, milk and salt.
2. Simmer mixture over low heat, stirring occasionally, for 30-35 minutes until mixture is the consistency of light syrup. Remove from heat.
3. In a medium bowl, whisk eggs.
4. Gradually add ½ cup (125 mL) coconut mixture to eggs.
5. Whisk egg mixture into remaining coconut mixture in saucepan.
6. Stir in vanilla and sherry. Return to heat.
7. Simmer mixture for 8-10 minutes, stirring constantly, until thickened. Remove from heat.
8. Allow mixture to cool.
9. Pour cooled mixture into a serving dish or 10 tall champagne glasses.
10. Cover with plastic wrap and chill for 12 hours.
11. Beat whipping cream until it holds soft peaks.
12. Garnish custard with whipped cream and toasted almonds.

10 servings

Approximate nutritional analysis per serving
Calories 410, Protein 8 g, Carbohydrates 37 g, Fat 26 g, Cholesterol 153 mg, Sodium 142 mg

Cocada

Lemon Bay Rice Pudding

Smooth and sensational, this recipe is a combination of unique flavors.

INGREDIENTS

1 cup	**(250 mL) scented Thai rice, uncooked**
2½ cups	**(625 mL) water**
3	**bay leaves**
pinch	**salt**
3 cups	**(750 mL) coconut milk**
½ cup	**(125 mL) sugar**
1 tsp	**(5 mL) lemon peel, grated**
1 tsp	**(5 mL) vanilla extract**
⅓ cup	**(75 mL) whipping cream**
2 tbsp	**(30 mL) icing sugar**

METHOD

1. In a large, heavy saucepan, mix rice and water.
2. Add bay leaves and salt. Bring to a boil over medium-high heat.
3. Reduce heat to low. Cover and cook for 10 minutes.
4. Remove saucepan from heat. Let sit, covered, for 5 minutes.
5. Stir coconut milk and sugar into rice. Return to heat.
6. Simmer over low heat, stirring occasionally, for 5 minutes until mixture is thick and creamy. Rice should be very soft.
7. Transfer rice to a large bowl. Stir in lemon peel and vanilla.
8. Cover with plastic wrap and refrigerate overnight. Do not remove bay leaves.
9. Place a medium bowl and beaters in freezer for 10 minutes.
10. Using chilled bowl and beaters, beat whipping cream and icing sugar until stiff peaks form.
11. Remove bay leaves from pudding.
12. Fold whipped cream into pudding.
13. Pour into 6 individual dishes and serve chilled.

6 servings

Approximate nutritional analysis per serving
Calories 463, Protein 5 g, Carbohydrates 49 g, Fat 29 g, Cholesterol 18 mg, Sodium 25 mg

Lemon Bay Rice Pudding

Lemon Soufflé Baskets

So pretty and refreshing.

INGREDIENTS

6	**large lemons**
3	**large egg yolks**
5 tbsp	**(75 mL) sugar**
1 tbsp	**(15 mL) lemon peel, grated**
4	**egg whites, room temperature**
pinch	**cream of tartar**

METHOD

1. Preheat oven to 375°F (190°C).
2. Slice lemons in half lengthwise.
3. With a spoon, remove pulp from lemon halves to form hollow shells.
4. Reserve 2 tbsp (30 mL) lemon juice from lemons. Discard pulp.
5. Cut a fine slice from base of each lemon half to prevent rolling.
6. In a medium bowl, beat egg yolks and 4 tbsp (60 mL) sugar with an electric mixer until thick.
7. Add reserved lemon juice and lemon peel.
8. In a clean, medium bowl, beat egg whites with cream of tartar.
9. Add remaining 1 tbsp (15 mL) sugar to egg whites. Beat until stiff peaks form.
10. Fold egg whites lightly into yolk mixture.
11. Fill lemon halves with soufflé mixture. Place on a baking sheet.
12. Bake 15-20 minutes, until tops are lightly browned.

6 servings

Raisin Bread Pudding

A traditional favorite.

INGREDIENTS

2 tbsp	**(30 mL) butter**
1 tsp	**(5 mL) cinnamon**
½ cup	**(125 mL) brown sugar, lightly packed**
½ cup	**(125 mL) raisins**
pinch	**salt**
4 cups	**(1 L) bread, cubed**
2½ cups	**(625 mL) milk**
2	**large eggs, lightly beaten**
1 tsp	**(5 mL) vanilla extract**

METHOD

1. Preheat oven to 350°F (175°C).
2. Butter an 8-inch (20 cm) round casserole dish.
3. In a small bowl, combine cinnamon, brown sugar, raisins and salt.
4. Sprinkle brown sugar mixture on bottom of casserole dish.
5. Place bread cubes in a large bowl.
6. In a medium bowl, combine milk, eggs and vanilla. Pour over bread cubes.
7. Stir mixture until well blended.
8. Pour bread mixture into prepared casserole dish.
9. Place a small rack in oven. Place a shallow pan on top of rack.
10. Place casserole dish into pan in oven.
11. Pour hot water into pan to a depth of 1 inch (2.5 cm).
12. Bake for 45 minutes, until a wooden pick inserted into center of pudding comes out clean.
13. Serve hot or cold with ice cream or butterscotch sauce.

6 servings

Approximate nutritional analysis per serving
Calories 272, Protein 8 g, Carbohydrates 38 g, Fat 10 g, Cholesterol 117 mg, Sodium 227 mg

◀ Approximate nutritional analysis per serving
Calories 84, Protein 4 g, Carbohydrates 12 g, Fat 3 g, Cholesterol 106 mg, Sodium 41 mg

Raisin Bread Pudding

Fruit-Filled Soufflé Omelettes

A creative variation on a simple recipe.

INGREDIENTS

8	**large eggs, separated**
1 tbsp	**(15 mL) sugar**
dash	**lemon juice**
pinch	**salt**
1 tbsp	**(15 mL) butter, melted**
1 cup	**(250 mL) strawberries, sliced**
1 cup	**(250 mL) blueberries**
1 tbsp	**(15 mL) icing sugar**

METHOD

1. Preheat oven to 350°F (175°C).
2. In a medium bowl, combine egg whites, sugar, lemon juice and salt.
3. Beat with an electric mixer just until soft peaks form.
4. In a medium bowl, beat egg yolks until light and fluffy.
5. Gently fold egg white mixture into egg yolks. Do not overmix.
6. Place butter in a small, cast iron pan. Heat over medium heat for 30 seconds.
7. Spread 1 cup (250 mL) egg mixture evenly over base of pan.
8. Cook for 1-2 minutes. Remove from heat.
9. Place pan in oven and bake for 5-7 minutes, until egg mixture begins to set.
10. Using oven mitts, carefully remove pan from oven. Handle will be very hot.
11. With a spatula, gently slide omelette onto a plate. Keep warm.
12. Repeat cooking and baking steps for remaining egg mixture.
13. In a medium bowl, lightly toss together strawberries and blueberries.
14. Place ½ cup (125 mL) berry mixture on top of each omelette.
15. Fold omelettes over filling.
16. Dust with icing sugar and serve.

4 servings

Approximate nutritional analysis per serving
Calories 230, Protein 13 g, Carbohydrates 14 g, Fat 14 g, Cholesterol 434 mg, Sodium 131 mg

Fruit-Filled Soufflé Omelettes

Strawberry Crêpe Delights

A wonderful choice for breakfast, brunch or dessert.

INGREDIENTS

Crêpes

3	**large eggs**
3	**large egg yolks**
¾ cup	**(175 mL) water**
1 cup	**(250 mL) milk**
½ tsp	**(2 mL) salt**
1½ cups	**(375 mL) all-purpose flour**
½ cup	**(125 mL) butter, melted**

Strawberry Topping

2 cups	**(500 mL) strawberries, sliced**
3 tbsp	**(45 mL) sugar**
1 tbsp	**(15 mL) lemon juice**
5	**fresh strawberries**

METHOD

1. In a medium bowl, whisk together first four ingredients until combined.
2. Whisk in salt and flour to make a smooth batter.
3. Stir in butter. Batter should be thin enough to coat the back of a metal spoon. If batter is too thick, add a small amount of milk.
4. Cover batter with plastic wrap and refrigerate for 1 hour.
5. In a medium bowl, combine strawberries, sugar and lemon juice.
6. Let strawberry mixture stand for 10 minutes at room temperature.
7. Toss strawberry mixture until syrup forms.
8. Wipe out an 8-inch (20 cm) non-stick crêpe pan with an oiled paper towel.
9. Heat crêpe pan over medium-high heat.
10. Holding pan off heat, add enough batter to coat base of pan.
11. Swirl batter to spread evenly over bottom of pan.
12. Return pan to heat. Cook until top of crêpe is dry, about 30 seconds.
13. Using a rubber or plastic spatula, flip crêpe over and cook for about 10 seconds.
14. Slide crêpe out of pan onto a dry surface. Keep warm.
15. Wipe out pan with oiled paper towel. Repeat steps until all of crêpe batter has been used.
16. Fold each crêpe in half twice to form a triangle. Place each crêpe on a serving plate.
17. Pour strawberry topping over warm crêpes.
18. Garnish with whole strawberries and serve.

5 servings

Variation:

- *Add 1 oz (30 mL) orange liqueur to strawberry mixture.*

Approximate nutritional analysis per serving
Calories 538, Protein 11 g, Carbohydrates 43 g, Fat 36 g, Cholesterol 319 mg, Sodium 277 mg

Strawberry Crêpe Delights

Minted Fruit with Lime and Candied Ginger

This mouth-watering dessert is light and satisfying.

INGREDIENTS

¾ cup	**(175 mL) sugar**
½ cup	**(125 mL) water**
1	**lime peel, cut into strips**
1 tsp	**(5 mL) crystallized ginger, chopped**
1 tbsp	**(15 mL) fresh mint leaves, shredded**
3 tbsp	**(45 mL) fresh lime juice**
1	**mango, peeled and sliced**
½	**small honeydew melon, peeled and sliced**

METHOD

1. Reserve 1 tbsp (15 mL) sugar.
2. In a medium saucepan, combine remaining sugar, water, half the lime peel and ginger.
3. Bring to a boil. Reduce heat to low, stirring until sugar has dissolved.
4. Simmer syrup for 10 minutes. Remove from heat.
5. Cool for 5 minutes.
6. Stir mint into syrup.
7. Strain syrup through a sieve into a small bowl. Discard lime peel and mint. Reserve ginger for garnish.
8. Add lime juice to syrup, stirring well to combine.
9. Cover with plastic wrap and refrigerate for 1 hour.
10. In a small bowl, toss remaining lime peel in reserved sugar.
11. Arrange mango and honeydew slices on a serving platter.
12. Pour syrup on top of fruit.
13. Garnish fruit with sugared lime peel and reserved ginger. Serve.

4 servings

Approximate nutritional analysis per serving
Calories 247, Protein 2 g, Carbohydrates 64 g, Fat 0 g, Cholesterol 0 mg, Sodium 24 mg

Minted Fruit with Lime and Candied Ginger

Baked Apples Extraordinaire

A hearty and healthy choice for dessert.

INGREDIENTS

4	**tart apples**
2 tbsp	**(30 mL) dried apricots, chopped**
2 tbsp	**(30 mL) currants**
2 tbsp	**(30 mL) raisins**
½ cup	**(125 mL) brown sugar, lightly packed**
1 tbsp	**(15 mL) cinnamon**
½ tsp	**(2 mL) lemon peel, grated**
½ tsp	**(2 mL) orange peel, grated**
1 tbsp	**(15 mL) butter**
1 cup	**(250 mL) hot water**
3 tbsp	**(45 mL) sugar**

Step 3. Trim a thin slice from the base of each apple.

Step 7. Remove cores and seeds from apple halves with a melon baller.

Step 8. Fill hollow center of each apple with fruit mixture.

METHOD

1. Preheat oven to 350°F (175°C).
2. Cut apples in half lengthwise.
3. Trim a thin slice from the base of each apple.
4. Soak apricots, currants and raisins in hot water for 8-10 minutes.
5. Drain water from fruit. Gently dry with paper towels.
6. In a medium bowl, mix fruit, brown sugar, cinnamon, lemon peel and orange peel.
7. Remove cores and seeds from apple halves with a melon baller.
8. Fill hollow center of each apple with fruit mixture.
9. Dot top of each filled apple with butter.
10. In a small saucepan, combine sugar and water. Cook over medium-high heat for 4 minutes, until mixture is the consistency of syrup. Remove from heat.
11. Pour syrup into bottom of a shallow baking dish.
12. Place filled apple halves in dish with syrup.
13. Cover. Bake for 45 minutes, until apples are tender.
14. Serve hot or cold.

4 servings

Approximate nutritional analysis per serving
Calories 300, Protein 1 g, Carbohydrates 72 g, Fat 4 g, Cholesterol 8 mg, Sodium 39 mg

Baked Apples E[illegible]naire

Cranberry Mango Cobbler

An old-fashioned favorite you'll want to prepare again and again.

INGREDIENTS

Fruit Filling

2	**ripe mangoes, peeled and diced into small pieces**
2 cups	**(500 mL) cranberries**
1½ cups	**(375 mL) sugar**
3 tbsp	**(45 mL) all-purpose flour**
½ tsp	**(2 mL) cinnamon**

Topping

1½ cups	**(375 mL) all-purpose flour**
1½ tbsp	**(25 mL) sugar**
2¼ tsp	**(11 mL) baking powder**
pinch	**nutmeg**
6 tbsp	**(90 mL) butter, room temperature**
¾ cup	**(175 mL) whipping cream**
2 tbsp	**(30 mL) milk**

METHOD

1. Preheat oven to 350°F (175°C).
2. In a medium bowl, combine mangoes, cranberries, sugar, flour and cinnamon.
3. Cover fruit filling with plastic wrap. Let stand while topping is being prepared.
4. In a medium bowl, mix flour, sugar, baking powder and nutmeg.
5. Cut butter into flour mixture until it is crumbly and resembles corn meal.
6. Add whipping cream and mix lightly to moisten dry ingredients.
7. Mix gently until mixture forms a ball and leaves the sides of the bowl.
8. Pour fruit filling into a 7-inch (18 cm) baking dish or 8 small baking dishes. Do not fill dishes more than half full.
9. Shape topping dough into ½-inch (1.3 cm) thick patties.
10. Place patties on top of fruit filling.
11. Brush top of dough patties with milk.
12. Bake for 35 minutes, until topping is golden brown.
13. Serve hot or cold with ice cream or whipped cream.

8 servings

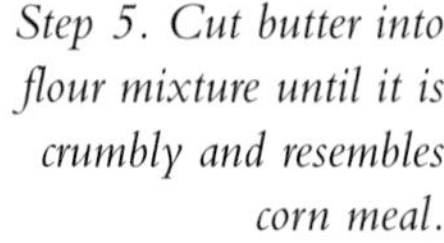

Step 5. Cut butter into flour mixture until it is crumbly and resembles corn meal.

Step 7. Mix gently until mixture forms a ball and leaves the sides of the bowl.

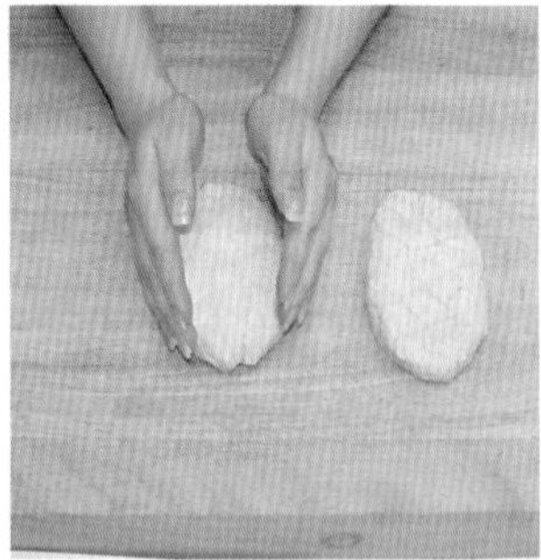

Step 9. Shape topping dough into ½-inch (1.3 cm) thick patties.

Approximate nutritional analysis per serving
Calories 584, Protein 4 g, Carbohydrates 108 g, Fat 17 g, Cholesterol 54 mg, Sodium 265 mg

Cranberry Mango Cobbler

Index

About the Author

John Butler was born in Scotland and served his chef's apprenticeship under Chef André Louis Meunière at the famous Le Coq d'Or in London. He is a Journeyman Red Seal Cook and Baker, and is a Master Chef as recognized by the Canadian Federation of Chefs and Cooks. John has gained recognition as a gold medal-winning team manager in national and international culinary competitions. Highly respected as a food stylist and designer, John's work has appeared in magazines, newspapers, cookbooks, film and video. John currently teaches culinary arts and resides with his wife and two daughters in St. Albert, Alberta, Canada.